I0608938

Dear Sallie is a rare collection of letters written by a Confederate private to his sister as she struggled to help maintain the family farm in rural Oglethorpe County, Georgia. Private James Jewel's candid thoughts and feelings provide a window to a bygone era as he tried to understand and assess the war's effect on himself, his family and his fellow soldiers. The War Between the States had already been underway for a year when he mustered into the Echols Light Artillery on May 3, 1862. The twenty-seven-year-old Jewel probably delayed enlisting because his wife was pregnant with their first child, but an April 1862 conscript law perhaps pushed him to join the war effort.

Like thousands of soldiers on both sides, Jewel exchanged letters with loved ones at home. The miracle is that 114 of James Jewel's letters have survived the ravages of time, and most of them were written to his younger sister, Sallie. A wit with a pen, Jewel used his keen eye to fill his letters with camp life information that involved officers and enlisted men. He noted the names of many Georgians and Floridians in his correspondence, and Gary Doster has painstakingly footnoted the genealogical background of many of these people.

Jewel had never been separated from his family before his arrival at Griffin, Georgia, for his initial training. His writings reflect his homesickness, especially after the birth of his daughter. Soon, Jewel and his fellow soldiers moved to Atlanta where they were responsible for guarding Union prisoners. In October 1862, men from the Echols Light Artillery scoured the Atlanta area in search of the escaped Andrews' Raiders.

Continued on next page

In January 1863, Jewel's unit moved to north Florida, where 68 of his letters present a new and unreported soldier's perspective from that area. While in the Florida Panhandle, these Georgians helped protect the "backdoor of the Confederacy" as they guarded the area's valuable salt works along the Gulf Coast. They also prevented Yankee gunboats from moving up the Apalachicola River and gaining access to northwest Florida and the interior of Alabama and Georgia. Jewel's Florida letters were written from Quincy, Tallahassee, Camp Brokaw, Camp Leon, Camp Limpkins, and Camp Sidney Johnston and make clear for the first time the location of these camps and their use in the Confederate war effort. His pen painted a vivid picture of life in Florida's wartime panhandle as he gave vivid descriptions of the land, the people and the homes. He also had much to say about his fellow soldiers, their living conditions, the weather, the food, sickness and the insects that plagued them almost constantly.

This book also contains eighteen letters written by Jewel's teenage sister Sallie and one letter by Jewel's wife, Eliza. Their correspondence reinforces our knowledge of the wartime difficulties endured by women and their families throughout the South.

Sadly, these letters follow the trail of James Jewel and his fellow artillerymen as they moved toward Jacksonville, Savannah and Charleston to help slow William Sherman's Union army in late 1864 and early 1865. The end would come for Private Jewel in March 1865 at Averasboro, North Carolina. Tragically, his family to this day has no idea what happened to him or where he is buried. They only know that the scanty Confederate records listed him as missing in action.

Gary Doster has provided a true service to students, historians and genealogists by first preserving and then transcribing these letters. Through painstaking detective work he has noted for the reader the background regarding the numerous people, places and things listed throughout the pages. Several appendices provide genealogical tables and obituary information for Jewel's family members, but the book also contains another valuable element – the first comprehensive roster ever published of Georgians who served in the Echols Light Artillery.

Dear Sallie...

...I would write more if I thought you would get it.

THE LETTERS OF
CONFEDERATE PRIVATE JAMES JEWEL

Echols Light Artillery, Oglethorpe County, Georgia

Edited by
GARY L. DOSTER

With foreword by
WILLIAM WARREN ROGERS

Angle Valley Press
Winchester, Virginia

Copyright © 2011 by Gary L. Doster

All rights reserved. No part of this publication may be reproduced, stored in a retrieval system, or transmitted, in any form or by any means, electronic, mechanical, photocopying, recording, or otherwise, without written permission from the publisher, except by a reviewer who may quote brief passages in a review.

For information contact:

Angle Valley Press, P.O. Box 4098, Winchester, VA 22604

www.AngleValleyPress.com

Designed & printed in the United States of America
First Edition, First Printing
14 13 12 11   4 3 2 1

Publisher's Cataloging-in-Publication Data

Jewel, James.
Dear Sallie: the letters of Confederate private James Jewel, Echols Light Artillery, Oglethorpe County, Georgia / edited by Gary L. Doster; with foreword by William Warren Rogers.

p. cm.

ISBN: 978-0-9711950-1-1

1. Florida—History—Civil War, 1861-1865—Personal narratives.   2. Confederate States of America. Army—Military life.   3. Soldiers—Florida—Correspondence.   4. Confederate States of America. Army. Georgia Artillery. Echols Light Artillery.   I. Doster, Gary L., ed. II. Title.
E559.4 .J49 2011
973.7—dc22

2011925102

For Faye
The best person I have ever known

ALSO BY GARY L. DOSTER

A Post Card History of Athens, Georgia

From Abbeville to Zebulon:
Early Post Card Views of Georgia

Northeast Georgia in Vintage Postcards

Northwest Georgia in Vintage Postcards

East Central Georgia in Vintage Postcards

West Central Georgia in Vintage Postcards

Southeast Georgia in Vintage Postcards

Southwest Georgia in Vintage Postcards

TABLE OF CONTENTS

ILLUSTRATIONS

ACKNOWLEDGMENTS

During the several years that I worked off and on researching and writing *Dear Sallie*, I became indebted to many people who helped in various ways. Some put forth considerable time and effort in doing actual work; others simply offered a cheerful word of encouragement. I am grateful to them all. I especially appreciate those listed below.

Carl Anderson – Good friend for more than 40 years. Carl spent untold hours in the Georgia Department of Archives and History searching census records, Compiled Military Service Records, Confederate Pension Records, and myriad other sources.

The late E. H. Armor – Greene County, Georgia, historian, friend, and grand raconteur. "H" led me over several miles of poorly marked trails and through many briar thickets guiding me to some obscure cemeteries where much valuable information was obtained from tombstones.

Dr. David J. Coles – Former archive supervisor at the Florida State Archives in Tallahassee, who went far beyond what was asked and expected of him. He directed me to many obscure records and maps that I would never have known existed if not for him. David is now associate professor of history at Longwood College in Farmville, Virginia.

Frances Greene – Descendant of Marshall Washington Edwards and Jane Jewel Edwards, who provided genealogical information on the family.

Gisela Gresham – Expert artist and illustrator. Gisela created three of the magnificent maps that add much to the book.

Tom Gresham – President of Historic Oglethorpe, Inc., who has done so much to promote and stimulate interest in the history of his adopted county. Tom immediately recognized the historic value of the Jewel letters and gave a great deal of encouragement, advice, and assistance with bringing the book to fruition. Tom also made the excellent photographs of Sallie's tombstone and the chimney of the Jewel homeplace.

Charlotte Thomas Marshall – Good friend and expert genealogist and historian. Charlotte read and reread various drafts of the manuscript and kept me from making some mistakes in identifying various individuals. She also helped prepare the genealogical charts, which make a valuable addition to the book.

Dr. George O. Marshall, Jr. – Another good friend who helped considerably. George gave me the same commitment and attention as if I had been one of his graduate students, yet treated me with the respect and consideration due a professional peer. He is unsurpassed at discovering inconsistencies, misspelled words, and grammatical errors.

Auvis Paradise – Oglethorpe County native who read a very early draft of the manuscript and supplied useful information regarding some of her family members mentioned in the book.

Glenn W. Paul – Another Oglethorpe County native, Glenn is an accomplished genealogist and historian who provided valuable information on several of his ancestors and others who served in the Echols Light Artillery.

William Reeves – A highly skilled designer and graphic artist who executed the typography and layout for *Dear Sallie*, prepared two of the five maps used as illustrations, and created the magnificent cover. Bill is a true master of his craft.

Dr. William Warren Rogers – A professional historian and friend who provided support and advice from the beginning and wrote the Foreword.

Patrick Segraves and Jeff West – Friends who discovered that the Jewel family letters were available, recognized their historic value, and put me in contact with the owner in order that I could acquire them.

Bill Smedlund – Fellow enthusiast for Georgia history, especially the War Between the States period. Bill provided me with numerous tidbits of information on the Echols Light Artillery that he gleaned from period newspapers. He also discovered the eight Jewel letters in the Emory University Library and directed me to them.

Former Georgia State Representative Bob Smith and his sister Mary Smith Mills – Bob and Mary shared information on their Colclough ancestors and helped identify some elusive individuals that I could not place in the family.

The late Susan Frances Barrow Tate – Sue Fan read a very early, rough draft of the manuscript, declared that it was worth publishing, and gave me valuable advice on how to go about it. She also shared some helpful information on several of her ancestors named in the Jewel letters.

Michelle Walker – A competent, hard working friend who invested a great deal of work in the early development of the manuscript. I greatly appreciate her inspiration and help but, most of all, I relish her pleasant and cheerful attitude.

Donna Wood – Longtime friend and master typist who is due considerable credit for the existence of *Dear Sallie.* During the earliest phase of this project Donna labored many hours typing the original transcriptions of the Jewel letters then taught me how to use the computer in order that I might finish the job.

Lonnie L. Williamson – Longtime friend who encouraged me along the way and who provided some valuable editing and proofing on some sections of the book.

Lastly, to Faye Thomas Doster, my sweetheart since 1956 and my wife since 1959, who in one way or another, is responsible for virtually everything I do, I offer my gratitude and my love.

Gary L. Doster, a native Georgian, has edited the Civil War letters of another native Georgian, Private James Jewel of Echols Light Artillery. In doing so, Doster has labored long and hard in bringing together the totally honest, day-to-day service letters of a young man but not a boy (Jewel was twenty-seven, and his wife, Eliza, was pregnant when he volunteered). Jewel's account of life as an enlisted man was rendered with no thoughts of future publication. Beyond their inherent value as historical documents, the letters describe the wartime milieu of an area about which little has been written: North Florida as centered around the state capital of Tallahassee. In fact, some of Jewel's revelations make clear for the first time the location and use of several Confederate camps and posts in the Florida counties of Leon, Gadsden, and Wakulla. Jewel's accounts from Georgia and South Carolina are also valuable.

The letters are an important find for several reasons. One is that the reader benefits from Private Jewel's talents as a keen observer. Because of his rural upbringing in Oglethorpe County in northeast Georgia, he closely describes weather, topography, animal, bird and insect life (his accounts of mosquitoes are vivid and humorous), trees, plants, and crops. In depicting his new surroundings, Jewel does so minutely to show the contrasts with Oglethorpe County, and the result is an engaging and highly informal environmental picture. There is no equivalent record in print.

The letters are additionally significant because they catalogue in colloquial and human terms the miseries and pleasures of life in the ranks and military duty in an area largely removed from the terror and excitement of battle. Food, clothing, and shelter receive their historic due from Jewel: they are basic to life, and their presence and level of quality determine how the young Georgian feels about a given day. He adds health to the fundamentals (historians of medicine will find his remarks of value).

Jewel was a pious Baptist. His letters reveal him as reflective but not morbidly introspective, concerned about himself but interested in his fellow soldiers, sympathetic to their trials, and always conscious of his family and their well-being. To read him in the present is to be attracted by his candidness and sharp insights, all couched in a straightforward narrative unfettered by the niceties of grammar or the demands of spelling. It is impossible to peruse the letters without becoming immersed in the setting they describe and without developing affection for Private Jewel.

Finally, Doster, a wildlife biologist by profession, has gone beyond the standard sources to discover facts about the lives of people central to the world of James Jewel. His editing of the letters is painstaking and exhibits first rate scholarship. It is clear that Doster identifies closely with his subject. Civil War experts will welcome the letters with their abundant and original detail. Beyond that, the correspondence will appeal to the general reader because unfolded here is the poignant and human story of a soldier away from familiar surroundings. James Jewel may not have understood the forces that brought him to North Florida with its humidity and palmetto undergrowth. He was no heroic figure, and when he felt put upon, he complained. There was never a time Jewel did not want to go home, but there was never a time when he failed to do his duty.

William Warren Rogers
Distinguished Teaching Professor of History, Emeritus
Florida State University
Tallahassee, Florida

INTRODUCTION

So much has been written about the American War Between the States that I am tempted to apologize for foisting yet another volume upon the reader. But the fascination for this period of our history continues with each generation, and James Jewel's story needs telling too. His personal account of the American tragedy is rendered with a sense of immediacy and unsophisticated detachment.

Jewel's view of the times and events diverges radically from the usual accounts of battles, strategy, troop movements, and political machinations – as interpreted by high-ranking officers and political leaders. Jewel was a yeoman farmer from rural Georgia who answered a new country's call to arms. He enlisted as a private and never rose above that rank. For most of his three years of service, Jewel was stationed far from the battlefronts and at one time jokingly referred to his unit as "the life insurance company." For the majority of his military experience he was as safe as if he had been a civilian. He saw combat only at the very end of the conflict. Yet what he wrote about has a compelling honesty: there is drama in the routine lives of soldiers serving in the backwaters of the Confederacy, far from enemy lines and the whizzing of bullets. He describes an area and milieu that have received little attention from fiction writers or historians.

Oglethorpe County, Georgia, provided four companies of 135 to 150 men each to the Confederate Army. Another 100 or more citizens served in other units. Soon after the firing on Fort Sumter on April 12, 1861, three of those companies — the Gilmer Blues,[1] the Oglethorpe Rifles,[2] and the Tom Cobb Infantry[3] – were pressed into service. As these patriotic young men of Oglethorpe County were formed into their various units and prepared to go off to a war, they no doubt expected to bring a hasty end to what they perceived as the "War of Northern Aggression."

The end did not come quickly. By 1862 it was apparent that the projected Confederate triumph was a distant goal. As harsh proof, there was a conscript law about to go into effect in April. Able-bodied men between the ages of 18 and 35 were to be liable for three years' service. Those who had not volunteered were to be drafted.

To avoid such a stigma on their patriotism, some of the remaining qualified men in Oglethorpe County formed an independent company of light artillery. The Echols Light Artillery was organized on the first of March 1862. It also is referred to in the records as Echols Battery, Georgia Light Artillery; Tiller's Battery, Georgia Light Artillery; and as Captain Tiller's Company (Echols Light Artillery), Georgia Volunteers. The company was named in honor of a distinguished local citizen, Joseph H. Echols, who later became a Confederate congressman. The first thirty volunteers departed on March 18 for the Camp of Instruction at Griffin, Georgia, to begin training and to acquire horses, guns, and other equipment. Others would follow until their ranks were filled. Twenty-seven-year-old James Jewel, Jr., was among these men. He enlisted May 3, 1862, for "three years or the war" and left home, probably for the first time in his life.

At Griffin, the Echols Artillery underwent the equivalent of basic training. The men learned to drill, to march and countermarch, and were taught to load and fire their cannons. Life at Griffin had little of severe military regime. The artillerymen had light duty, good living quarters, plenty to eat, and regular contact with home and family. In late June 1862, James's wife Eliza, pregnant with their first child, visited him there, and he was allowed to accompany her back home for a short visit.

The Echols Artillery spent three months at Griffin, training and waiting their turn to be sent to the battlefields of Virginia or other states further north. Instead, in mid-August they were moved only fifty miles north to Atlanta. Their main duty was to help guard Union prisoners of war. The most exciting thing that happened was when fourteen of the Yankees escaped from the stockade. The Echols Artillery participated in the attempt to recapture them. Although Jewel and the pursing Confederates did not realize it, some of the escapees were part of the audacious Andrews' Raiders.

Still enjoying the same leisure that had existed at Griffin, Jewel was allowed a short furlough. He went home to be with Eliza when their daughter, Martha "Mattie" Elizabeth, was born August 31,

1862. A few months later in December 1862, Eliza brought Mattie to camp for a visit. The war seemed far away.

After six months' duty in Atlanta, the Echols Artillery was removed even farther from the war front. The first week of January 1863 the men were transferred to northwest Florida to help guard the "back door" of the Confederacy from attack and protect the valuable saltworks along the Gulf coast. Jewel and his comrades began their Florida duty at "a place called quincy about fifteen miles from Tallahassa." For the next two years they were at various camps at or near Quincy, St. Marks, and Tallahassee.

Florida was divided into two military divisions: the Middle District of Florida, with headquarters at Quincy and the District of East Florida, with headquarters at Lake City. Both Districts were under the Department of South Carolina, Georgia, and Florida, with Headquarters at Charleston, South Carolina. The Middle District was successively commanded by Brigadier General Howell Cobb, Colonel William J. McGill, and Brigadier General William M. Gardner. The Eastern District was under the command of Brigadier General Joseph Finegan. The Middle and East Districts were eventually combined and placed under the command of Major General James Patton Anderson.

Having never been far from home before, Jewel was greatly interested in his new surroundings. For him, most of the things he saw were exotic. He wrote long, newsy letters describing in detail the countryside, the homes and gardens, farming practices, and the people. On first marching into "Tallahassa," he announced in a letter to his sister Sallie that he "had the pleasure once in my life of passing through the capitol of a state" (obviously, he had never been to Milledgeville, then the capital of Georgia and less than seventy miles from his home). He saw his first lake when the company camped a few miles north of Tallahassee at Lake Jackson. He reported seeing "a good many ponds in the neighborhood... some of them large enough for allegators." Later, after being nearer the coast for a while, he learned first hand what the term "flat as a flounder" meant and gave Sallie a minute description of that curiosity, as well as his first impression of a palm tree and other native vegetation. His letters also contained many comments about his fellow soldiers from Oglethorpe County.

Although Jewel and his comrades were in no danger from Yankee bullets, they suffered many of the same privations as their brothers and friends on the battlefields of the upper South. They were usually short of food and medical supplies, had inferior living quarters, and at one time they went for more than a year without pay. Even when the soldiers had money, there often was little available to buy, and what was available was offered at exorbitant war-inflated prices. Jewel was a devout Baptist and was particularly dismayed by not having the opportunity to attend regular church services.

When glanders, a bacterial disease, killed most of their horses in the Spring of 1864, an earlier fear was realized: the Echols Artillery was transformed into an infantry company. After their first short march with an infantryman's accouterments, Jewel wrote, "I have seen enough of the infantry to know I will not like it."

Summers in Florida seemed endless. The steaming heat and hordes of biting and stinging insects were almost unbearable at times. Worst of all, there was the constant threat of malaria. The fever's symptoms and effects were obvious, but the disease itself had not been identified. Virtually every man stationed in the area was infected with the malady that they knew as miasma or miasmatic fever. It was commonly believed that the disease emanated from the soil or swamps (which was partly true, since much of the area was ideal habitat for producing the mosquitos that served as the vector for the malaria organism). Regular attacks by the chills and fever of malaria, the "bowel complaint," and other ailments kept a large number of men incapacitated much of the time. At one time there were only six men in Jewel's company well enough to stand duty.

Almost as bad as the physical illnesses was being homesick for loved ones and the comforts of familiar surroundings. The remoteness of northwestern Florida at that time made travel difficult. An eighteen-mile railroad connected Tallahassee with St. Marks to the South. East-West connections were to Jacksonville and to Quincy, but there was no line north to Georgia. Most travel had to be by foot, horseback, or stagecoach. Furloughs seemed to be reserved for officers. Enlisted men stayed on duty unless they were seriously ill and became eligible for medical leave. Or so it seemed to Private Jewel. When Jewel's letters ended, it had been almost 2 1/2 years since he had been home and 27 months since he had seen his wife and then 3-month-old baby when they visited him in camp at Atlanta.

In December 1864, Union General William T. Sherman's army of more than 60,000 soldiers neared the end of its infamous invasion of Georgia and approached Savannah. The Echols Artillery, along with every other available Confederate soldier, was placed under the command of General William J. Hardee and moved into position in a frantic effort to fortify the town. Only 10,000 strong, their efforts were futile. After a 10-day siege, the overwhelming Yankee forces took the city and drove the meager Confederate defenders across the Savannah River into South Carolina. Sherman presented Savannah to Lincoln as a Christmas present.

After a brief stay at Hardeeville, the Confederate forces were moved by railroad to Pocataligo where they spent a few days before going to James Island near Charleston. Here they spent seven cold, wet, miserable weeks without relief. Food and firewood were scarce and the ever present closeness of the enemy forced them to remain in constant battle readiness. It was from James Island on February 13, 1865, that Jewel wrote his last letter home. In a short note of a few sentences he informed Sallie that the Yankees had captured the railroad and cut communications and he doubted that his letter would reach her.

THE JEWEL FAMILY

James Jewel's family was not of the wealthy, aristocratic planter class. Yet the Jewels and their kin were substantial farmers. James's father, James Jewel, Sr., owned 635 acres of land, and the Georgia Slave Census of 1860 indicated that he owned 21 slaves. James Jr., only 25, owned one slave. By the time of the War Between the States the Jewels had been long-time residents of the Hermon Community on either side of the geographic line dividing the Falling Creek and

Wolfskin Militia districts of Oglethorpe County, Georgia, on what is now named Bull Bray Road. The county was formed in 1793 out of part of Wilkes County, and Lexington is the county seat. James's parents were native Georgians, and he and his brothers and sisters were all born in Georgia, probably in or near Oglethorpe County.

James Jewel, Sr., was the son of Joseph and Jane Jewel, early residents of Oglethorpe County. Joseph Jewel is listed in the 1790 census of Wilkes County as the owner of 170 acres of land in that section of the county that was to become Oglethorpe County in 1793. When Joseph Jewel died in 1809 he lived on a 218-acre tract of land on Little River in the southeastern corner of Oglethorpe County. He also owned an additional 286 acres in Oglethorpe County, some of which was identified as being located on Big Creek, which is in the Wolfskin District. Jane Jewel lived until 1823.

In addition to James, Sr., the other children of Joseph and Jane Jewel were Elizabeth, Margaret, Martha, Polly, Sarah, and William.

James Jewel, Sr.'s wife Rebecca Bell was the daughter of John Bell. Rebecca's brothers and sisters were Elizabeth (married to William Jewel, brother to James Jewel, Sr.), James, Jesse, John A., Sylvanus, Nancy, and Patsy. At the time of his death, John Bell was married to Mary, but it is not known if she was the mother of his children.

James Jewel, Sr., was born March 15, 1788, and Rebecca Bell on August 6, 1802 (the age disparity of 14 years was not uncommon). They were married in Oglethorpe County on February 3, 1819, and over the next 26 years had nine children, the last two being James, Jr., and Sara Rebecca (Sallie), the writer and the recipient of most of these letters.

On December 1, 1859, James married Eliza Cordelia Colclough (his senior by one year, which was unusual). Eliza was from the nearby Penfield District of adjoining Greene County. At the beginning of the war James and Eliza lived on his father's land and farmed. When James joined the Confederate Army, Eliza, pregnant with their first and only child, moved back home with her parents to await the birth of the baby and the return of James.

Editorial Considerations

James's letters began May 16, 1862, with a letter to his father giving a report of his safe arrival at Griffin, Georgia's Camp Stephens via Atlanta. When that letter and his next correspondence of May 22 remained unanswered, he began directing his letters to his 17-year-old sister Sallie. Sallie soon became unofficial correspondent for the entire family.

Just over 100 of James's letters have survived. Three of these were written to his father, four to his brother William, and one each to his wife Eliza and his niece Mary Crowley. The rest were to Sallie. In addition, 20 of the letters that James received from home also have been preserved. Dated from February 7, 1863, through July 17, 1863, 19 letters were from sister Sallie and one was from his wife, Eliza. Although few in number and spanning less than six months, they nevertheless contain valuable information relative to family, friends, and local events. James's letters are presented in chronological order and comprise the first eight chapters. Originally, Sallie and Eliza's letters were to be interspersed with James's letters chronologically, but it was thought that this might disrupt the flow of his letters and make them difficult to follow. Consequently, Sallie and Eliza's letters are presented separately as the final chapter.

I did not attempt a detailed genealogical search on every person mentioned in the letters. I only wanted to determine who each one was in relation to the Jewels and their immediate families. Occasionally a great deal of information was easily available on some individuals, but some mentioned only once were difficult to identify and were not pursued. More prominent family members and friends who were regularly included in the correspondence are identified in more detail.

One problem often encountered was Sallie's practice of referring to individuals as "cousin," "uncle," and "aunt," even when they were not relatives. As was the common custom among many southern families at that time, when a cousin married, not only did the cousin's spouse become a "cousin," but any and all brothers and sisters as well! This also extended to the parents of the family, who became "uncle" and "aunt." Uncle and aunt also were sometimes used as titles of respect for older family friends and neighbors, as well as longtime family slaves. One need look no further than the Jewel letters to discover the importance of family among antebellum southerners.

In presenting the Jewel letters, I felt obligated to leave them in their original form as much as possible. Only minor changes involving the insertion of punctuation, which Jewel, like many of his contemporaries, rarely used, have been made. In the interest of readability the text has been divided into paragraphs. The changes have been made without editorial notation so as to avoid changing the flavor and mood of Jewel's style.

Misspellings have been corrected only when it was thought that the reader might find it difficult to decipher the word. Brackets indicate the insertion of missing words. The letters appear with little deletion, and footnotes are added to identify as many of the people and events mentioned as possible.

The Federal census records, published rosters of soldiers, official records, newspapers, personal memoirs, and a wide variety of record sources were invaluable in lending accuracy to this study. Several identities were made or confirmed by visiting family cemeteries in Greene, Oconee, and Oglethorpe counties. Other unpublished Jewel family letters in the author's possession helped identity some individuals.

The family name is alternately spelled Jewel and Jewell in correspondence and various sources and even on the headstones in the family cemetery. Jewel is used herein because that was the form consistently used by James.

Eight of the letters are in the Special Collection Department of the Robert W. Woodruff Library at Emory University. Each is identified as it appears in the text. The remaining letters are in my personal collection.

1   The Gilmer Blues were officially designated as Company K, 6th Regiment, Georgia Volunteer Infantry, Army of Tennessee. The company was named for former Georgia governor and Oglethorpe County resident George Rockingham Gilmer. The company was formed in Lexington, Georgia, in 1860 and was mustered into service in the Confederate Army in May 1861.

2   The Oglethorpe Rifles were mustered into service in Maxeys, Georgia, May 15, 1861, as Company K, 8th Regiment, Georgia Volunteer Infantry, Army of Northern Virginia.

3   The Tom Cobb Infantry was formed in September 1861 and was mustered into service in October as Company E, 38th Regiment, Georgia Volunteer Infantry, Army of Northern Virginia. The unit was named for Brigadier General Thomas Reade Rootes Cobb of Athens, Georgia, brother of Major General Howell Cobb, who was former governor of Georgia and had been Secretary of the Treasury in the cabinet of President James Buchanan. T.R.R. Cobb played an important role in the formation of the Confederate government and was the author of the Confederate Constitution. He was married to Marion McHenry Lumpkin, daughter of Joseph Henry Lumpkin and Callender Cunningham Grieve Lumpkin of Oglethorpe County.

CHAPTER I

Near Griffin, Georgia

"Sallie you have no idea how glad I would be to hear from home"

CAMP STEPHENS
MAY 16/62

Dear Pa

We arrived in Atlanta just before dark. I thought I never saw as many men as was there that night, mostly soldiers going off to different parts of the world.

We slept in the tavern and eat our cold vituals for supper and breakfast. Left there abot six Oclock with two long trains full of soldiers. Some going to Savannah and one company to our camps from green and Talifaro counties [Georgia]. Jack Colclough[1] is here close by us.

As to day is the day set apart for humilation and prayer, we have holiday so that all those who chose might go to town to preaching. I went to the Baptist church where we had a very good sermon and as good singing as I ever heard, I think, any where.

The battallion that was here when we was here before, left for Savanah the day we got here. Two or three days before they left, other companies commenced coming in, about three a day. there is a company just got here since I commence writing and Two more will be here directly, so I understand. I think there is about fifteen companies at this camp now.

They are a going to form two regiments in a few days, which will take about twenty six hundred [men]. There is two or three other camps in the neighborhood of Griffin. They are forming two regiments of cavelry at Camp Ector one mile from griffin on the other side from here.[2]

We have got four guns[3] and will get two more in a day or two, I suppose. We had them tested yesterday evening by a gentleman from Rome [Georgia]. we dismounted the pieces and loaded them with three pounds of powder and a six pound ball with a tight wad on it and fired them by a fuze like blowing rock so as to give everybody a chance to get out of the way if they should burst. I had but very [little] idea of how a cannon was fixed before. they weigh about nine hundred pounds. they are placed on the hind wheels of the carriage and the amunition box on the front ones. The wheels are heavier than the strongest kind of cart wheels. Then we have a carriage of the same kind to each gun with three boxes called caisson and a moveable blacksmith shop.

May 17th. As I did not finish this yesterday I will close this morning. I fell very well this morning and hope you are all well.

The amount of comissary stores burnt in Atlanta was small. I do not know exactly [how much]. It was rumored here that there had been another fire there the day before but I don't know how true it is. They have declared martial law in that citty

I must come to a close as G.W. Martin[4] is mailboy to day and will have to start now soon over to Griffin. I wrote to Eliza day before yesterday thinking that Dock was going home but he did not get off.[5] he will leave this morning Tell Sallie[6] she must write soon and give me all the news.

all of you mus write as soon you can. Give my love to all the friends. Your Son James

PS Direct your letters to Camp Stephens Griffin Ga
Echols Artillery in care of Capt. Tiller[7]

1 Jack Colclough was John F. Colclough, first cousin of Jewel's wife Eliza. John Colclough enlisted in the Confederate Army October 13, 1861, as a Private in Co. D, 2nd Battalion, Georgia State Troops. He was promoted to 3rd Corporal December 30, 1861. Colclough was mustered out of service at Camp Brown near Savannah April 28, 1862, but reenlisted May 5,

1862, as a Private in Co. B, 55th Regiment Georgia Volunteer Infantry and was appointed 4th Sergeant in June 1863. Colclough was captured at Cumberland, Tennessee, September 9, 1863, and died in prison at Camp Douglas, Illinois, January 1864.

2   Griffin is the county seat of Spalding County, Georgia, located about 50 miles south of Atlanta. Camp Ector undoubtedly was named in honor of Colonel Walton Ector of the Meriwether Volunteers, which was Co. B, 13th Regiment, Georgia Volunteer Infantry, Evans Brigade, Gordon's Division, Army of Northern Virginia. Colonel Ector was a veteran of the Mexican War of 1846-1848.

3   Since their's was an artillery company, Jewel was referring to cannons.

4   George Wynn Martin joined the Echols Artillery as a Private in March 1862. His younger brother Tom would join a year later. The 1860 Georgia census identifies George W. Martin as a 26-year-old farmer in the household of his parents, John and Nancy L. Martin, in the Wolfskin District of Oglethorpe County.

5   Eliza was Jewel's wife, Eliza Cordelia Colclough Jewel, and Dock was the nickname of her younger brother Franklin W. Colclough. Colclough was appointed 4th Corporal of Co. D, 2nd Battalion, Georgia State Troops, on October 31, 1861. He mustered out at Camp Brown near Savannah April 28, 1862, but rejoined the army and was appointed 4th Corporal, Co. B, 55th Regiment, Georgia Volunteer Infantry.

6   Sallie was Jewel's younger sister, Sara Rebecca Jewel.

7   Captain John Hopson Tiller organized the Echols Artillery and was its commanding officer. The 1860 Georgia census lists Tiller as a 33-year-old farmer in the Glade District of Oglethorpe County, along with his 27-year-old wife Mary and four children.

CAMP STEPHENS
MAY 22/62

Dear Father

I have been examined by the physician of our company Dr Ham[1] and received fifty dollars bounty which I send to you to keep for Eliza untill she comes home. I send it in care of John P. Tiller[2] to Antioch,[3] there to be left with G.R. Marcum.[4]

I am not as well to day as I have been. I have had a slight head ache, which I think is only caused from cold. John[5] is well. he has gone over to town to stay all night. Some of the boys in camps have the mumps, but none of them are very bad off, I think.

Dr Ham was elected the other day company surgeon. We have moved from where we were when I wrote to you before. we are now encamped on a hill about a half a mile from and in full view of Griffin. we have a very pleasant place and very good water. We are by our selves and the gentleman that owns the land say that he will not let any other company come here. I have no idea how long we will stay here or where we will go. I hope that we will not have to [move] much farther from home, but the prospects look very gloomy now. we have only got four guns [cannons] yet. I do not know whether we will get any more or not but we should have two more, so say the Capt.

We have got a very good tent and have it fixed up in stile with a plank floor in it high enough to put our trunk and other bagage under out of the way at night. We [must] be at the roll calling in the morning a little before sun rise, then get breakfast. [We are] called again at seven Oclock to Drill till ten, then get dinner. then called out at three and drill two hours and sometimes longer, but not often.

If you want any money for your own use, or if you can lone it out in good hands, I would like very well for you to do so, for I don't think I will need it soon. As for my comeing home, I can not say when that will be.

Write as soon as you receive this and let me know whether it got home safe or not. Tell Sallie to write in your place which will do as well if you have not time and let me know how you all are getting along. I received a letter from Eliza today and will answer it tomorrow morning. Dirc [direct] your letters to the same place.

Camp Stephens Griffin
Echols Artillery
Care of Capt. Tiller

Give my love to all the family and friends

I remain your son James Jewel

1   Dr. William G. Ham was listed in the 1860 census as a 29-year-old physician in the Glade District of Oglethorpe County, Georgia, along with his wife Elizabeth and two young sons. Dr. Ham enlisted in the Echols Artillery as a Private March 4, 1862, and was discharged August 20, 1862, by hiring a substitute, John R. Bowers.

2   John P. Tiller was identified in the 1860 census as a 47-year-old farmer in the Simston District of Oglethorpe County, Georgia. Others in the household were Martha, 42, and six children ranging in age from 1 to 18.

3   Antioch was the name of a community in Oglethorpe County, Georgia, between Lexington and Union Point, named for the Antioch Baptist Church established there in 1827. The settlement was renamed Stephens in honor of Alexander H. Stephens, vice-president of the Confederacy and governor of Georgia.

4   George R. Marcum was identified in the 1860 census as a 40-year-old merchant in Maxeys, Georgia, a small community just south of Antioch. Marcum was the Postmaster for the Antioch community from January 20, 1859, to April 19, 1866.

5   John was James Jewel's cousin, John Anderson Jewel. John was the son of William Jewel, brother to James Jewel, Sr. James Jewel, Sr., and his brother William were married to sisters, Rebecca and Elizabeth Bell. Because James Jewel, Sr., also had a son named William, hereafter they will be referred to as William Jewel, I and William Jewel, II. The 1860 Georgia census lists William Jewel, I as a 63-year-old farmer in the Goose Pond District of Oglethorpe County. Others in the household were his wife Elizabeth, 54, and 3 of their 4 sons: George, 32; John, 20; and Mark, 17. Their other son, Edgar, and their two daughters, Emmialy and Camilla, are cited elsewhere.

CAMP STEPHENS
MAY 26TH/62

To: S.R. Jewel

Dear Sallie,

I [have] written two letters home to Pa and I thought some of you would have written before now. Sallie you have no idea how glad I would be to hear from home. I received one last week from Eliza and one from John.[1] I think every day I surely will get a letter by the next mail. I am tolerable well this morning, one of my teeth feels sore like it might be going to ache. I have nearly got well of my cold. The boys in our mess are all well. Cousin John is getting along finely. he seems to enjoy himself very well with Miss Sallie Jorden[2] and Miss Ophelia Colwell[3] over in Griffin. They came over to our camps Saturday evening. he goes out to see them every sunday and sometimes in the week. I went to preaching in town yesterday. There is three churches there, Baptist, Methodist, and Presbiterian. They have [preaching] twice a day at each church. Mr. Vanhoof[4] is the paster of the baptist church.

Some of the boys in this company have the mumps, a good many of them complaining. some one complaint, and some another. Lieut Gibson[5] is sick, he has what is called the roseola, I suppose it resembles the measles. that is what some people call the camp measles, or having them the second time. I sent my bounty money home friday by John P. Tiller, and I am very anxious to know whether Pa has got it or not.[6] Jack Edwards[7] and G.W. Martin sent theirs also. Mine was two 20 and one 10 dollar bills.

Buntin[8] has taken our measures to cut out [our] uniform suit. he is to leave to day or tomorrow for Lexington[9] to get help to cut them out, and then they are to be sent out in the country to be made up. I donot know how long it will be before they will get mine cut. Some body will have to go to town to get it. if any of the neighbors goes there Buntin says he will send them out. the triming will be furnished.

The coats are to be trimmed with red on the outside of the collar and red cuffs. Stripes on the outer seams of the pants. tell the girls to be sure to make pockets in my coat and pants, whether the taylor marks them or not.

We are allowed twenty five dollars for the suit. The Capt says it will cost about fifteen dollars. The cloth cost one dollar and fifty cents per yard. If that is the case I think we will have a cheap Suit.

Frank Collier[10] is going home to morrow and I thought it would be a good chance for me to send this letter and save a postage stamp as they are getting scarce here.

We are improving in cooking a gooddeal. Simon[11] has learned to cook very good biscuit. We had some of the best last night I have seen since the soda give out at home. we have a bench to beat the dough on. Our meat is not of the best but will do to eat. We are saving some of our meat we brought from home for hard times. The comissary brought some here saturday that was spoilt and the capt sent it back [to] town and got more. They sold seven thousand pounds of bacon in Griffin saturday from five to ten cents. I did not see any of it but I think it must have been badly spoilt. so much so that the soldiers would not have it.

We have nearly got through with our butter that we brought from home. I recon we will have to do without till Frank comes back from home. he say he will bring some with him. I look for a letter from Brother Marshal[12] tomorrow by Charlie Sims.[13] You must write as soon as you can when you get this. if you have not written, sit down and write without delay. we get the mail here every day, sunday not excepted, at half past nine Oclock. Tell Mary and Mat[14] they must write and I will answer them as soon as I can. Give my love to all the friends. I remain you affectionate brother James

P.S. Tell Pa when he settles with Wm Edwards[15] pay him fifty cents for me for Shoeing Brother Marshals horse as I forgot it when I left home.

James Jewel

1 It is not clear to which John he refers; however, it most likely was his wife's younger brother John Colclough.

2 Sarah Jordan was listed in the 1860 Georgia census as the 17-year-old daughter of Methodist preacher Willis Jordan of Griffin. Among others in the household was her younger sister Martha, age 14 (cited elsewhere).

3 Ophelia Colwell is unidentified.

4 Azor Vanhoose [not Vanhoof] was listed in the 1860 Georgia census as a Baptist minister in Griffin, Georgia. The census indicates that he was born in Tennessee.

5 John Glenn Gibson enlisted in the Echols Artillery March 4, 1862, as a 2nd Lieutenant. He was eventually promoted to First Lieutenant and served until the end of the war. Gibson was listed in the 1860 Georgia census as a 28-year-old "Student of Law" in the household of Martha J. Hartsfield, a farmer, in the Glade District of Oglethorpe County. Gibson was born in Morgan County, Alabama, March 29, 1832, and moved to Oglethorpe County as a teenager. He attended Oglethorpe County schools and studied law under John T. Loften of Lexington. Before the war he served as Clerk of the Inferior and Superior Courts. After the war he was Judge of the County Court. He became an ordained Baptist minister in 1865 and served as pastor for several Oglethorpe County churches. Gibson died in 1900.

6   Each of the volunteers of the Echols Artillery was paid $50.00 bounty upon enlisting in the Confederate Army.

7   Private Thomas Jack Edwards was the company bugler. T.J. Edwards, Jr., also served as a Private in the Echols Artillery. Though probably related, they were not father and son.

8   Fourth Corporal John Bunting was listed in the 1860 Georgia census as a 29-year-old merchant/tailor living with the Thomas Stewart family in Lexington, Georgia. Bunting, Stewart, and Stewart's wife Margaret, were identified as born in Ireland. The oldest of Stewart's eight children was born in New York, and the rest were born in Georgia.

9   Lexington is the county seat of Oglethorpe County, Georgia, settled in the the late eighteenth century and incorporated in 1806.

10   Frank P. Collier enlisted in the Echols Artillery as a Private May 3, 1862, and served until the end of the war. Collier is listed in the 1860 Georgia census as a 23-year-old school teacher in Maxeys, Georgia, living with the H.C. Parrish family.

11   Simon was a slave of cousin John A. Jewel. It was common practice during the War Between the States for soldiers to have slaves accompany them into service to act as cooks and manservants. The 1862 Tax Digest for Oglethorpe County showed that John Jewel's father, William, I, owned 47 slaves.

12   Marshall W. Edwards was married to Jewel's older sister, Jane. Marshall Edwards' parents were Lemuel and Mary Johnson Edwards. The 1860 Georgia census lists him as a 39-year-old farmer in the Buck Branch District of Clarke County, along with Jane, 34, Lemuel J., 11, Rebecca, 5, and George M., 3 months. Edwards also was a Baptist minister.

13   Charles W. Sims is listed in the 1860 Georgia census as age 19 and living in the household of John Sims, 78, and Martha Sims, 60, in the Beaver Dam District of Oglethorpe County. Sims enlisted in the Echols Artillery as a Private but was soon promoted to Corporal. He was discharged November 11, 1862, by hiring a substitute, D.E. Stinson.

14   Mary and Margaret were Jewel's twin sisters born November 23, 1827. Neither ever married. Mary died February 24, 1887, and Margaret died September 1, 1912.

15   This probably was the William Edwards listed in the 1860 Georgia census as a 58-year-old farmer who lived near the Jewels in the Wolfskin District of Oglethorpe County. Also in the Edwards household, in addition to his wife Narcissus W., age 53, were eight other individuals with the surnames Edwards, Ellis, and Harrison.

CAMP STEPHENS
MAY 29, 1862

Dear Sister

As I have a little leasure time I thought I would write a few lines in answer to yours sent by Cob Davis[1] which I received Tuesday morning. I am in very good health. I have nearly got well of my cold I had when I wrote to you last. Tell Ma I have not taken any of the salts yet for I have not needed anything of that sort. I have take one dram of the brandy I brought with me and that is all that has been taken out of the bottle yet. I told the boys in my mess when I brought it here that it was well understood that it was not to be used unless in case of sickness and they don't say any thing about it. my wine has not been opened yet. I would be glad if it was so that I could have a dram some times of a morning, but if I had it to use it would soon be found out and would be gone before you could turn round twice.

Capt Tiller left here yesterday at twelve Oclock for richmond. he has gone on some business, I donot know exactly what Some of the company say to see something about getting horses. I expect it is to see something about where we are to go from here. Lieutenant William Smith[2] is officer in command while he is gone. The captain addressed the company yesterday morning before he left, which was a fine thing for some of the boys. he sayed that some of them had violated his rules as though they cared nothing for them at all by getting permission to [go into] town in the morning and to be back by three Oclock, but staying all night and coming back drunk. he sayed he thought that it was doing injustice to those who was disposed to do right to let such go unpunished. Therefore it would not be done any more. He said that he would be obliged to stop giving furloughs to go home for every day there was some body wanting a furlough which kept so many out of the company that we would never learn to drill as we should. That part of it I, for one, you may guess, did not like so well. for I want to go home but I am not the only one that want to get home. but still I have [not]

sayed any thing to him about going. I think if we stay here long I
will stand a chance of getting back again, I hope so at least. Frank
Collier took a notion last sunday that he would go home as he had
not been and went to the capt for a furlough which was granted
for seven days. The capt told him to wait about a month [and] he
could get a furlough for twenty five days, so he declined going at
that time.

The crowd that went home when Cob Davis did stayed two days
over their time and some of them have not come back yet. I think
there is three missing. I recon they are sick. When I come here I
talked to the Capt about getting off from his company and was in
hopes of getting off but he sayed that there was no chance unless a
regular discharge. If I could get a contract for making canteens I
would [be] transfered from here by the government. I see no other
chance but to take what come, let it be what it maybe. I feel that I
have as much right to fight for my country as a great many that have
already gone although it is very sad for me to think of the loved
ones at home. somehow or other, I can not tell why, I think we all
will meet again before long. Sometime I think of the war going on
three or four years. O how dredful it is to think of. None but the all
wise providence knows and I feel thankfull that it is so.

We have received news here for several day the tide is turned in
our favor in virginia   Stone Wall Jackson has completely routed
the yankie army near winchester. The reports say that he has
captured all their baggag, amunitions, and a great many guns,
and they are now crossing the Potomac in to Maryland. I hope
it is true. General Beauregard is still waiting for them at Cornith
[Mississippi]. We all are listening to hear of a big fight at Richmond
every day. I understand that president Davis says that he is going to
try [to] defend Richmond at all hazards. I would not be surprised
to hear that it was evacuated by our people.

You sayed Ma wanted to [know] who was in the mess with me
and what we eat. If I could see her I could tell her all about it better
than I can write. There is Cousin John, Jack Edwards, Frank Collier,
George Martin, Josep Armstron,[3] and McKinebrew.[4] They are all
very steady clever sort of fellows. I think we have the best mess in
the company without any exception, all the others are mixed up
with some wicked fellows.

We take it turn about in cooking. two to help Sci[5] get breakfast and two at dinner and [two] to get Supper. I and Jack Edwards attend to getting supper. We have biscuit, coffee, fried meat, and some times corn bread for breakfast. I can fry meat and potatoes very well and make very good rye coffee. I dont know how it will be when our rye gives out. McKinebrew brought about a bushel of potatoes with him so we have had a plenty of them untill [now]. We have bacon and dry peas for dinner when the boys fell like cooking them. The bacon we get is not of the best but we have enough to get some that will do to eat. We have had fresh beef twice since we have been here. We boil it and then make hash. We have biscuit like common   sometime they are very good and sometimes tolerable flat   I have made a bench and mall to beat dough with.

Our vituals eats a bout as well to us I recon as it commonly does at home, not that I think that it is as good, but I recond we have a better appetite for it. We have had a plenty of butter all the time untill now. We were near about out day before yesterday when we received a small bottle full from aunt Betsy[6] and a pone of light bread. we will finish our butter to night and then I recon we will have to do with out and eat gravy. our meat is fat enough to make gravy. We have been saving our gravy to put in biscuit so as to save our lard as long as we could. Some of them brought lard with them when they come. we have not used a greatdeal of it yet.

Sallie I thought every [since] I have commenced writing this I would take more time and write all the news but would get in a hurry to send it off. So I thought I [would] try and write this sheet but I donot know whether I will get through or not.   I saw a young lady last week up here that didnot have any arms nor never had any at all. She looked like any one withe their armes cut off smooth with their shoulders. She can do almost any kind of work such as braeding hair. I cannot tell how she does it.

The ladies visit our camp very often. Two Miss Jordan, two Miss Turners and a Miss Ware[7] of Griffin. McKinebrew's wife[8] is boarding here in town about as far from camps as from our house to mrs Lumpkins,[9] so he can go [there] after supper and get back to breakfast. Lieut Gibson was taken sick sunday with some thing like the measles but he says he has had the measles a long time ago. he went over to town to stay untill he got well. As

I cannot finish this to day I will to morrow morning.

May 30th   I slept very well last night and have been to roll call this morning. breakfast is not ready yet. Cous. John is well. Some of the boys in the company have the mumps but none of them is very bad off. Martial law has been declared in town to take effect this morning. Two from our company have been orderd to go to stand guard. Joseph Armstrong and a man by the name of Amosson[10] is going to day.

I received a letter from John yesterday and one from Eliza tuesday and wrote to her wednesday. I wrote to you that Buntin was going home monday. he has not gone yet. he told me last night that he did not know when he would go. I will let you all know so you can get my clothes to make. I think [that he] has not got the money to pay for the cloth that has been sent to Atlanta and they will not let him have it on credit. I must close. I thought I would write with a pencil as it is more convenient. Write soon and let me know whether Pa has got my bounty money or not. Give my love to all enquireing friends. I remain your affectionat brother   James.

So good bye

1   This was Howell Cobb Davis, son of William J. and Angelina Lumpkin Davis. Cobb Davis' mother died November 10, 1847, and his father died September 8, 1857. Cobb and some of his younger siblings lived with his older brother, Middleton Pope Davis, who married Mary Frances Thompson. Cobb Davis entered service in the Echols Artillery on March 4, 1862, as a Corporal but was later promoted to Sergeant.

2   Lieutenant William M. Smith was instrumental in the formation of the Echols Artillery and was among the first to join the company on March 4, 1862. He resigned December 12, 1862, due to poor health. He was listed in the 1860 census as a 31-year-old lawyer in Lexington, Georgia.

3   Joseph W. Armstrong enlisted in the Echols Artillery as a Private on May 3, 1862, and served until the end of the war.

4   McKinebrew apparently was Jewel's nickname for Marcus B. Kinnebrew, listed in the 1860 Georgia census as the 22-year-old overseer on the farm of his father, C.D. Kinnebrew. Among the seven others in the household was his 17-year-old brother John, a Sergeant in the Echols Artillery (cited elsewhere).

5   Cousin John's slave Simon.

6   Aunt Betsy was Elizabeth Bell Jewel, Cousin John Jewel's mother.

7 The two Jordans were probably Sarah Jordan (previously identified) and her younger sister Martha Jordan. The Turners were probably Margaret A. Turner and Martha Green Turner, teenaged daughters of Levi Hancock Turner and Frances Bibb Harper Turner of McDonough, Georgia, in Henry County. Miss Ware is unidentified.

8 Marcus B. Kinnebrew had married Julia M. Edmondson in Greene County, May 9, 1862. She is listed in the 1860 Georgia census as the 16-year-old daughter of William and Matilda Edmondson, farmers in the Woodville District of Greene County.

9 Lucy Lumpkin lived near the Jewels in Oglethorpe County with her sons, M.W. Johnson, 24, and W.W. Johnson, 22. She was born Lucy Deupree, February 17, 1801. On May 13, 1817, she married James Johnson, who had been previously married to Polly George and had five children. Lucy had eight children by Johnson before he died in November 1839. She married Samuel Lumpkin 5 years later on December 6, 1844. She died August 8, 1871.

10 Manoah Bolton Amason [not Amosson] was listed on the muster roll of the Echols Artillery as 2nd Corporal. His name also appears as Amerson.

CAMP TILLER
JUNE 2ND 62

Dear Sister

I received two letters from you [since I have] written. the last one relieved me as you might suppose. Frank Collier was taken sick Friday. his Uncle came over saturday morning and took him to his house. he is getting well again [and] he will be back to camp to morrow.

I went with George Martin [to] Uncle Richard Sims'es and [to] Mr Threlkeld's[1] saturday. we went to Mr Threldkeld to supper and then [went] back to Mr. Sims'es, which is but a short distance [and] stayed untill eight Oclock Sunday morning. we then came to town and staye a little while and went back to Mr Threlkeld to dinner. Miss mollie and her mother[2] and Mrs Sims came over to our camps Friday morning and brought us some english peas, beets, light bread, and butter milk. They told us we must send Sci out there to morrow and they would send us some vegetables and buttermilk. We will have rough living this week if there is not an alteration. Our meat that we have is badly spoilt and have only half allowance of sugar. we have some lard yet but no butter. Lieut Wm Smith has gone to town to try to get some better meat for us. I hope he will succed. They have a great deal of Spoilt meat in Griffin. they Sold eight thousand pounds that was spoilt saturday to the country people.

They have received some Glorious news here to day by telegraph, if [it] be true. Stone wall Jackson has crossed the Potomac on his way to washington and our forces had whipped the yankeys badly at Richmond. I am really in hopes this [is] true but I cannot tell whether it is or not.³ I have heard that Capt Tiller went home last week and was going to start to Richmond to day. He said when he left here that he would be in Richmond and would get back here this week if he could, but I cant tell how long he will be gone.

Martial law is in effect now in Griffin. We have to send two from our company to guard 24 hours at a time. They have to stand at their post two hours and rest four hours out of the twenty four hours. All the boys that had the mumps are getting well again. There is a fellow here who has been down for nearly four weeks. The most of them that get sick go home. I dont know why he did not unless he got to sick to travel. Frank Collier come to camp today but went back again. he says he is going to try [to get] a furlough to go home now. If he does I will let you [know] before he comes back from home.

Eliza wrote to me yesterday that Doc [Franklin W. Colclough] is comeing up here the tenth of this month and her Pa talkes of comeing. if he does she is comeing with him. if they come I want you all to send us a box of provisions. you must let Aunt Betsy know of it. When you send us any, let it be something that will keep. Butter, egg, light bread or cracker, gingercakes, or any thing of that sort. Chickens are worth from thirty to fifty cent here and very scarce at that.

Buntin has not gone home yet he says he has no idea when he will, not before the Capt comes back I recon. I thought if I had time betwen this and tomorrow morning I would writ a little to Mary Crowley.⁴ if I dont I will try and write to her some time this week. I will stop and write a line or two in the morning to let you know how I am.

June 3rd   I am well this morning. It is raining this morning. I think it [rained] nearly all night. It rained a little here sunday evening with a little hail Jack Edwards went to his cousin in henry county. he says the ground was covered with hail and the wind blowed down the wheat. the wheat is sorry here. Some have cut their wheat about here. corn is very small but is growing finely. I have not seen any cotton in some time. I dont know whether it is growing or not.

One of our company Henry Firkron[5] went to town saturday evening and did not get back to roll call. So Lieut Smith thought he would punish him by making him go on guard sunday. So he stayed all day and night and forgot to come back monday morning. The officers sent four men after him and had him arrested and brough to camps and Still have him under arrest. I don't know what they will do with him. I must come to a close. write soon. If you see Mary tell her I will write to [her] soon.

Lieut Smith called on the company last night for them to raise eight hundred and fifty to pay for the cloth to make our uniform. The Capt has not drawn the money for us yet. They have sent 800 yards to Atlanta and they want the money, that is the Roswell factory.[6] Nothin more at present.

Give [my love] to all enquirin friends. Your Brother James

1   Richard H. Sims is identified in the 1860 Georgia census as a cotton broker in Griffin. Others in the household were Amanda A., 27, four children, and Emily L. Owens, 20. Mr. Threlkeld was Thomas Threlkeld, listed in the census as a 50-year-old Baptist preacher, along with his wife Elizabeth, 47, and Mary J. Threlkeld, 16. The census noted that Thomas Threlkeld was born in South Carolina.

2   Miss Mollie was Mary J. Threlkeld and her mother was Elizabeth Threlkeld (cited above).

3   Confederate forces under General Robert E. Lee successfully defended Richmond against invasion by the Union Army under General George B. McClellan for several weeks during late May and June 1862. Confederate General Thomas J. "Stonewall" Jackson did not join Lee in the fighting around Richmond until the end of June, but his activities in the northern Shenandoah Valley in late May and early June played an important roll in the defense of the Confederate capital; Jackson's army of about 17,000 men kept 40-60,000 Union troops occupied for weeks with the threat of an invasion of Washington but did not cross the Potomac River at that time.

4   Mary Crowley was Jewel's niece, daughter of his older sister Elizabeth and her husband Benajah Crowley. Jewel always used her surname in his letters to distinguish her from his sister Mary.

5   H.C. Furcron (not Firkron) enrolled in the Echols Artillery as a Private on May 3, 1862, and served until the end of the war. His name also appears on the muster roll as Fircron.

6   Roswell Factory was established by Roswell King and his son Barrington soon after the community of Roswell was settled by the King family in Cobb County [now Fulton], Georgia, in the late 1830s. The factory became a successful cotton manufacturing plant, and by the time of the War Between the States the operation consisted of two cotton mills and one woolen mill. The mills were important in the production of goods for the Confederacy. When General William T. Sherman captured Atlanta in July 1864, the owners were flying a French flag in hope of appearing neutral and avoiding the destruction of the buildings. In addition to knowing that the facilities were a tremendous asset to the Confederate cause, Sherman was so enraged by the flying of the French flag that not only were the buildings and machinery burned, but he ordered the owners and the 400 women employees to be arrested, charged with treason, and sent North. They were carried by railroad to Jeffersonville, Ohio, and released. Some eventually returned home, but some settled and remained in Ohio.

CAMP TILLER
JUNE 14/62
7-OCLOCK.P.M.

Dear Sister.

I went to town this evening as I had not heard from the box that was to be sent by Doc. I thought I would inquire at the express office and see if it was there, thinking that I was not going to get and lo it was there. Sallie you dont know how glad I was. So there was a wagon going to camps with provisions so I put my box on and jumped up on it and rode to the camps as proud as you need want to see any body, and some of the boys in my mess were nere about as glad as I was. I have not been exactly well this week. I feel well to day. I have a sore mouth and my toung has been a little sore which I think is caused by some tobacco I bought last week in town so I have quit useing [it] to see if my mouth wont get well. Sallie I liked to forgot to tell you how the things was in the box. every thing come perfectly safe just as it was put up. The fried chickens was not so good as fresh, but we can eat it. The bottle of brandy peaches is very good.

I dont know how long the box had been at the depot for I had not inquired. I went there thursday and thought I would be sure to see Doc but he did not come. five of the company came up here after their tents and other equipage. I asked Billie Davison[1] about Doc. he sayed that he left him at home and Thomas[2] had joined their company and come on with them. The company stopped in Atlanta until those that come here got back there. They got here at half past eight Oclock and left at half after one, then I commenced writing. I thought I would write a few lines before dark and finish in the morning. so good night.

Sunday morning. Dear Sister I have eat a hearty breakfast this morning and now I will write you a few more lines if I can think of any thing to write. I do not know hardly what to write. I and Jack Edward are alone in the [tent] both writing. Joseph Armstrong has gone aroung to see some of the rest of them.

George Martin come from his Uncles friday morning sick and lay about here untill evening, when Mrs Sims, his wife, and Mit[3] come to our camps and spent a part of the evening and George went home with them. he has not come back yet. I saw John Edwards[4] yesterday going to camp McDonald. all the regiment has gone. they all went on their horses but a few, to take charge of the baggage and the sick that were carried on the [railroad] cars. John says he dont think they will stay there long before they will have to go to Camp Randolph about seventy five miles up the railroad towards chattanooga.

One of the Yankey prisoners was buried over in town yesterday evening. They are here yet. I have not seen them since the day they were brought here. Our company has been relieved from guard duty entirely now from town and all. if it had not been so I recon I should have seen the yankeys again before this time. some of the boys go there most every day. I am affraid some of them will [catch] lice from them and bring them to our camps.

I recon some of you will see cousin John before he comes [back here]. he told me if he did not see any of you he would go to our house. If you see him he can give you all the news. I have paid out fourteen dollars toward my uniform suit and I hope I wont have to pay any more untill I get it. Smith told us the other day all that wanted their coats wadded in the front would have to write to Buntin about it I wont you all to make mine in the common Stile of Military coats. Capt Tiller has not got back here yet. I recon when the capt gets back he will get the money to pay for our clothes. the buttons cost $1.75 per dozen. the company had raised money to pay for them before we could have them sent to Lexington.

I had my hair cut the other day and send you some. you must give Eliza a lock of it. I must [close] for the present as I want to go to church to day and it is nearly time for me to get ready. Tell Bud⁵ when you see him he must write to me. You must all write when you can. if Eliza is not home you must let me know. so good bye Sallie.

I remain your affectionate brother James

P.S.

You did not date your [letter] sent in the box, consequently I could not tell when it was written. I am glad you sent me the Testament.

1   William Davison [also seen as Davidson] is listed in the 1860 Georgia census as the 16-year-old son of James M. Davison, a farmer in the Woodville District of Greene County. James M. Davison was born in Ireland. William Davison enlisted January 10, 1862, as a Private in Co. D, 2nd Battalion, Georgia State Troops. He was mustered out of service at Camp Brown near Savannah April 28, 1862. He reentered service May 5, 1862, as 2nd Sergeant of Co. B, 55th Regiment, Georgia Volunteer Infantry. Davison was discharged with a disability in June 1862 but reenlisted in June 1864.

2   Thomas was another of Jewel's brothers-in-law, Thomas F. Colclough, older brother of Jewel's wife Eliza. Colclough enlisted May 5, 1862, as a Private in Co. B, 55th Regiment, Georgia Volunteer Infantry.

3   Mit was George Martin's sister Lucinda J. Camp (cited elsewhere).

4   John Edwards is unidentified, but he may have been related to Jewel's brother-in-law Marshall Washington Edwards.

5   Bud was Jewel's older brother William, II.

CAMP TILLER
JUNE 24TH 1862

Dear Sister.

I went to Atlanta yesterday evening and met Eliza and Cousin John[1] They got along [on their trip] very well. we came here this morning, and we are now at Mr Jordans[2] We are both well. it was very dusty traveling on the cars.

Sallie I wish you could have been along too. I got to Atlanta at four Oclock so I went in to the tavern and engaged a room, and then I went out to Hammochs & Langston store[3] and stayed with them a little and then walked about over town.

I began to get very impatient waiting for the train to come from the Point,[4] but a little after sundown I heard the whistle blow and dont you recon I was glad. I got where I could see and saw Eliza before the cars stopped and I knew where she was. if I had not seen her then it might have been sometime before I could have found her in the crowd that was there.

Sallie I have no news of any importance to write. I put on my uniform and wore it over to the camps to day. The boy were very much taken with it. my coat is a little tight across the shoulders and I think most too short in the waist. it will do very well I recon. the stripe on the pants should have been a cord put in like my blue ones at home. they fit very nice I think. When the company all gets their suits I think it will be worth looking at. I will close for the present as I must go to camp & write a little more in the morning.

June 25th I have just eat breakfast at camps [and] it is now about six oclock. we are both well, Eliza is not complaining at all. Jack Edwards has got the bowel complaint pretty bad. the rest of our mess is well. some few of the company are sick but not many. James Johnson[5] has got about again. We have not got any horses yet, nor I dont know when we will get any. It is very dry here. the corn is suffering. There is some prospects of rain this morning but you know all signs fail in dry weather. I am at a loss to know what to write. The flies pester me so bad I have to keep knocking at them to keep them out of my face so I can write. I dont think I ever saw them worse than they are here. Cousin John has not been to see Sallie[6] yet. she was very much disappointed at his not comeing into see her when he come. he went in the piazza but did not go into the room where she was and from what she said to me she was badly disappointed. Sallie you must excuse bad writing as I have a bad pen and sorry ink. You must write soon

Next week we will have to pay ten cents postage a letter[7] and I expect some of us will have to stop writing so much.

Give my love to all the friends. Jack Edwards sends his best respects to you all for the cake you sent me.

I remain your affectionate brother James

1   Jewel's wife Eliza, who was 6 months pregnant with their first child, had come for a visit, accompanied by Cousin John. Jewel had taken the train to Atlanta to meet her and accompany her to camp in Griffin. When her visit of about 12 days ended, Jewel escorted her home and had a short furlough.

2   Probably Reverend Willis Jordan (already identified).

3   Hammocks & Langstons store actually was Langston, Crane, & Hammock, a dry goods store on the corner of Whitehall and Alabama Streets in Atlanta. Thomas L. Langston, Benjamin E. Crane, and Cicero C. Hammock were all listed in the 1860 Georgia census as residents of Oglethorpe County. At that time, Langston and Crane were identified as merchants and lived in the same household. Hammock was the Clerk of Court for Oglethorpe County. All three became prominent in business and civic affairs, and Crane and Hammock both served terms as mayor of Atlanta in the 1870s and 1880s.

4   The Point was Union Point, a community on the Georgia Railroad in Greene County, Georgia. It was named Union Point because it was the place where a spur line of the railroad to Athens united with the main line which ran from Augusta to Atlanta and other points west.

5   James T. Johnson joined the Echols Artillery as a Private May 5, 1862, and served until the end of the war. Johnson is identified in the 1860 Georgia census as a 39-year-old merchant in Lexington, Georgia.

6   Jewel probably was referring to Sarah Jordan (already identified).

7   The rate for a standard letter for delivery up to 500 miles was doubled by the Confederate Postal Service July 1, 1862.

CAMP TILLER
JUNE 29TH/62

Dear Sallie

I have been thinking all day I would write to you but I did not have any paper to write on without going over to camps to get it. It was so hot & I was so lazy I put it off till late this evening. I am very well myself. Eliza is complaining a little with the toothache. We have heard some good [news] yesterday and to day. Our forces have whipped the Yankeys at Richmond and have completely surrounded McClellands army. We have taken a great many prisoners. One hundred commissioned officers and three Brigadier Generals. it is said to be a more complete victory than that of Manassas.[1] If they can get McClelland prisoner and distroy his army I think you will hear talk of peace soon, or at least I hope so anyhow.

We had a very pretty shower of rain friday evening just before night and another still better yesterday evening.

I did not have time to write much before supper and I put it off untill after drill hours to day which is monday and it is now half past nine oclock. I do not feel so well this morning as I have done. Eliza was sick last night but she is up this [morning] and tolerable well. I reckon when she gets home she will have something to tell you all, perhaps more than you would have found out any other way in a great while. I have not heard any news this morning. I have not been up in town yet, I expect to go soon. It was telegraphed here last night that the seventh & eight Ga reg. suffered very much in the fight.

Sallie I thought I would be certain to get a letter from some of you yesterday. tell Mary Crowley I recon she has forgotten me entirely. I thought when she wrote to me if I would answer her letter she would write again, but it has been so long and now the postage will be double, I will now give up the idea of seeing a letter from her. You must all recollect that there is a great many at home

that I want to write to but I cannot write to every one. if I did it
would take all my time and money too. Sallie I expect to write
to some of you at home as often as once a week as long as I have
money and the chance to do so and I want you all to do the same.
If I cant be at home to see any thing there nor hear from there, how
do you reckon I would feel. why I can tell you I would feel like I had
no home nor friends either for a while.

I am going to try to get off to come with Eliza home next friday
as I expect she will Start that day and get home saturday evening.
I think it is very doubtful whether capt. Tiller will let me off to go
with her any further than Atlanta or not. he has refused to let some
of them go with their wives home and I expect he will treat me the
same way. We will have time to look around in Atlanta two or three
hour when we get there.

I must close with my love to you all.

I remain your affectionate brother James Jewel

PS. Cousin John got a letter from Mark[2] last friday   he was well but
no telling where [he] is now   J.J.

---

1   Jewel was probably referring to Confederate General J.E.B. Stuart's famous 4-day "ride
around McClellan's army" during a reconnaissance mission June 12-15, 1862. Although
Confederate General Robert E. Lee was considered victorious in defending Richmond in
several major battles in Virginia in May and June 1862, he did not capture McClellan and
both sides suffered heavy losses.

2   Mark was Cousin John Jewel's younger brother, Marcus de Lafayette Jewel. Mark Jewel
joined the Oglethorpe Rifles as a Private on May 28, 1861, and served until the end of the war.

CAMP TILLER
JULY 9TH/62

Dear Sallie

I left Greensborough monday night at nine Oclock and come to Atlanta with a company of soldiers from Augusta going to Chatanooga belonging to Major Capers Battallion.[1] I got to Atlanta at two Oclock in the night and I went into the ladies saloon. there was three or four ladies in there and a few soldiers. I lay down on the seats and took a short nap of sleep. I saw a man in there that was wounded by the cars at Ringold [Georgia]. I reckon you have heard of the accident [there] last sunday. You heard that Major Capers battallion was to pass the Unionpoint satturday going to chatanooga. Ivens Lawrence, Billy Howard, and Jim Calloway[2] belonged to a company in the Battallion. Sunday when they got up about Ringold Station a little this side of Chatanooga they very unexpectingly met a train coming down and the engineers did not see each other untill they were very close to gether. one of them was blown into pieces and the other one killed also. seven negroes and five soldiers killed and thirty six or seven soldiers wounded, a good many scalded by the engine. from what I have heard it was a complete smash up of the two trains.[3] I have not heard any news from Richmond of any consequence since I left home.

It was cloudy this morning and looked like rain but the clouds have nearly all disappeared and it is very warm. Cousin John and Jack Edwards have got the bowel complaint again. several of the company have it. I cant tell what can be the cause of so much of it. George Martin and his wife went home yesterday. he received a letter stating his mother was sick and wanted him to come home. I will write the [back] page of this to Eliza as she expects to be with you all friday.

I remain your affectionate brother James

1   Major Capers was Henry D. Capers of the 12th Battalion of Georgia Artillery.

2   Evan (not Ivens) H. Lawrence and William T. Howard enlisted as Privates in Co. A, 12th Battalion, Georgia Light Artillery, April 10, 1862. Both transferred to Co. A, 63rd Regiment, Georgia Volunteer Infantry, in October 1862. Lawrence served until the end of the war and was paroled at New Bern, North Carolina, in April 1865. Howard was captured at Kennesaw Mountain, Georgia, and sent to a prison in Louisville, Kentucky, July 14, 1864, and was transferred to Camp Douglas, Illinois, July 16, 1864. Howard was released June 16, 1865. Jim Calloway is unidentified.

3   The train wreck occurred July 6, 1862. A combination mail/passenger/troop train traveling north from Atlanta to Chattanooga hit a freight train headed south. Engineer Sylvester Cannon was killed.

CAMP TILLER
JULY 9 1862

Dear Wife

According to promis I will write you a few lines to let you know I arrived safe at camps yesterday morning and am now enjoying very good health. I met with Mr James Hall Sr[1] in Greensborough and he treated me very kindly. I went in the store and asked him for a piece of tobacco and offered to pay him for it but he would not have it. I talked with him a while and then we went out to his boarding house to supper. I came all the way to Atlanta without seeing a man that I was acquainted with. McKinebrew did not come till this morning. Mat Pass[2] got back this morning.

When I got to Griffin Cousin John met me there and told me there had been a fuss raised in the company and they had not drill any since I left. Wm Smith had said that Dr Jerrell[3] our 1st Sargent was an under minding sort of a fellow and he had been trying to get the company against Dr Ham so they would turn him out of his office so that he could take his place. Dr Jerrell attacked Smith about it and told him he would have to give some satisfaction about it and if he did not give it now he would have it to do when they both got upon an equality. Smith got scared and left sunday without telling any of them where he was going. he has not got back yet.

I dont think there is one of the Privates in the company that does not like Dr Jerrell as well as any one. Gibson has gone to Richmon to see his brother that was wounded in the fight there, so the third Lieut has command of the company. I am sorry that this thing has taken place. I recon there will be a report about it in Oglethorpe soon.

We have got nine horses here and I expect will have some more. I thought when I commenced writing I would write a little and finish in the morning so if I do I will have to add a little more paper so I will stop for the present as it is nearly four Oclock. [James]

1　James F. Hall, Sr., is listed in the 1860 Georgia census as a clerk in Greene County, living in the household of B.F. Green, a merchant.

2　Matthew J.H. Pass enrolled in the Echols Artillery May 3, 1862, as a Private and served until the end of the war. Pass is listed in the 1860 Georgia census as the 20-year-old son of M.J. and Nancy Pass, residents of the Buck Branch District of Clarke County and neighbors to Marshall and Jane Edwards. At the time of the 1850 census, the family lived in Oglethorpe County.

3　Dr. William H. Jarrell and his brothers Jesse Lewis Jarrell and John Warner Jarrell all served in the Echols Artillery. They were the sons of Stinson S. Jarrell and Susan Thompson Davenport of what is now Oconee County, Georgia. Dr. Jarrell had been a student at Jefferson Medical College at Philadelphia before the war, but he and other southern students left that school at the time of John Brown's raid at Harper's Ferry, Virginia. Dr. Jarrell continued his studies at Augusta, Georgia, and received his medical degree. After the war he practiced medicine in Oglethorpe County and died in Lexington in 1884.

CAMP TILLER
JULY 17TH 1862

Dear Sallie

I received your letter of the 12 inst last tuesday morning and thought I would have answered it before now, but I thought I would write to Eliza and then to you as soon as I had an opportunity. I received a letter from Mary Crowley yesterday by G.W. Martin and one from Eliza to day. Eliza is not very well, she says she has a pain in her neck and Shoulders. This leaves me in very good health. our mess is all well, and getting along very well. We are living very well at present and have been since I came from home. George Martin brought a box with him yesterday. he brought some peaches and a few apples and irish potatoes.

Last tuesday Mr Thomas Edwards and his wife[1] come to see us and dined with us. I recon you will think very strange of it. the first lady that has ever eat at our table. you ought to have seen how we were fixed up. Sallie, I will tell you what she brought with her and then you may guess whether we was glad to see them or not. She brought us a nice piece of boiled ham, a pone of lightbread, about ten pounds of very nice butter, a big jug full of butter milk, and some as nice ginger cakes as I ever eat. After dinner Mr James Edwards and his wife[2] came over. They are cousins to Jack Edwards and live in Henry County about twelve miles from here. they gave me and cousin John a special invitation to come out and see them in a week or two and we could have as many peaches and watermelons as we could eat.

I think we will try to go out there about next saturday week and stay untill sunday evening if we Stay here. I dont know how long we will stay here, no more than [I knew] when I was at home.

We have thirty one horses besides three for the Lieut and two mules. The officers horses were brought from home. Capt Tiller sent nine here yesterday from home. The others were bought up in Griffin and Atlanta, by the quarter masters of those places.

I have understood that the Capt will be here tomorrow with some more but I dont know how many. Lieut D. Smith our third Lieut[3] is in command yet. I wrote to you that Lieut Wm Smith had gone home he come back saturday and gave orders that there should be no more furloughs granted under no considerations untill the Capt came back and all that has gone home were to be here by friday.

I dont know what is going to happen, that day is tomorrow. He left monday and I have not heard from him since. some of the company say he has gone to savanah. There is great deal of dissatisfaction in the company about the way some of them have done lately. Dr Ham has quit us and gone to Atlanta to the hospital. that is what I call another Lumpkin scrape right over.

So now we are left without a surgeon in our company. I recon we will elect one soon as we have three Doctors in the company, but they have no medicines, nor wont have until we elect one of them.

I recon you are tired of this so I will stop it for the present. You wrote that you wanted to know something about fixing up a box of provisions. you all may send any thing in the line of vegetables you have. I dont suppose you have much as it has been so dry. Lightbread & butter is very acceptable. I would be glad to have some peaches but I [think] we had better wait untill they get ripe good. I would like some rosenears[4] to eat. I and Eliza was talking while I was at home, I told her I didnt think they would [keep] well but McKinebrew brought some with him and they kept several days. you must not send me any unless you let me know before you start it from home.

I must close as my paper is about come to a point. You must write as often as once a week if you can. It is getting cloudy and looks like it might rain soon. the crops are very fine here. if the people dont make corn here I think it will be because it has not been worked right as it has not suffered any.

Give my love to all the family and friends. I hope I will get the chance to come to see you all again before long, but I dont [know] that it will be so. a short visit is better than none at all. I remain your affectionate brother James

---

1   Thomas J. Edwards is listed in the 1860 Georgia Census as a 40-year-old resident of Henry County, Georgia. Also in the household were Martha T., age 31, and six children.

2   James W. Edwards was an older brother of Thomas J. Edwards, and they owned adjoining plantations on Bear Creek in Henry County, Georgia. In the 1860 census, James was listed as 44 years old, along with Sarah, 40, and six children.

3   Daniel C. Smith entered service in the Echols Artillery as a Lieutenant on May 4, 1862. He was discharged February 7, 1863, upon being authorized by Confederate officials to organize a cavalry company at Atlanta.

4   Roasting ears of corn.

CAMP TILLER
JULY 24TH

Dear Sister

I have just received your [letter] date the 23rd, also one from Eliza. I was very glad to hear that you all had rain. I heard tuesday morning of the rain there but I did not know how much there had been. Eliza writes that she is not very well but I hope she will get better soon. as for myself I am enjoying uncomonly good health. I think if we all ly about here much longer we will get to be a very lazy crowd. It is very warm and dry here now, [but] there is some little appearance of rain to day. I am sorry to hear that it is dry down about Buds and Mr Colcloughs.[1] Joseph Armstrong received a letter from Mrs E. Edwards at Dr Landrums.[2] She says it is very dry there. Jack Edwards has not come back yet. I looked for him here tuesday as his furlough was out but he is staying over his time. I recon he will be here in a day or two.

I have no idea when we will leave here. we here a great many report about leaving here but they all prove to be false so far. I heard this morning that the quarter master of Griffin sayed yesterday he had been ordered to Macon. of course if that be the case we will hear rumors enough about moving for a while and we may hear it in earness soon for what I know. we have not got horses enough yet. we have about fifty five, some are what I call very sorry stock. We have not drilled any with them yet.

Capt Tiller has not come back yet. some of the boys come yesterday with some horses [and] they sayed the Capt was sick. Wm Smith has not come to camps, he is over in town. says he is sick. Lieut Gibson arrived here yesterday. Miss Sallie Jorden has got well of the measles. there is no new cases there. I went with George Martin to Mr Threldkelds night before last and got a bate of nice peaches and eat supper and came back to camp. I expect to go there a gain to night.

Sallie I expect to send this letter by a man going home to day so I will not have time to write any more. I have no news of any importance. You must write as soon as you can. I wish I had time to write more, I will write to you when I hear we are going to leave here, so you all need not think we are gone untill I tell you so. Give my regards to all enquiring friends and to all the folke at home. you must [excuse this] bad writing as it is done in a hurry.

Tell all howdy for me.

I remain you affectionate brother James

1   Bud was Jewel's brother William, II.   Mr. Colclough was Jewel's father-in-law, John Colclough, Sr. William Jewel and John Colclough lived in the same section of Greene County. John Colclough is identified in the 1860 Georgia census as a 60-year-old farmer in the Penfield District of Greene County, along with his wife Nancy, 50, and their seven youngest children. The three oldest children, including James Jewel's wife Eliza, were married and lived elsewhere. The census further identifies John Colclough as having been born in North Carolina. The inscription on his tombstone in the family cemetery in the Penfield District of Greene County gives his birth date as December 8, 1800, and his death as March 13, 1868.

2   Dr. Thomas H. Landrum, 28, and his wife Mary A. Landrum, 20, were listed in the 1860 Georgia census as residents of the Scull Shoals District of Greene County.   Mrs. E. Edwards may have been Elizabeth, widow of Thomas Edwards. She was identified in the 1860 Georgia census as a 52-year-old resident of the Simston District of Oglethorpe County, along with nine children, age 10 to 24. Elizabeth Edwards was born in South Carolina.

CAMP TILLER
JULY 26TH 1862

Dear Sister

I have been busy this evening drawing our rations for the next week and I am through with it. I thought I would write you a few lines to let you know that I am well. our mess are all well. Cousin John and McKinebrew has gone over to town. We received the box sent to us yesterday. it was in a very bad condition when it got to the depot. it had been split open from one end to the other and a piece nailed across the bottom and one end, and the other end piece was nearly out. I dont [know] whether there was any thing taken out or [not]. if there had been any thing in it that would brake it would have been smash to pieces.

I will tell what was received and you all will know if any thing was taken out. there was one large pone of light bread and two small ones & [a] bucket of butter, two baskets of peaches, irish potatoes, and apples, a piece of meat and about a dozen years of corn and some crackers in a pillow case. you did wrong in shucking the corn. the air got to it and and it has swiveled, which makes it almost too hard to cook. it ought to have been sent with the shuck all on just like it was pulled off the stalk. I did not get any flour this evening and of course we will not have any biscuit. we have been having two cornbreads to one biscuit for some time so now we will have it all the time I reckon. flour is very high here, it is twelve and half a hundred or twenty five dollars a barrel. Sallie you know what it is to have to go out and get supper. So all the boys have squandered off but me and I will have to attend if it is done, so I will close untill to morrow morning.

So Good Bye

CAMP TILLER
JULY 27, 1862
SUNDAY MORNING

Dear Sallie

I have taken a seat to try to write a few more lines to inform you that I am still well. Cousin John is well. The weather is cool for the season. [The] wind [is] from the east this morning and [there is] some appearance of rain which would be very acceptable in this country [as] it is dry and dusty. We have been drilling with our horses three days and if it does not rain soon our drill groung will get to be very dusty and disagreeable drilling. I think we will get along with the horses without much trouble as far as breaking [them is] concerned.

I have never heard when we will leave here. I would not be supprised if we were to receive a call at any time. There is so much artillery all ready in the field that they are not in a hurry to receive any more. There is a great deal of sickness in the town here. I heard Mr Sims say there was five corpse there last thursday that died in the town, mostly from the typhoid fever. There is some few of our company sick, but nothing more than common.

I must close as I have nothing more of importance to write. I sent you a letter the same day I received yours by one of the members of this company and I heard that there was one going home to day, so I thought I would write again. Jack Edwards has not come back yet. he got a furlough for four day and this is the tenth day. If he has not left home you can find out when he is comeing and write by him.

Write when you have the chance. tell Bud when you see him he must write to me. Give my love to all.

I remain your affectionate brother untill death.   James Jewel

CAMP TILLER
JULY 31, 1862

Dear Sallie

I received your kind letter yesterday by the hands of Mr Edwards also one from Mary crowley   I was not expecting such a thing. I went to the Depot tuesday morning and thought I would be sure to meet him there but he did not come so I quit looking for him.

This leaves me well. Cousin John is also well. the health of our company is tolerable good at present. James Bolton[1] & James T. Johnson have the Measles   they have been tolerable sick with them but they are both on the mend. If you recollect I wrote to you about both of them having the mumps at the same time & Johnson was the worst off. They both took the measles at same time in the same tent. We had about a dozen ladies out here yesterday evening I was not acquainted with but two of them.

We have all of our horses and are putting them through drilling. our drill ground is getting very dry and dusty. I do hope it will rain soon there has been [rain] all around but did not get here. there is still some appearance about this morning.

There is a talk of our moving to Atlanta soon, but we have not received any official orders yet, nor I don't know that we will. but we are listening for it every day. It is said here that the company that has been left there to guard the citty has been ordered to leave there and of course there will be some body sent there as guards If we get there we will be a little nearer home, but I dont know that it will be of much [benefit] for us taking everything in consideration, unless the home folkes will come to see us oftener.

Sallie I have no news of any importance I reckon you have heard of the Murfreys Borrough [Tennessee] fight.[2] John Edwards had his horse shot down under him, he was not hurt him self. several of his company was killed and some wounded.

Cousin John and Joseph Armstrong went over to Mrs Dunns[3] yesterday evening and stayed till bedtime. Cousin John does not visit Dr Jordens near as much as he did sometime ago. I think he has seen and heard enough to satisfied him at that place.

Capt Tiller came to camps tuesday, but he is not well enough to take command of the company. he is going to Atlanta to day on some business and says he will go home again or to the Indian springs.[4] Lieut Wm Smith has not come back yet I dont know where he is, some say he has gone to the springs for his health. he has been absent from the company the most of the time for the last two months. it seems he is in bad health.

You must tell Eliza she must not encourage me to tell such stories for I might be caught in them like some of them here. there was one of our company told the Capt that his wife was sick and he let him go home and it was found to be all false so the Capt has set his veto on him, as the saying is he will not get the chance to go home any more on such terms as that I want to write to Bud and send it with this if I have time. I expect to send this by hand as I have heard one of the company is going home. I would be very glad to be at Antioch but I cannot get there write to me next week let me hear the news   Give my love to all the family and friends. Your affectionate   Brother James

1   James L. Bolton enlisted in the Echols Artillery as a Private on May 3, 1862, and served until the end of the war. Bolton is identified in the 1860 census as a 22-year-old farmer in Madison County, Georgia, along with his wife, 18-year-old Martha E.

2   A Confederate force of about 1,400 men under command of Brigadier General Nathan Bedford Forrest captured an entire Union supply garrison of about 900 men under command of Brigadier General Thomas T. Crittenden at Murfreesboro, Tennessee, July 13, 1862. A report filed by General Forrest soon after the battle stated that about 25 Confederates were killed and 40-60 were wounded. He put the Union losses at about 75 killed and 125 wounded. Later information stated that Confederate casualties totaled an estimated 150 killed and wounded.

3   The 1860 Georgia census listed Mary P. Dunn, age 62, as a farmer and head of the household in the Union District of Spalding County. Others in the home and assumed to be her children or their spouses were: Martha E., age 28, a "Common School Teacher"; John V., 27; Mary R., 25; James S., 20; Mintora L., 15; George L., 13; Lorenza C., 12; Howard, 7; and Elizabeth, 4.

4   Indian Springs in Butts County, Georgia, was a famous health resort. It was believed that the mineral waters there had medicinal value.

CAMP TILLER
AUGUST 7TH 62

Dear Sister

I received your letter this morning also one from Bud   I was glad to hear that you all were well. I received a letter from Eliza tuesday and a box of peaches from John Colclough. They got a letter from Mr Colclough last friday. he said he thought Doc and Thomas was both taking the fever. he expects to come home soon he will bring them with him if he can get them off. I think it is very doubtful whether they can get a furlough now or not.

I have not heard any thing more about our leaving here since I wrote to you last   from the way they bring the fodder in here it looks like we might stay here some time. Some of the boys had a fine time here to day. they went off in the woods and had a barbecue of two sheep and a turkey goblar. I suppose they bought them yesterday and had them brought here last night. they tried to keep it a secret but before they got ready to eat I think every one in camps knew it. I did not get any to eat. I dont know how they come out.

One of the negroes in the mess next to ours took a notion he wanted some fresh meat and killed a shoat.[1] he cleaned it and carried it down and put in the branch in a camp kettle. some of the boys was out that way and found it. they took the meat out and put some sand in the bucket to sink it and then hid themselves where they could watch it. Soon after, a cloud came up and [it] looked like [it might] rain so the owner of the bucket thought it might get washed away so he went down after it and then he was caught. I have been thinking that it would be a wonder if some of these nice fat shoats about here were not taken off by some of them.

Sallie, Jack Edwards got permission from Lieut Gibson for himself, me, Cousin John, and Mat Norton[2] to go to his Cousins tomorrow evening to go a fishing and to get watermelons. he was here yesterday and brought us a basket of peaches and a jug of sider. he gave us a very pressing invitation to come. he will be fixed up for us I recon. Capt Tiller come back from the springs. he is mending some but looks bad yet. He will take command now, so I think it doubtful whether we get to go. I will find out by morning and let you know if we go.

We have to drill a goodeal now a days so as to get our horses trained. I will close untill morning.

Friday morning. I have been to rollcall. I am well. Cousin John is also well there [are] some cases of the measles yet. Dr Ham has come here with a substitute. the hospital he was going in has busted up so he was compelled to come back to the company. there has been a good many applications a head of him, so if the Capt acts honestly he will come into ranks. George Martin has bargained with two men in Griffin as substitutes. one at a thousand and the other six hundred dollars. he spoke to [the] Capt to get one but he could not get him in several months.

I can tell you now where the report started about our going to Atlanta as the Capt told the company last night. Col Lee[3] of Atlanta wrote to Genl Mercer[4] [that] he wanted our company there. we may go or may not, I cant tell. Tell Mary Crowley I will write before long. I must close write as soon as you [can and] let me know how Pa come out making blackberry brandy.

Cousin John sends his love to all. Give my love to all.

I remain your affectionate brother James

Dear Sallie,

I closed my letter before I found out certain that we would go. we are expecting to have a fine time out there. I expected to send this by mail untill a little while ago. One of Capt Loftens[5] company, Wm Waller,[6] was wounded at Richmond. he has been here to see his brother [Cpl T. J. Waller], so I thought I would send it by him. write when you have the chance. Tell Bud I will write to him as soon as I have a chance. We all have holiday to day except the drivers, they are drilling with their horses.

Yours truely, JJ

1   A shoat is a young pig, usually less than 1 year old.

2   James M. Norton is listed in the 1860 Georgia census as a 20-year-old farmer in the home of his parents James and Calender Norton in the Lexington District of Oglethorpe County. There were eight other children in the household, including William J. Norton (cited elsewhere). James M. Norton enlisted as a Private in the Echols Artillery on March 1, 1863, and served until the end of the war.

3   Colonel Lee was George W. Lee who served successively with the 25th Battalion, Georgia Cavalry (Provost Battalion); 38th Georgia Infantry (Wrights Legion); and 3rd Battalion, Georgia State Guards (Atlanta Fire Battalion).

4   Brigadier General Hugh Weedon Mercer.

5   John T. Lofton is identified in the 1860 census as a 28-year-old lawyer in Lexington, Georgia. He began his service in the Confederate Army May 28, 1861, as a Captain in the Gilmer Blues. He was elected Colonel September 17, 1862, and was killed at Fort Fisher, Virginia, January 13, 1865.

6   William Waller is listed in the 1860 Georgia census as an 18-year-old son of Benjamin and Louisa Waller, farmers in the Simston District of Oglethorpe County. Also in the household were two younger brothers and four younger sisters. Waller enlisted as a Private in the Gilmer Blues May 28, 1861, and served until the end of the war.

CAMP STEPHENS
AUGUST 12, 1862

Dear Sister

I have just received a letter from Eliza   She is well. they were all well except her mother, [but] she is getting better. she wrote that she had been very uneasy about me. She heard that you had received a letter from cousin John stating that we were going to Savannah, which of course would cause any one that was interested in our welfare to be troubled about us. I am happy to tell you that we are well at present and we are at the same place and I dont know how long we will stay here. Capt Tiller told us last week that he would not be supprised if we had to leave here soon but we might stay here some time. I was very much in hopes that I would get a letter from you this morning.

Sallie I wrote to you that I was going out to Mr. Thomas Edwards'es. Jack, Mat Norton, Cousin John, and myself went there friday evening. we got there about four Oclock. we had some good sider, peaches, and watermelons, and then went out to the river about seven miles and stayed all night and had a fish fry for breakfast. We caught some nice fish. you [ought] to have seen us eat fish. we fished till nearly twelve Oclock, then went to James Edwards'es to dinner. the two Edwards'es and two of their boys was with us. The way we drank sider and eat peaches and watermelons you dont know. I was afraid some of us would make ourselves sick eating so much. besides the fruit, we had a plenty of good vituals to eat. We enjoyed our trip the best sort untill we got to the depot and the cars come by and did not stop at all, so we had to foot it for twelve miles to camps. it was very hot. I forgot to tell you when we started back to camps. it was yesterday morning at eight Oclock when we left the depot. It was a right smart undertaking to walk that far and it so hot, but we thought we would try it. we got tolerable tired by the time we got to camps. as we came on we would Stop once and awhile, get water, and rest in the shade. So [we] got home about twelve oclock. if we had gone back to Mr. Edwardes I expect he would have sent us home, or a part of the way at least.

Mr Thomas Edwards and his wife promised us they would come down to see us this week about thursday or friday. I reckon you begin to think by my writing that I have become some what attached to them. They are the right sort of folks they have a plenty of property to live well on and besides, they are very accomidating people.

We went to a Methodist church sunday. They had two sermons such as you dont hear at home. it was what I call real backwood preaching. I think if some of the people that was there ever sees either of us again they will know us from the way they looked at us. I reckon you are getting tired of such as this but I have no news of any importance to write. Tell Mary Crowley I have not forgot her yet. I will write to her before long. I thought as I had a chance to send a letter to day by hand I would write as I expect it will be the only chance this week. if I was to undertake to keep up correspondence with you all by mail it would soon take all the money I have. I must close as it is dinner time the boys are all eating. You must write as often as you have the chance. Give my love to all.

Tell Bud and Mat howdy when you see them. I will write to them soon.

I remain your affectionate brother James.

Dear Brother

I received your letter last week and thought I would [have] written to you before this time but I have been closely engaged so hope you will excuse me for the present. I am not as well this morning as I have been for some time, but still I cant say that I am sick. We are all getting tolerable well. there is some few casses of the measles in the company. It seem to me they suffer more with them here than people do generally at home. I recon it is for the want of proper attention

Me and Cousin John, Jack Edwards, and Mat Norton went out in Henry County to Jack Edwardes Cousin's Mr Thomas Edwards friday evening and stayed untill monday morning. We had as many watermelons and peaches as we wanted to eat and sider to drink all the time. We went seven miles from there to [the] Flint river a fishing and stayed all night down on the bank of the river. we caught as many fish as we wanted for breakfast and carried enough home for supper. that was the first fish fry that I ever was at. Mr Edwards Cooked them and I tell you they were good. we enjoyed our trip finely till it come to walking back to camps Monday morning. we came to the depot to take the cars and they did not stop for us to get on, so we had to take it a foot twelve miles between eight and twelve Oclock and it was very hot. We took it moderate and rested several times on the road. I would not care to take another such walk as that.

I have no news worth writing to you but I will write what I can. We are improving some with our horses drilling. the weather is so hot and dry and our drill ground so dusty it is very disagreeable drilling. When we first commenced with the horses I thought we would be troubled with them. several of the teams would baugh [balk] so much that we could not get along hardly atall, but they have got so they do very well now.

Since writing the above I eat dinner. we got two boxes of provisions from home yesterday. Jos Armstrong brought one and Jack Edwards'es wife sent him one. Sis Jane sent me a bag of beans and irish potatoes and some nice apples, also a nice piece of ham. we will have a plenty to eat two or three days. We have have not drawed any flour in three weeks. last week we got meal bolted for flour.[1] We can get along very well as long as we get a plenty of corn bread and fat midling meat and get a little butter from home once and awhile. William Blanton[2] sent Meed here with a load of watermelons wednesday. they were long and nice. I tried to get Meed to give me one but I could [not] get it. He sold them out at very good prices, all but what some of the boys stole from him.

I was thinking about writing some thing about the reports about our leaving here when the trumpet was sounded for us to fall in line and the Capt read to us orders from General Mercer of Savanah that we must go to Atlanta. so we will leave here tuesday morning without a doubt. I must close you must write when we get there.

I remain your affectionate brother James Jewel

1   Bolting refers to sifting ground wheat through a fine-mesh sieve or cloth to produce flour. Since there was no wheat from which to make flour, finely ground corn meal was used as a substitute.

2   William M. Blanton is identified in the 1860 census as a farmer in the Mt. Zion District of Spalding County, Georgia. Also in the household were his wife Julia and eight children. Meed probably was William Blanton's hired hand but may have been his slave.

CHAPTER I

CHAPTER 11

Duty In Atlanta

"I am very sorry to inform you we have received marching orders"

Dear Sister

I guess it will suprise you to hear that I was carried to jail yesterday evening at six Oclock and kept there untill two this evening. It was the first time that I was carried to jail and I would't care if was the last time. but there was one consolation, there was several clever boys with me. We were carried there to guard the prisoners. the house is paled in with plank about ten feet high and so close together you can scarcely see through it atall, and a very small door to go in we were carried in there and the key turned on us till morning. there was nine of us and three had to guard two hours at a time.

Sallie as we were going on I heard the sad news of Thomas Colcloughs[1] death and John [Colclough] was at the depot with his corps. I asked Dr Smith, he being the officer of the guard, to let me go to see him, but his reply was you cant go, although we had to go by there and stoped about a half an hour on the road before we got there. You cant imagine how I felt passing in about fifty yards of them and knowing that my brotherinlaw was a corps lying there and I could not go there. I find that we have not seen anything of the soldiers life before. We are stationed about three quarters of a mile from the pasenger depot out in between the Macon and Chatanooga railroad.

We have a very pleasant place for a camp ground but water is scarce. there is three or four families close by and we have to go into their yards to their wells to get water. from here we can see the engine house and the portion of town that extends along the chatanooga railroad, but it is very little pleasure to stand off and look at the town and cant be alowed the privilidge of going there. The other company that is here [has] guards stationed around this side of the depot so that a soldier cannot pass unless he has a pass from his Capt, and Col Lee has ordered the capts not to give the men leave to [go except] on special business. I thought when we come here that we would have a chance to go out to the depot so we could see some of our friends passing on the cars sometimes. Mr & Mrs Martin passed here yesterday evening going up to see Frank.[2] he is likely to die. Mr Mell[3] come to see us a few minutes last Wednesday. You may depend I was glad to see him. he said he could not stay long with us but he thought he would come and see us any how Preacher Harbin[4] was here the same day.

Since we come here they give us flour a plenty and something I did not expect to see again as long as the war lasted and that was a little coffee. I thought there would be no more coffee for the soldiers. it is said that flour is selling at eighteen dollars a hundred. I have been thinging for some time that I would get a chance to come home afterwhile and see you all, but I am afraid now the chance is bad. Capt Tiller says he has received orders from Col Lee not to grant any more furloughs to this company. all the sick are to be sent to the hospital. there is seven or eight of our company there. I was very sorry to hear of the death of McKinnebrews wife. he has not come back to camps yet. I want to try to get to work in the navy yard if I can find out who to apply to. if I can get in there, I can be transfered from this company. you must not let ever body know this.

It is too late for me to send this letter off this evening but I will be on guard from eight oclock in the morning till eight the next day so I will not have a chance to write. we have to stand [guard] every other day and some of them two days in succession. I wish some of you would write, I have not heard a word from home since I came here. I have written twice to Eliza but have not heard a word from her. I hope you will write soon. You must not say any thing to her about my not coming home untill I see how it will be. I am going to try [even] if I fail. write soon.

I remain your affectionate brother JJ

1 Jewel's brother-in-law Thomas F. Colclough died of measles at Lookout Mountain, Tennessee, in August 1862.

2 John Franklin Martin was the son of John and Nancy Martin and brother of George W. Martin and Thomas Martin, all cited elsewhere. Franklin Martin is listed in the 1860 Georgia census as a 22-year-old farmer in the Woodville District of Greene County, along with his 19-year-old wife, Adaline C. [Malone], whom he married December 7, 1858. According to the inscription on his tombstone in the family cemetery in the Wolfskin District of Oglethorpe County, John Franklin Martin was born April 9, 1836, and died August 22, 1862.

3 Patrick Hues Mell was a professor at the University of Georgia in Athens and one of the leading Baptists in the state. He was the pastor of a number of local churches, including Antioch Baptist Church in Oglethorpe County, which he served for 26 years.

4 Preacher Harbin is unidentified.

Dear Sister

As I came into town this morning your letter of the 19th was handed me by frank Collier. I also received one from Eliza yesterday evening late, written the same day. She wrote for me to be certain to come home by the last of the week. I went to the Capt and [asked] him for a furlough. he said he would see Col Lee to day and try to let me off for a few days. I am on guard today, but he promised me this morning if he could permission for me to go, he would let me [off in] time enough for me to leave on the seven oclock train this evening. if I get off I will go to Greensborough to night and from there to Mr. Colcloughs. I think there is some uncertainty about my comeing, though I hope I may get off.[1] no more at present.

Your brother James Jewel

1 Jewel did receive a furlough and was at home when his baby, Martha (Mattie) Elizabeth, was born August 31, 1862.

SEPT 9TH 1862

Dear Sister

I arrived here safe saturday evening in a little before sunset and it was dark when I got to camps and our mess were all out on guard but Jack Edwards. I am well and hope these few lines may find you all enjoying the same blessing.

I went to the hospital soon sunday morning. I found Doc[1] very bad off. I thought there was but little hopes of his ever recovering. I dont know whether you were aware that William[2] was with him or not. he came up here last wednesday. I spent a good part of the day with him yesterday and have just come from there this morning. The Dr says he is a good deal better and I think there is a great difference on him. Matilda and Sarah Ann[3] come up last night and are with him to day. they told me that my baby was sick yesterday. Eliza is about as common. I was sorry to hear that the little creature was sick. Miss Lucy Moore[4] pass me on the street last night. she liked to have passed me before I found her out. she told me she saw you all at meeting sunday. She is going to Marietta[5] while she is up here.

I recon you have seen cousin Billie Campbell[6] before this time. I met him at the Point as I came up here, but I did not have time to talk much with him. he said he thought he would stay about with you all two or three weeks.

The boys have had a pretty tight time of it since I left. they have been standing guard two days at a time and off one. I did not go out till yesterday morning and was relieved this morning. I was close to the hospital where Doc was so when I went on post I would go in and stay with him so as to let William rest a little. I recon he will stay with him untill he gets better than he is now. Any one that is very sick and has none of his friends with him fares but middling I tell you.

There is another company come in here to help us so we will not have to be out more than every other day I recon. Sallie I have heard some good news to day. it is reported that Genl Stewart[7] is near Cinsinatta in Ohio and has demanded the surrender of of the Citty. It is thought from his position he can take it very easy. I do hope it is true. From what I can learn there has been another great battle at Manassas and our forces are near Arlington heights and the Yanks have evacuated Winchester. It is reported a part of our forces have crossed the Potomac river. I dont [know if any of it is true] it is rather doubtful.

I must close. I want to write another letter and go over and see Doc this evening. You all must go and see Eliza as often as you can and try and cheer her up, they are all in low spirits down there. I am afraid she want get along. Write soon   I remain your affectionate brother James

1   Franklin W. (Doc) Colclough died September 16, 1862, just 6 weeks after his brother Thomas had died.

2   William was William A. Colclough, older brother of Franklin and Thomas. William was listed in the 1860 Georgia census as a 33-year-old retail merchant in the Penfield District of Greene County, along with his wife Matilda, age 27, Tallulah, 4, William A, Jr., 1, and an unnamed male infant, 1 month old (John).

3   Matilda J. Moore married William A. Colclough November 12, 1854.   Sara Ann [Colclough] was a younger sister to William, Franklin, Thomas, and Eliza. She never married and died April 26, 1914.

4   Lucy Moore is listed in the 1860 Georgia census as the 15-year-old daughter of Burnett and Martha Moore (cited elsewhere), farmers in the Falling Creek District of Oglethorpe County, along with four other children.

5   Marietta, Georgia, a few miles northwest of Atlanta.

6   This was William B. Campbell, son of Franklin C. and Clementine Campbell. He probably was not really a cousin, but his uncle, William Campbell, was married to Jewel's aunt, Elizabeth Jewel. The Campbells were located in Oglethorpe County, Georgia, at the time of the 1850 census but had moved to Carroll County, Georgia, by the time the 1860 census was taken.

7   Brigadier General Alexander Peter Stewart.

ATLANTA
SEPT 14TH 1862

Dear Sister

I received your letter day before yesterday. I was glad to hear that you all were well. I am not very well [but] I feel better this morning than I did yesterday. I went out on guard friday and I was taken with a headache and it continued to ache till last night. I took some pills that McKinebrew had yesterday morning and they did not operate so I took some salts before breakfast this morning and I have had two operations this morning so I think I will get well now. If I dont I will try Oil the next time. I have not seen Doc since thursday evening. he seemed to be a goodeal better than he did the first of the week. Cousin John saw him yesterday evening. he sayed he was getting better. Jos Armstrong says he heard from him this morning and he was not as well as he had been.

There was some good news last night, our fources have crossed the Potomac and taken possession of Baltimore. I dont [know] that it is true, I am afraid it is like a good many other reports we hear. We heard here the first of the week that Earby Smith had taken Cinsinatta in Ohio, but it was only published about one day and that is the last that I have heard of it.[1]

I saw a list of the wounded in the Oglethorpe rifles.[2] Capt Phinizy was acting as Major and was killed.[3] Berry Bowling[4] was [wounded] and Mark [Jewel],[5] John and Davy Christopher,[6] Thomas Gilham,[7] John Butler,[8] and several others that I dont recollect their names [were wounded]. I heard that there was seventeen wounded, the same number that was wounded there last year on the twenty first of July. I did not learn how many of them was killed, I would like very well to know. Cousin John is well, he is out on guard. George Martin is complaining today, there is a good many of the company that is complaining. I think a many one of them do it in order to get off from standing guard.

We drawed our wages last week up to the first of July and twenty five dollars comutation money. If the Capt. is as long about making out the parole [payroll] and drawing the money as he has been this time, I reckon it will be christmas when [we] get any more. the first of next month will be the time for us to be paied off again. There is some talk of our moveing our camp ground where we can have a better chance to get water. I dont know when it will be. it is thought by some that we will [stay] here at Atlanta during the war, but I think it is very uncertain where we will be next christmas. Capt Tiller has gone home again. Lieut Wm. Smith has not been here since the first of July. Uncle Billy told me the day I left home he saw him a day or two before [and that was] the first time I had heard from him in a long time. Some of the boys say they have seen him several time over in town this week.

I must close. You must write as often as you can   I remain your affectionate brother James

1   Jewel was referring to Major General Edmund Kirby Smith. The rumor was untrue. Actually, General Smith with an army of 7,000 had proceeded from Knoxville, Tennessee, to Richmond, Kentucky, where they routed 6,500 Union troops and then occupied Lexington, Kentucky. Although Cincinnati was fortified with thousands of Ohio and Kentucky militia in anticipation of an attack by General Smith, it never took place.

2   The Oglethorpe Rifles had been engaged in the Second Battle of Manassas (Bull Run) which took place August 28-30, 1862.

3   Jacob Phinizy is listed in the 1860 Georgia census as a 36-year-old farmer in the Beaverdam District of Oglethorpe County. He joined the Oglethorpe Rifles as 1st Lieutenant upon its formation May 15, 1861. He was promoted to Captain in August 1861 and was killed August 30, 1862.

4   Thornbury J. Bowling was a neighbor to the Jewels in Oglethorpe County, Georgia. The 1860 census lists him as a 26-year-old farmer in the household of his mother, 67-year-old Mary Bowling, along with his wife, 18-year-old Elizabeth, whom he married March 29, 1860. Elizabeth was the daughter of Joseph and Harriett Smith and the granddaughter of Paschal and Polly Jewel Smith, sister of James Jewel, Sr. Bowling joined the Oglethorpe Rifles as 2nd Corporal May 15, 1861. He was soon promoted to Lieutenant and was elected Captain upon the death of Jacob Phinizy. Bowling survived his wound at Second Manassas and was wounded twice more during the war: at Gettysburg, July 2, 1863, and at Deep Bottom, Virginia, August 16, 1864. Despite being wounded three times during the war, Berry Bowling lived to the advanced age of 85 and died November 7, 1919.

5   This was Mark L. Jewel, Cousin John Jewel's younger brother, already identified. Mark Jewel was wounded again and captured at the Battle of the Wilderness on May 6, 1864, and was paroled at the end of the war.

6   John A. Christopher and his brother David both joined the Oglethorpe Rifles as Privates in April 1862. John was married to Mary R. Campbell, daughter of Franklin C. and Clementine Campbell. The Christophers and the Campbells had previously lived in Oglethorpe County, but at the time of the 1860 census, John and Mary lived next to her parents in Carroll County. John was discharged after the Second Battle of Manassas due to his wound. David Christopher was married to Sarah A. Parris, daughter of Nathan H. and Sarah Jewel Parris, sister of James Jewel, Sr. David and Sarah Christopher lived next to his parents, Richard and Martha Christopher, in the Wolfskin District of Oglethorpe County. David Christopher survived his wound at Second Manassas but was killed at Spotsylvania Court House, Virginia, on May 10, 1864.

7   Thomas D. Gilham joined the Oglethorpe Rifles May 15, 1861, as a Private but was later elected 2nd Lieutenant. He saw action in several major battles of the war and was wounded again at Darbytown Road, Virginia, October 7, 1864, which resulted in the loss of his right arm. His brother Benjamin F. Gilham, cited elsewhere, also served in the Oglethorpe Rifles. Thomas and Benjamin were the sons of William Gilham, 52, and Isabella Gilham, listed in the 1860 Georgia census as farmers in the Bowling Green District of Oglethorpe County.

8   John Butler enlisted as a Private in the Oglethorpe Rifles April 23, 1862. He lost a leg at the Second Battle of Manassas and soon died. The 1860 census identified Butler as a 29-year-old farmer and neighbor of the Jewels in the Wolfskin District of Oglethorpe County.

ATLANTA
SEPT 23RD 1862

Dear Sallie

I have been looking for a letter from you for several days, but I have not heard from you all, only from Eliza, in nearly two week. Eliza wrote to me that Beck and Sci[1] had been up to see you and you had been up to Brother Marshals and sis Jane was comeing down the first sunday. I have not [heard] of any of you going to see Eliza since she has been sick. you must go to see her if you can. I have not been in very good health since I wrote to you last. some days I fell tolerable well and then for a day or two my bowels are effected but I feel tolerable well to day, but still I dont feel as stout as I did some time ago.

I was on guard yesterday and last night and I recon I wont go out again before Thursday. we dont have to send out so many men as we did sometime ago. we only have to send out twenty one a day now. there is a good many of them complaining yet, but they are always ready when eating time comes on and some of them can frolick about as much as any body else. when I get sick I dont feel [like] cutting up such capers as some of them. I know it is wrong to say they are not sick, neither do I say so, but I do [say] this much, they act very strange for sick folks. out of one hundred fifty there is only about sixty or seventy that do any thing except to eat. George Martin is still complaining, he has been quite sick for several days. he complains of haveing chills every day or two he has been [sick] about ten days. he is not confined to his bed but he does not eat but very little and begins to look badly.

Sallie, I am now twenty eight years old and I never knew what it was to be where I could not get some thing to [eat] till to day. at dinner time we did not have a mouth full of meat, nothing but cornmeal and a little rice for dinner and not a particle of grease to put in it. five of our mess went to town to get their [rations?]. I, Jack Edwards, and Frank Collier stayed here. I got some meat from one and some peas from another so I mad out very well. we have sent to town and got meat enogh to do till tomorrow then I recon we will draw some. We did not draw but half allowance last wednesday and the balance was to be made out in beef and they have not brought the beef. We used up the butter that I brought from home and cousin John sent back last week. I was in hopes they would send us some butter by the first of this week but I have not heard from Aunt Bettsy, and when she sends it I am a going to try to get some of the other boys to send home for some. I dont think it is right for us to furnish butter all the time. some of the boys have had boxes brought, but none that I have seen seemed to do any good but one that Frank Collier had sent to him full of beans week before last and some chickens. I dont recon there is enough meat in camps for twenty men for supper. we have got a small shoulder of bacon which cost about Six dollars. that is dear meat I think. Tell Pa I want him to lay in a claim for Eliza for some of governor Browns salt if there is such a thing going on there.[2] all Soldiers wives are allowed a bushel of salt for one dollar. it is now selling for fifty cents a pound.

I have been making an effort to get nearer home, that is to get into the armory at Athens.[3] I have written to Mr. Barrow.[4] Walker

Brooks [5] was here and stayed with us last thursday night. he come up here to get him some tools to go there to work. he went there yesterday, or at least he said he agreed to go Monday. he says they want a great many hands and pay them good wages. I can do any work as good as the government work is done about here. there is nothing nice about the houses. I think it very doubtful whether I get [on] there or not.

I recon you have heard the news about Jackson taking Harpers ferry with ten thousand prisoners. it has been confirmed in the papers and another part of them have gone through Maryland and near the line of Pennsylvania. They sayed here that they met with as hearty a welcome as they would have done at home.

I reckon you will think that this a very dirty sheet of paper to write [on]. I put it in my pocket yesterday to carry with me to write, but I did not use it. I thought it would not do to throw it away and it would not do to writ with a pen and ink, so [I thought I] would use a pencil. I must close as it is nearly night. you must write and let me hear from you all as soon as you can. I dont [know] whether you can read this or not. If you cant you must guess at it the best you can.

I remain your affectionate brother

James Jewel

---

1   Beck was Rebecca D. Colclough, younger sister of James Jewel's wife Eliza; Sci was Simon, the slave who had accompanied Cousin John Jewel earlier in the war.

2   The Georgia Legislature appropriated funds for the purchase or manufacture of salt for Georgia citizens. Georgia Governor Joseph Emerson Brown had a plan of distribution whereby 1/2 bushel of salt would be given to the widows or families of soldiers who died in service, and 1/2 bushel could be sold to each family of a soldier for $1.00. After these needs were supplied, heads of families could each purchase one bushel for $4.50. There was never enough salt available to carry out the plan.

3   Soon after the outbreak of the War Between the States, brothers Ferdinand W.C. and Francis L. Cook had established an armory in New Orleans for the production of arms for the Confederacy. When the capture of New Orleans was imminent, the machinery of the armory was moved to Athens, Georgia, where a new building was constructed to house the factory.

4   This was Colonel David Crenshaw Barrow, Sr., prominent and influential former neighbor of the Jewels in Oglethorpe County. Barrow had moved his family to Athens in

January 1861. In 1838, Barrow had married Sarah Eliza Pope, granddaughter of former Georgia Governor Wilson Lumpkin. Jewel no doubt hoped that Colonel Barrow would assist him in getting discharged and assigned to the armory.

5   This probably was W.W. Brooks, identified in the 1860 Georgia census as a farmer in the Falling Creek District of Oglethorpe County.

Atlanta
Sept 27th 1862

Dear Sister

I received your letter this morning without any date. I suppose it has been written some time since the twenty third of this month. I read it over and I thought it was written on the twenty third, but I found I was mistaken. I and cousin John and Evans[1] hitched up a team and went to the express office, but we could not find it [a box of provisions from home]. we then went to the freight depot but did not find it there, so we had to turn around and come back without it. if we dont get it this evening we will wait till monday. We have got some thing to eat now. we drew our rations last wednesday, the next day after I wrote to you. I think we will have enough to do us this week. the reason we got out last week, we did not get our full allowance. our mess has always had a plenty while some of them are very often out.

We have had a great deal better time this week about guard duty than we had before. I was off three days in succession. I was out yesterday and last night and I expect to be on guard tomorrow. Fifteen of our company were sent to Delonega in Lumpkin [County, Georgia] yester evening with orders to be there this morning and it is about sixty five or seventy miles from here. so they had to travel all night. they went horseback. it is said by some that they went to bring the mint and all the coin here to this place and some say they are gone after the Gold and silver for they are fearful that it will be taken by the Union men up there if it is not moved away soon.[2] they will not be back until monday or Tuesday. and besides that, Col Lee has given us another post to guard. he has about twenty or twenty five men from his battallion around the pasenger depot to guard that place and I have been there and I never can see one single thing they do, only when the trains start off they get at the doors to see that all the pasengers have passes. Cousin Billy [Campbell] come up and stayed with us two nights and one day. he intended staying only till three Oclock in the morning but we persuaded him to stay till the next night. he brought me your letter. he says he will be here again in about two weeks and he will bring my hat, if he does not send it before that time.[3] I told him I thought we would stay here til he come back by here, though I do not know. it is so uncertain about what will take place no one can tell when or where they are going. we may stay here till christmas and again for what I know we may not be here a week. There has been a talk of our being attached to Lee's battallion. if that is done it is likely we will stay here sometime. I was in hopes I would get to Athens but I thought it doubtful, for it is a hard mater for any one to get off from a company now. I recon maybe the war will close after a while and some of us may get home.

You wanted to know what the Baby was named. I would have written to you but I thought you had heard it. I named her Martha Elizabeth, as they all were so anxious for me to name her something. I dont know but what I may take a notion to change it after a while, but that will do for the present. I wish I could see the little thing but I dont [know] when that will be. Eliza says she is bound to come up here after a while if I stay here long enough. some of the boys are complaining of being tired of this place. they say they had rather be any where than here, but they have never been any where but here and at Griffin, yet if they had to spend the winter in Virgina they would be willing to stay here as long as the war lasts. As for my part, if I cant get to go nearer home I dont care about leaving here.

Tell Mary[4] that I dont know that I could do her any good if I was there but I do hope she will never give up untill she has been pardoned for her sins. I do hope that she may find Jesus precious to her soul before she will ever be satisfied again. I dout whether I can get the chance to send this letter off this evening or not. if I dont I will write a little more tomorrow. You must write soon.

I remain your affectionate brother James

1   N.H. Evans joined the Echols Artillery as a Private on March 1, 1862, and served until the end of the war.

2   A United States branch mint was established in Dahlonega, Georgia, in 1838 and produced gold coins from that date until 1861. There were also branch mints in Charlotte, North Carolina, and New Orleans, Louisiana. Just before Union forces occupied New Orleans in April 1862, Confederate authorities transferred the gold and silver bullion from there to Jackson, Mississippi. In July 1862, 973 ounces of gold and 17,736 ounces of silver were shipped from Jackson to Dahlonega. This bullion, and probably that on hand at Dahlonega, was melted and cast into 17 gold bars, 196 silver bars, and 3 bars of gold and silver. On October 1, 1862, Confederate military authorities arrived in Dahlonega and took possession of the bullion for delivery to a depository in Augusta.

3   Jewel had recently returned from home where he had been with Eliza when their first child was born August 31, 1862, and had left his hat there.

4   Mary Jewel, James Jewel's older sister.

ATLANTA
SEPT 29TH/62

Dear Sister,

I seat myself to write you a few lines to inform you that we have received the box you all sent to us today. It was brought on as freight and did not get here till saturday evening. Cousin John and I went to the depot this morning and found it. It had just been taken out of the car and put in the depot. The agents at the express office and the depot are so careless if any one dont look for themselves it is uncertain whether they will find it or not. I went in this morning and asked if there was a box there for Jewel and the agent told me no. he said there was a man here saturday after a box for him. I told him if he was he did not get it and then he commenced looking over the freight list and found [it] at the same time cousin John and Jack Edwards was in the other room looking for it and found it. it only cost twenty five cents freight. it would have cost about a dollar and a half by express. as there was nothing in it easy to spoil it done just as well sent that [way]. as I wrote to you saturday evening that we had not received it I thought I would let you know that we had received it to day.

I am getting a long very well now. I have felt better yesterday and to day than I have done in two weeks. it has been a hard mater for me to get my bowels regular for some time, but I hope they wont be any more trouble to me soon.

I received a letter from Eliza which contained some good news to me. She said it done her so much good when she heard it that she could hardly write and what do you recon it was. William had been to Athens and had just got back and told her he had got me a situation in the armoury there. They sent me a written agreement to give me employment in the armoury by the eight of november, but the worst of the work is to do yet. that is to get off from this company. I dont know whether I can be detailed from the service to go there, and more than that, i dont expect that Capt. Tiller will want to let me off if he could. it is a very hard mater for some of them to get transfers to other companies there has been several that has tried to get transfers but [only] one has succeeded [as] yet and that was Ples Roberson, Alven's son.[1] he got off from here and put in a substitute and gone home. and what acount will he be when he gets there. just such men can get a chance to go home that is no count there. I have not said any thing to the Capt. yet. I want to find out if I can how to commence with him. if I dont, he will be apt to give me no satisfaction about it. he has received George Pace[2] of Lexington in the company again. he discharged him some time ago but I suppose he could not stand the conscript.

There is a lot of soldiers passing here this evening going to Kentucky. about four thousand of Genl [John C.] Breckenridges army from the west. I would not be surprised if we had to leave here before long for Savanah or Charleston, but I dont know that we will leave before christmas. It [is] rumoured that Genl. [Braxton] Bragg has taken Louisville Ky. John Gilham[3] of Tennessee come in to see us to day. he is employed on the train from Chatanooga to Nashvill. he says there is a very small force of yankey in Nashvill and but very few union men in that part of Tennessee. they all left when the yankey army left.

I have not time to write any more. you must write soon. Cousin

John is well. George Martin is about the same. he dont seem to improve much. he has been complaining of being chilly and has been taking quineine for some time. by the time I write again I will find out some thing more about going to Athens. I do wish I could leave here before we are ordered some where else but I reckon maybe I can if I got off at all. The boys have not come back from Dalton yet. Nothing more at present. Give my love to all

I remain your affectionate brother James

1   Pleasant P. Robertson enlisted in the Echols Artillery March 3, 1862, and was discharged June 6, 1862, by furnishing a substitute. Robertson is listed in the 1860 Georgia census as the 17-year-old son of Alvin M. Robertson and Mary Robertson, farmers in the Goose Pond District of Oglethorpe County.

2   There is no record that George Pace served in the Echols Artillery, but he was a Private in Co. A, 64th Regiment, Georgia Volunteer Infantry. Jewel must have confused him with an older brother, John Howard Pace, who was a Sergeant in the Echols Artillery.

3   John Gilham of Tennessee is unidentified.

Dear Sallie

I wrote to you yesterday and intended to send it by George Martin but I was at the race tract and did not get a chance to send it to camps last night. Cousin John was quite sick last night but he is better to day. he is up this evening. I am well.

We have got a plenty to eat now. John Kinebrew[1] brought a box last night and one for Jack Edwards and Mr Martin passed here and left one with George and he has gone home. I think they brough three bushels of potatoes and Jack Edwards had about a half a bushel of shelled peas sent to him. It looks [like] when we do get anything from home it all comes at once so there is a goodeal of it wasted. We will [get you to] send a box before long, but you must wait till we let you know before you send it. There was two or three more of the Oglethorpe folks come in last night. some of them will leave tomorrow if they [do not] leave soon we will have a crowd here soon.

There is another train of soldiers come in this evening from the west. I suppose they belong to Breckenridges division. We are looking for John smith[2] back from Calhoun to night. he said he would come and stay till monday. if [he] does, we will try to get him to take a box with him and leave it at the depot.

I reckon Eliza has got the letter I wrote to her thursday. All of our officers has left us but the Capt. Lieut. D. Smith has been appointed enrolling officer in this Dept. He got back from Delonega yesterday and left today for Camp Randolp, so I reckon we will have a Capt. and 2nd Lieut in our company. there is still men wanting to join us. if I can get off, some one may have my place.

Nothing more at present. Give my love to all. Write soon and give me all the news of the day. I remain as ever your affectionate brother James   Oct 4th 62

P.S.

I recon you will think this is badly written but as it [is] not very long, may be you can make out to read the most of it and guess at the rest. You must write. I wrote to Bud about two weeks ago but have not heard from him. tell him to write once and a while.

Give my love to all. I reckon Eliza has come up to see you all. I remain your affectionate brother, James

1   John H. Kinnebrew joined the Echols Artillery as a Sergeant in March 1862. He is listed in the 1860 Georgia census as the 17-year-old son of C.D. Kinnebrew, along with his older brother, Marcus B. Kinnebrew, whom Jewel called McKinebrew (already cited).

2   John Smith is unidentified.

ATLANTA
OCT. 19TH 1862

Dear Sister

I received your letter from Cousin John yesterday morning but I did not feel like writing after I had wrote to Eliza. I reckon you have heard of the prisoners getting out of jail Thursday evening.[1] a little after sunset fourteen of the yankey prisoners got out of jail and twelve of them made their escape. one was caught before he got over the pailings and one fell from the top of them and broke his leg. another one was taken up friday night which leaves eleven out yet. we have had a great time hunting for them. fifteen or twenty of our company are out now. one of them came in this morning after help. he sayed they were on tract of six of them over on the Chatahoochee river.

Now I will tell you of my trip and you wont wonder at my feeling a little tired   I was at the car shed when I heard the news. I and Cousin J. and four others had been appointed for scouting duty that day, and I was waiting for George Martin to come up on the train and soon after the train got there Col Lee came to me and says I want your scouting party at the jail as quick as you can get there. I did not [know] what was the matter so I looked about and could not find any [one] but cousin John and we started right off. it was about a half a mile and soon as I got there he told me to go to our camps and send out forty men on horses, so that was another mile to go in a great hurry. and then we had to go over and knock about in town awhile, so I did not get [a] chance to sleep but very little that night. and in the morning twenty more of us had to start out. ten of us went out to Decatur and then went out a south coars [course] from there untill about twelve oclock. I rode one of the meanest horses I ever rode in my life. I could not get it to walk a step. we rode a good part of the way in a gallop. I swoped horses with one of the fellows at twelve Oclock and then rode on till dark when a part of us got back to town. I did not [feel] so much weried, but the next morning I felt as sore as if I had [been] bruised all over. I feel better to day but my legs and feet feel quite sore yet. I reckon I will get over it in a day or two.

Cousin John and Jos Armstrong went out yesterday morning and have not come back yet. I reckon they are with the crowd that is in persuit of the yankeys. that deserter that was brought from delonega is one that has escaped so far.

I had like to have for got to tell you how they got out of jail. as the jailer went in to carry their supper, one or two of them gathered hold on him and took the keys and unlocked the door and went out. one of the guards was standing at the door and they took his gun away from him and carried it off with them. I think my self the guard must have been very careless. it takes six men there and they were all gone but two. the other four had gone to their camps to get their supper. when our company guarded there, we had nine men, three on post at the time and the others was not allowed to go out side of the pailings, or at least not more than one or two at the time. if the guards had all been there they could have stoped several of them before they got over the pailings. Some people about here blame our company with being there and letting them out but they are very much mistaken. we have not had to gard the jail since about the first of september. it is Capt. Echols[2] company instead of the Echols Artillery. there is a very good chance for us to be misrepresented. I [am] sorry that such a mistake has been made but I reckon it will all come straight after awhile.

I will close for the present as it is nearly time for the mail to leave here. You must write as soon as you can. I received the pants and bottle of brandy sent by George martin but I could not keep it, for so many found it out it was drank up directly. Give my love to all the family and brothers folks. tell them to write. I remain as ever your affectionate brother James

1   On April 12, 1862, Union spy James J. Andrews, another civilian, and 19 Union soldiers from an Ohio unit had stolen the locomotive, The General, at Big Shanty near Atlanta, and headed north toward Chattanooga, attempting to burn bridges and destroy tracks along the way. Their mission was to sever the main line of transportation between Chattanooga and Atlanta, but they met with failure and were all captured. Seven of the raiders, including their leader, were hanged. Eight of the Andrews crew, along with some other prisoners, escaped October 16, 1862, and all eight were successful in reaching Union lines. The remaining

six raiders were transferred to Libby Prison in Richmond, Virginia, and were exchanged as prisoners of war March 18, 1863. Six of the Ohio soldiers were the first recipients of the U.S. Congressional Medal of Honor recently created by Congress and President Lincoln. The remaining 13 soldiers later received the medal. James J. Andrews was not eligible to receive the Medal of Honor because he was a civilian.

2   Captain Echols was Thomas J. Echols of Co. B, 25th Battalion, Georgia Infantry (Provost Guards) of Atlanta.

ATLANTA
OCT 21ST 1862

Dear Sallie,

I just now learned that Billy Norton & Gabe Britain[1] was going home in the morning and it is nearly dark, but I thought I would write you a few lines to let you all know that I am well except a slight cold. Cousin John is complaining of being tired from riding. he has been out three days. Only one more of the prisoners have been caught since I wrote to you. there is ten of them out yet   some of them have been seen down about Griffin and some have crossed the Chatahoochee river. I received a letter from Eliza this morning, they are all well but her Gran Ma,[2] she was a little better.

One of our company, R.N. Reed,[3] asked yesterday to write to you all to know if you would make him six yards of nice white flannel. he wants it fine and nice. he has seen some that Dr. Jerrel bought at two dollars a yard. he says he will [pay] two and half for some rather than miss it. he wants it for shirts and drawers   he asked me what I thought he could get it at and I told him I had no idea whether he could get it or not. as wool and factory yarn was very high, of course the cloth would be high. if you cant get fine warp and have it nice I dont expect he will take it, but if you all feel disposed to try it, if he dont [buy it] some of the [rest] of them will about here. I dont care about anymore clothes now. I have been thinking about getting some of you to make me an over coat with a cape on it, longer than the one I have got. mine is not quite long enough to come down to my knees, but I reckon we had [just] as well wait a while untill I see whether I will need it or not. I think I will get me an oil cloth one here for six dollars. I dont like them much, they are most too sticky.

I dont [know] whether you can read this or not as the other side was written in the dark and this by a very dim light. Nothing more at present. Give my [love] to all.

write soon and let hear the news.

I remain your affectionate brother James

P.S. Let me know about the flannel the first time you write.

1   This probably was William J. Norton and Jabez Mercer Brittain of the Tom Cobb Infantry. Norton was 3rd Sergeant and Brittain was Lieutenant. Norton is listed in the 1860 Georgia census as a 20-year-old mechanic who lived with his parents, James and Calender Norton, and his younger brother, James M. Norton, all previously cited. Brittain is listed in the 1860 Georgia census as the 18-year-old son of Henry and Louisa Brittain, farmers in the Lexington District of Oglethorpe County. The elder Brittain was born in Virginia. Jabez Brittain joined the Tom Cobb Infantry as 1st Sergeant September 29, 1861, and was soon promoted to Lieutenant. He was appointed Chaplain June 16, 1863, and resigned from the army July 12, 1863, to accept an appointment from the Southern Baptist Board of Missions as missionary to the Army of Northern Virginia.

2   Eliza's maternal grandmother was Sallie (also Sally) Nelms. The inscription on her tombstone in the Colclough family cemetery in Greene County, Georgia, gives her birth as November 18, 1792, and the date of her death as November 6, 1862.

3   Robert N. Reed [also seen as Read] enlisted in the Echols Artillery on May 4, 1862, and was discharged February 1, 1863, by furnishing J.P. Tiller as a substitute.

ATLANTA
OCT 24TH 62

Dear Sister

I received your letter this morning and was glad to hear from you all. I was very glad to see that letter from Mark [Jewel]. I have not heard from him before in a good while. I think Cousin John must have been very careless about fixing up his letters when he wrote to his sweet heart the last time. that I think will be a lesson to him hereafter. I think he will be more particular the next time he writes two letters at the same time.

I have no news of importance to write but I thought I would try to write a little as some more of our company is going home tomorrow morning. As you said, I reckon we will all get home after awhile. I dont think there is but about twenty five of the company at home now and the most of them are on sick furloughs and five more are to go to morrow. Jim Hurt[1] went home on three days furlough because his Mother was sick and I suppose he has been [sick] a little, and has wrote here that he was not able to come back. I heard this morning that he had been to Augusta to try to get a discharge. he certainly [must have] got bad off since he left here. he was in very good health when he left here and [I] think he was as well as he ever was in his life. I reckon he will get a discharge when the war closes.

Frank Collier has gone home to day on a ten days furlough but there is no telling when he will come back, as very few of them come back when their furlough is out. he promised to write to me so I could let you all know when to send that box. We are getting along very well in the eating line. we have potatoes the most of the time. Evens come back from home wednesday and Jack Edwards come yesterday. his wife is with him. they brought some potatoes and peas and onions. I reckon he left before you heard of it. If any of you have any thing you want to sell send it up here. Chickens are selling at 75 cnts butter 60 to 70, buttermilk .20 a quart, potatoes three dollars a bushel, goobers .20 a quart. Coperas is selling for $1.50 a pound. if you all want any at that price let me know and I will send it to you. Common brown sugar is .50. Sallie I want some chesnuts if you have got a plenty of them. George Martin told me there was none at their house.

We have not caught any more of the prisoners that I know of. Some of our company are out hunting for them yet. Four men from one of the companies here went out in search of the yankey last tuesday and instead of hunting for them, they got on the train and went to Marrietta and got drunk and killed a young man that was at home on furlough who was standing off looking on. I suppose the one that shot did not shoot at him. They are all in jail but one and he ran away. they are searching for him now. they were great men to be out hunting Yankeys, dont you think. Jack Edwardes wife is here at camps this evening. I will close. you must write as often as you can. give my love to all the family and friends.

Your affectionate brother James

1   James Hurt joined the Echols Artillery as a Private in March 1862, and served until the end of the war. He is listed in the 1860 Georgia census as 26 years old in the home of Joel and Mary Hurt, farmers in the Bowling Green District of Oglethorpe County. Also in the household was James Hurt's brother F.A. Hurt (cited elsewhere).

ATLANTA
OCTOBER 28TH/62

Dear Sister

I thought I would write you a few lines to let you that I am well as I had a chance to send it by hand. Tom Martin[1] & Billy Smith[2] stayed with us last night and will be here untill tomorrow morning. Tom is going home. I have not heard Billy say when he will go. They have got a discharge clearing them from the conscript law, also Gus Hurt[3] and Jim Young.[4] they went back last night. Jim Hurt sent up a certificate to have his furlough extended fifteen days.

I received a letter from Eliza this morning written the 20th. she was complaining with the toothache. the baby is well and getting along finely from what she writes. I reckon I will get the chance to see you all in a week or two. William has fixed up for me to be detailed from here to Athens. he saw Stephens[5] and he told [William] there was no difficulty in the matter now and has written to the secretary of war and he will write to Capt Tiller to send me there. Sallie that is good news to me you may be sure. I expect to [be] closely confined there, but I reckon may be I can get the chance to go to church sundays and that is more than I can get here. I got permission to go one sunday since I have been here and I got sick before I got there and [had] to come back. I have not heard a surmon preached since the third sunday in August at Griffin. while we was there I went to preaching every sunday, and as winter is coming on our guard duty is not so very pleasant.

Saturday night it rained a little and the wind blew from the north west cold   sunday morning it commenced sleeting but it did not last long. it [has been] cloudy all day and looks like it was nearly cold enough to freez. I was out on guard that night from four till six oclock in the evening and from ten till twelve and four to six monday morning. there was plenty of ice in the water buckets. I was well wrapped up with clothes but I could not keep warm. there was a big white frost this morning. It is very pleasant today in the sun. Frank Collier will return to camps next monday. you must send us some potatoes and butter if Ma has got a plenty to spare. I have been talking to the boys about sending for butter and they all say they have not got it to spare & I would be glad to have some but there is nine in our mess and you [know] it would take a lot to do them when they all love butter as well as any fellows you ever saw. Cousin John and I have had twenty or twenty five pounds and all the rest together have not had as much as ten pounds since we have been in Atlanta, so I dont care much whether you send any or not unless Ma has it to spare.

You must let me know about that flannel for Mr. Reed as [soon as] you can.   he is very anxious to know if you have any to spare. send me a sample and the price as soon as you can. If you send that, put in some potatoes and some dry peas and any thing else you please. Nothing more at present. write when you have the chance. Give my love to all. I remain your affectionate Brother James

1   Elijah Thomas Martin was the younger brother of George W. Martin, mentioned often in Jewel's letters. He is listed in the 1860 Georgia census as the 19-year-old son of John and Nancy L. Martin, farmers in the Wolfskin District of Oglethorpe County. Tom joined the Echols Artillery April 30, 1863, as a Private, and was discharged early in 1864 when he was elected constable of Oglethorpe County.

2   Billy Smith probably was William Franklin Smith, son of Joseph Benjamin Smith and grandson of Paschal Smith and Polly Jewel Smith. Polly was a sister to James Jewel, Sr.

3   Gus Hurt was Franklin Augustus Hurt, brother to James Hurt (already cited). In the 1860 census Gus Hurt's age was listed as 23.

4 James C. Young joined the Echols Artillery as a Private on March 1, 1862, and served until the end of the war. He is listed in the 1860 Georgia census as a 32-year-old farmer in the Bowling Green District of Oglethorpe County, along with his wife Sarah, and two young sons.

5 Alexander H. Stephens, vice-president of the Confederacy, from adjoining Taliaferro County.

ATLANTA
NOV. 14TH 1862

Dear Sister

I received your letter yesterday morning and was glad to hear that you all was well. this leaves me in very good health. I think I am beginning to fatten up a little as the fall of the year has come in and I get a plenty of tough beef to eat. we get a half a pound of bacon apiece for ten days. we get along finely as long as we get so many potatoes from home. Frank Collier come back to camps tuesday and brought a box full with him. he sayed he was sorry he could not bring any butter for they did not have it. Butter is worth a dollar and twenty five cents a pound here and eggs one dollar a dozen. I thought I had heard of them being high before but I never heard of such prices here before. There was a great many soldiers brought here day before yesterday from the hospitals at Knoxville Tennessee. there was about a thousand so I have understood. lots of them was not able to travel with out help.

There was a fire broke out in an old house last night about two Oclock. there was nothing lost of any consequence but the building. it was an old tavern on the same block with the Washington Hall and has been used for a hospital for some time but there was no soldiers in it.

The Chattanooga train ran off the tract at Kingston last night and did not come down till eleven Oclock to day instead of comeing at four this morning. one of our company was there at the time. he said there was nobody hurt but they had not got the engine on the tract when he left. it was caused by the switch being left wrong.

You wrote some thing about Jim Hurts returning to camps but you was mistaken. he has not got here yet. I heard he sent a certificate last week for twenty [days]. that is, he would not be able for duty in less time than that. I dont look for him any more soon unless he is ordered back by the Capt. I think from what I can hear he has never had any thing to keep him from [coming] to camps long ago. I reckon he is trying to get a discharge yet.

Lieut. Gibson has returned to his command again. Lieut Wm Smith was here yesterday. he has been knocking about here several times recently but dont pretend to do any thing more than if he was a stranger to the company. It was reported last week he was going to resign his office but I hear today that he is going to hold on to it, and is now gone up to Chattanooga to buy corn to speculate on. I have not sold that flannel yet. Reed has been gone ever since I got it untill yesterday and I was on guard. he put in a substitute and left this morning. he will be back to night and if he dont like it there is a plenty of them here that I think will [buy it] at two dollars a yard. I thought about keeping it myself if he did not take it if I had to stay here. but if you all got a plenty, I will sell this and send after more if I dont get to come home. I dont care to get in the habit of wearing flannel if I can get along well without it. I have not heard any thing from the war department yet.

There was a case of small pox reported to be here the first of the week and the family were all moved out of town. I have not [heard] certain whether it was the smallpox or not. Our company has all been ordered to be vaxinated, [those] that has not been here before. I reckon you have heard that Mrs Daniel[1] hung herself last monday, I believe it was. I have not heard from Eliza this week. I am looking for a letter every day from her.

I expect to send this letter by hand tomorrow so I will wait till night to see if George Martin comes.

Dear Sallie George Martin has come and brought the potatoes safe and your letter. we have got about five bushels of potatoes now. George got a letter from his mother. she said that John Lumkin[2] was going to start home sunday and she is comeing with him. she did not say any thing about Brother. I reckon they were well when they left there. it is reported that there is twenty cases of smallpox here but I have no idea that it is so. you must write soon as you can.

Give my love to all the family. I remain as ever your brother JJ

1   Mrs. Daniel is unidentified.

2   John Lumpkin is unidentified.

ATLANTA
NOV 28TH/62

Dear Sallie

I received your welcome letter this morning. I did not know what had become of you. I had not heard from you [and] I am glad to hear that you all are well   this leaves me in very good health. I am just as hearty as a pig [and] can eat any thing that I can get.

Cousin John has a bad cough. with that exception he is well. The health of the company is tolerable good. we have to be on duty about two thirds of our time   [We are] on guard one day and night and the next day, on scout the next, and some time rest the next. The deputy Sheriff J.P. Tiller is a substitute here for Reed[1]   I sold him that piece of flannel for $12. We have drawed two monts wages and comutation money which was forty nine dollars.

I went to the hog pen today where they are killing hogs for the government. I think they can kill, clean, and cut up four hundred a day at the last calculation   any body that never saw such fixing cant imagine how they get along. they have big knives that they use with both hand. they can cut up a hole hog at about five licks and it is the smoothest cut I ever saw. The government is buying hogs in Tenn and bring them here and carring a great many down the country to fatten and kill to bacon up for the army. Pork sells for thirty cent [a pound] here. they ask ten cents [a pound] for back bones and ribs at the hog pen. haslets [are] fifteen cents a piece.[2]

Sallie you said I must come home. you know I would be very glad to come, but as some of the boys say, I dont live on the same side of the county that the Capt does, there fore I will have to wait till I get a chance to come. he will give me leave of absence for one day, but I cant come home and back in that time. If Eliza comes up here I expect to meet her at Greensboro and go back with her that far, but I will not be allowed to go home with her unless we were to go down on the night train and get conveyance from Greensboro that night to her Pas, and then I could stay there all day and come back the next night.

There is some that can go home any time almost, and others that cant get home hardly at all. I think we will stay here this winter and may be I will get home some time next spring. As my paper is about to give out I must close give my love to all. Tell Mary C to write. you must write often. I remain as ever your brother James

<hr>

1   John P. Tiller's Compiled Service Record indicates that he joined the Echol's Artillery February 17, 1863, but it appears from this letter that he was in the unit much earlier. Tiller died of "congestion" in the hospital in Tallahassee, Florida, August 11, 1864

2   Haslets include the heart, liver, and other edible viscera.

ATLANTA
SUNDAY DEC 14TH 62

Dear Sister

I have just received your letter this morning. I was glad to hear from you all   I had concluded to write home to day to know how you all were getting along, as it had been two weeks since I had heard from there. I wrote to you last wednesday and sent the letter by Isham Cheatham[1] and told him to be sure to send it to Brother Marshall's. he said he would be certain to see him thursday.

This leaves me enjoying very good health. Cousin John is mending. he was out here at camps yesterday, he expects to start home tomorrow morning. he will not be at home before tuesday or wednesday. he is going to stop in Madison a day or two. I think you will hear of his being about three mile down the railroad in a few day after he gets home. I think if he could get to see Sallie[2] he would almost forget his head had ever been hurt. Some of us have been telling him that he wanted to get a furlough to go home to get married, but he says he dont expect to marry as long as he has to stay in the war.

We had a general review yesterday evening, by Col Lee and two of Genl Johnson's staff of Tenn. I dont know what could be the object of their coming here unless is was to see if we were worth caring [carrying] up to Tennessee. It is thought by the most of the people here that there will be a battle about Murfreysborough before a great while. It seems that all the armies have been still for some time and I will not be supprised to hear of some move soon. I have no doubt but it will be reported all over Oglethorpe County in a few days that we are going to Tennessee. but we will never know where we are going only a few days before we have to start. I think myself we will stay here sometime yet. I do hope I will not have to stay here much longer but that is very uncertain.

Well, Sallie it will soon be christmas and how do you reckon we will all like to spend our christmas here at this place. You all must fix us something to send us. You must try to save some eggs so we can have an eggnog at least. I expect we will have more guard duty to do then than any other time. Tell Pa if I dont get the chance to come home by that time I want to hire Leathy[3] out some where if he dont want her, if he can get anything for her worth while. I received a letter from Eliza the other day. she said she got home safe and without any trouble. she says her Pa has sent one of his negro men down to the coast.

You want me to tell you who Mattie favors. I cant tell who she favors the most. I will tell you more about that after a while. Some of us are fixing up winter quarters. Our mess have dug a cave. We have dug deep enough for a fireplace on the upper side of the hill and are trying to get plank to fix it up but have not got it yet. I must close as I have nothing of importance to write, hoping that I may see you all soon. write as often as you can. Give my love to all.

excuse bad writing as it was done with a bad pen. I remain as ever your affectionate brother James

1   This probably was John Isham Cheatham, who joined the Echols Artillery as a Private on May 3, 1862, and served until the end of the war. Cheatham is listed in the 1860 Georgia census as a 33-year-old farmer from Madison County. Also in the household were Rhoday, age 35, and 9 children, some with interesting names: David I., 13; Nancy C.P., 11; Roday E., 10; Georgia Ann, 8; Jacob B.J.J., 6; Rispan J., 5; Riley C., 4; James J.A., 3; and Mildred S.G.P.C., 4 months.

2   Miss Sarah F. (Sallie) Stevens, Cousin John's sweetheart, lived at Maxeys, Georgia. She was the daughter of Joseph B. and Celestia McWhorter Stevens. John and Sallie were married March 3, 1864.

3   Leathy was Jewel's slave. In the 1860 Georgia Slave census, James Jewel, Jr., was listed as the owner of one 17-year-old female slave.

ATLANTA
DEC 18TH 62

Dear Sister

I received your letter yesterday, but as I was on guard I [could not go] to the express office to see if my box had come. [When I went] I did not find it. I was glad to hear from you all. I was looking for a letter from Eliza as she was with you. I reckon she did not write. Isham Cheatham has come back to our company again, so I heard from the letter I sent to you by him. he sent it to Daniels Ville[1] and sent there the next day after it. I backed it to you in the care of M.W. Edwards, Athens. I think he must have been very careless or very much excited about having to leave home. You said you hoped it would rain and turn cold. I dont know whether it is cold where you are or not, but I thought it was very cold here last night, and the night before was not much better.

Col Lee, Capt Tiller and a capt from the Battallion, and twenty five of our company went out patrolling and was out till eleven oclock. Some fellow come in from the country and told Col Lee that the negroes were having gathering of all sorts and somebody ought to patroll, but we did not see anything amiss.

Well Sallie, I have been over to the depot again and got my box and opened it after eating my dinner, but I eat two biscuits and two pieces of sausage. dont you reckon I would be glad to be at home to live high now. We have some back bones and ribs once and awhile, but we have to pay fifteen cents a pound which I think is dear living. I have a bate of light bread and sausage for supper to night. I carried a box to the depot when I went after the other one. there is seven bottles in it that I have picked up about here. one of them is full of buckshot for Pa. I promised to let Brother have some of them if they would suit his gun and the large ball will do to mold over again. The checked pillow case belongs to Mrs Colclough.[2] Eliza told to get some iron to send to her Mother to make copperas. I gathered some this morning at the State shop and put it in a bag in the box. I reckon there will be some passing so they can get it. When you go to open the box look at the right hand corner and you will see a little string with a knot on the outside which is tied to the key inside the box.

There is a goodeal of talk about the battle that has taken place at Fredricksburg, but we have not learned the particulars yet. Genl Thomas Cobb[3] was killed. Genl Hooker of the U.S. army is reported killed.[4]

President Davis[5] and Genl Joseph Johnston[6] stayed Monday night. I was very anxious to see them but I did not get the chance to see the Gentlemen. They told Col Lee that there was not men enough here so I understood, and there is to be another company sent here and our company is to be changed to cavelry. Genl Johnston says he considers this a very important place and wants it well guarded. We do actually have more to do here than we would if we were in Virginia or Tenn. but then we are not so much exposed. I had rather stay here my self but some of the boys talk like they want to leave here. Capt Tiller says he will have to get forty more horses so as to mount about a hundred men. The talk is that we will be exempt from guard duty and have to scout all the time while we stay here and if we are called off we will take our guns again. My notion is that if we are changed to a cavelry company we will not stay here long.

I reckon Cousin John has got home before this time. he left here monday morning. I would like to hear how he is getting along. I got a letter for him from his Pa the next day after he left [and] he sayed Mrs Perkins[7] & Sallie was there. they come up to see him I reckon, as they were looking for him home.

Well Sallie, you wrote about killing Mas hogs but you did not say what they weighed. [I] though you said you would send the weights.

Well now, let me tell you about our nice little house. you never saw just such a house as we have any where. We dug about three feet in the groung and made a fire place and got an old engine chimney and turned it bottom upwards for the chimney, then put up post and weather boarded and covered it with plank. it is ten feet wide and eighteen long. Oh, it is so much better than a tent without any fire these cold nights. since we put up ours, nearly all the boys have gone to work.

I must close, maybe I can tell you something more the next time I write. you must write soon. Give my love to all.

I hope to see you all before long. I remain as ever, your affectionat brother James

1   Danielsville, the county seat of Madison County, Georgia, is a few miles north of Athens.

2   This was Nancy Nelms Colclough, Eliza's mother and James Jewel's mother-in-law. The inscription on her tombstone in the family cemetery in the Penfield District of Greene County gives her birth date as February 14, 1812, and her death as February 14, 1892.

3   General Thomas Reade Rootes Cobb of Athens, brother of General Howell Cobb, was killed at the battle of Fredricksburg, Virginia, December 13, 1862.

4   This was a false rumor. Major General Joseph "Fighting Joe" Hooker was not killed during the War Between the States.

5   Jefferson Davis, President of the Confederate States of America.

6   General Joseph Eggleston Johnston.

7   Mrs. Perkins was Permelia S. Perkins. She is listed in the 1860 Georgia census as 55 years old and living in the household next to the family of Sarah F. Stevens (already cited) and may have been a relative.

ATLANTA
DEC 22ND 62

Dear Sallie

I take my seat to write you a few lines to let you know that I am still enjoying good health, as I have an opportunity of sending [a letter] by hand. William Norton is here and going home tomorrow. I have no news of importance to write the health of our company is generally good.   One of the boys, Nathan Eberheart,[1] got his shoulder put out of joint yesterday evening by falling from the fence some where between here and the race tract, so he says. he is badly hurt.

I believe I wrote to you about our being changed to a cavelry company but I have not heard any thing about it in two or three days. it looks more like changeing to infantry because they have given nearly all the company guns last saturday.[2] we only had about thirty guns for the company before. The guard duty will be very hard on us during christmas I think from what I can see now. a week ago we had enough men for three reliefs so we would not be on guard oftener than every third day, but for several days now we never miss more than a day and night   I was out last night. the weather has moderated a goodeal, it is pleasant knocking about to day. I am in hopes it will be warm for a while now. There is a lot of soldiers pass in here now. One Brigade of Genl Bragg's going to Jackson Miss., so it is said. There must be some expectation of a battle there by them moveing the troops there.

Well Sallie if you could see our little house and see how we can cook in it you would [wonder] why we did not build one long ago. You must excuse this short letter as I havent time to write any more

I hope to hear from you soon. I have not heard from Cousin John since he left. I hope you may have a mery christmas. Write soon. Give my love to all the family and connections. I remain as ever your affectionate brother James

1   Nathan M. Eberhart joined the Echols Artillery as a Private on March 1, 1862. He is listed in the 1860 Georgia census as the 17-year-old son of John and Sarah Eberhart of the Goose Pond District of Oglethorpe County.

2   It was well over a year before a change was made. In March 1864 glanders, a bacterial disease, killed most of their horses and the Echols Artillery was changed to an infantry company.

ATLANTA
JANUARY 2ND 1863

Dear Pa

I am very sorry to inform you that we have received marching orders. We are to leave here next tuesday morning for florida. we are going to a place called quincy about fifteen miles from Tallahassa and report to Brg: Genl H. Cobb.[1] It has been reported in camps for several days that we would have to leave, but none of us put any confidence in the reports. We have just put us up a good house to stay in (our mess), and liked a few hours work of having [it] completed when we heard the orders. we put up one a week or two ago but it was not quite large enough and the government furnished us some more plank, and now we have to leave it. The ladies of the citty gave the company a nice dinner to day. I did not think they would be liberal these hard times. I have not time to write, but as I had to go out on a scout to night over the citty and it is now after eleven oclock and I will be on guard tomorrow night, I will have to send all my things home, only what I can toat. We will go through Macon and Albany, from which place we will have to march about eighty miles. I will write again the first opportunity.

This leaves me in very good health. I weigh one hundred and sixty pounds, which is more than than I ever weighed before. My love to all. I remain your affectionate son James

1   Brigadier General (later Major General) Howell Cobb of Athens was the older brother of Brigadier General T.R.R. Cobb and was the governor of Georgia from 1851 to 1853. Howell Cobb was Secretary of the Treasury in President James Buchanan's cabinet, but he resigned his post and returned home to support the South when secession was imminent. He served as President of the Confederate Provisional Congress, which met in Montgomery, Alabama, in February 1861 to form the Confederate Government. Cobb was placed in command of Confederate forces in the Middle Florida Military District when it was formed in November 1862. The District extended from the Suwannee River in the east to the Choctawhatchee River in the west. Headquarters were in Quincy. Brigadier General Joseph Finegan commanded the District of East Florida, which extended from the Suwannee eastward to the coast.

   In August 1863, Cobb was ordered to Atlanta to organize the State Militia and other state forces for the defense of Georgia. He was temporarily replaced by Colonel William J. McGill, but when Cobb was ordered to remain in Atlanta, General Finegan assumed command of both the Middle and East Districts of Florida on September 8, 1863. On October 30, 1863, Brigadier General William M. Gardner was placed in command of the Middle District.

CHAPTER III

The Move to Florida

"This is the first time that I have been off of Georgia soil"

*[This letter is in the collection of the
Robert W. Woodruff Library at Emory University]*

QUINCY FLA:
JANUARY 15TH 1863

Dear Sallie

I have taken a seat to write you a few lines. We are in camps about a mile below the above named town in the piny wood, which resembles an old piny field. the most of the large timber has been cut down. I thought when we come here we would find an army stationed here but there is none nearer that the Chatahoochee river and that is about twenty miles from here. We are not stationed yet. Genl Cobb told Capt Tiller that he would keep us here two or three weeks and we will go to the junction of the Flint and Chatahoochee rivers at the arcenell [arsenal][1] which is about the georgia line. This is the first time that I have been off of georgia soil.

I will give you a short history of our travels. We packed up early wednesday morning and left our old camp ground and marched over to town [Griffin] and put our plunder on the cars and thought we would leave at ten oclock but there was some misunderstanding about the transportation so we did not leave till six oclock that night. We got to Macon about three oclock where we stayed till twelve when we left for Albany and landed there about nine at [the] end of the railroad. Friday we went out about three miles to the blue spring. it runs a small river from the spring it is about eighty feet deep where it boils up and as clear as water can be. I saw a many a large fish in the spring. One of George Martins Wifes uncles brought us enough fresh meat to last our mess down here. We left there early the next mornin and travelled about twenty five miles and half of the day in the rain. I eat dinner monday at John Edwards. They were all well.

The ladies of bainbridge heard that we were comeing through there so they wrote to the Capt by the stage driver to know when we would get there. he sent them word that we would get there monday evening. You ought to have seen every man woman and child was out to meet us with their drums and flag and I guess you never heard such hollowing in your life. they could not have made much more to do over us if we had went from there and come back home. so we camped in the edge of the town and a great many of them went out with us and soon had the [area] strewed around with baskets of vituals for our supper and the next morning they were sent out again with enough for breakfast. if all the people were all to treat the soldiers with as much hospitality as they did it would be a poor soldier that would not fight for them. James Barrow[2] and Frank Pope[3] belong to Genl Cobbs staff. we met James Barrow on his way to Richmond, on some business I suppose. I would be glad to write more but the mail boy has come around and says he is going to carry the mail this evening. We will only get the mail here every other day. You must write as soon as you receive this as it will be several days before I will hear from you all. Give my love to all. I must close. you must excuse mistakes as it was written in a hurry. I remain as ever you affectionate brother James

Direct your letter to Quincy Gadsden County Florida

1   The U.S. Arsenal at Chattahoochee, Florida, was built over a several-year period in the 1830s. The main complex, which covered 4 acres and included 9 buildings, was enclosed by a 12-foot-high brick wall, 2 1/2 feet thick. There also were 4 buildings outside the enclosure. Bricks for the buildings and wall were made locally from alluvial clay tempered with sand. Granite sills, caps, and coping were brought from Maine. The arsenal saw only limited use and by the late 1850s was considerably deteriorated. After the war, the facilities were used for a state penitentiary and later were converted to a state mental hospital, which still occupies the site.

2   James Barrow was the son of David Crenshaw Barrow, Sr., the Jewels' former neighbor in Oglethorpe County. He had resigned from the Military Academy at West Point when Georgia seceded from the union and accepted a commission in the Confederate Army. James Barrow was killed at the Battle of Olustee, Florida, February 20, 1864. He was 22 years old at the time

and was one of the youngest soldiers in the Confederate Army to hold the rank of Lieutenant Colonel.

3   Alexander Franklin Pope was a 2nd Lieutenant in the Troup Artillery under his brother-in-law, Captain Marcellus Stanley. The company had been formed in Athens, Georgia, and named in honor of former Georgia Governor George M. Troup. Pope was the son of General Burwell Pope, who had begun his military career during the War of 1812.

QUINCY, GADSDEN
COUNTY FLA
FEB 17TH 1863

Dear Sallie

I received your letter yesterday written the 9th. I was very glad to hear from you all. I began to think you had not received my letter that I wrote in answer to yours of the 20 of January. I was about to start to church to a night meeting when it was handed to me so I was obliged to read it before I left and I would have read it if it had been five times as long before I would have gone. although I cannot tell how you all are, I can tell how you was ten day ago. I cannot tell why it is that some of the letters are so long comeing to hand when a letter will go from here to Lexington in three days or from there here sometimes. I think it must be carelessness at some of the post offices.

I am glad that I can still say to you that I am enjoy good health. I heard the other day it was reported in Oglethorpe that some of our company had the chill and fever. that is a mistake. there is not a man in camps sick. There is one over in town that is a little, but he will be out in a day or two I reckon. Cobb Davis was left at John Edwards'es as we came down here. he was very sick for a while. the last account I had of him he was going to Georgees to stay a while. that has been two weeks or more. in short, the health of the company is better than it ever has been since I came into camps.

Well Sallie I will give you [the] history of our trip to Tallahassa last week, but before I commence that, I will tell you of something that happened the night before we left. Monday Morning Capt Till. received a ticket inviting our company to a party given by the ladies of Quincy. There was a new company in camps near here so they had to go or be slighted. so forty of them come over and went with us. there was about 150 in the crowd [that] went over and went upstairs in the female Academy where the ladies were where we were addressed by the Rev Mr Andrews on the part of the ladies. he was replied to by Capt Tiller and Lieut Gibson, after which we called on Genl Cobb. he gave us a short speech complimenting the women very highly for what they had done for the soldiers during the war. We then marched out across the street to an old church where the table was set. I tell you it was nice. it was dressed off like a wedding table and a plenty of every thing that was good on it. All that wished were invited to return and keep company with the ladies. the supper did not come off till ten Oclock.

Tuesday morning we started with the battery for Tallahassa for a review. the route we had to go was about twenty six miles. that night we camped at lake Jackson, the first lake that I ever saw. it is five or six miles long and from one to three miles wide. There is a good many ponds in the neighborhood of the lake, some of them large enough for allegators.

I had the pleasure once in my life of passing through the capital of a state. From what I could see I thought Tallahassa to be a small town, though I [illegible] as to the size of Quincy when I first come here. it is a nice little town. Well we camped a mile below Tallahassa untill friday morning. thursday we went on the field where there was 3 companies of infantry, 3 of cavelry and a Artillery company that was made up in the neighborhood of Tala [Talahassee]. [They] never have been off from home and [have] been in service for twelve months and nothing to do but to drill. Their horses look a great deal better than ours but Genl Cobb says we beat them drilling. one of the company, Dr Glenn,[1] got thrown from one of the wagons and his arm broken at the rist joint. Genl Cobb gave him a furlough of sixty day to go home.

We came through Tallahassa again Friday morning on the way to camps and landed here saturday morning. I dont think I ever saw as many foggy mornings before and such heavy dews while we were gone. I could hear the water dripping off the trees like it was raining. Sallie I saw some of the greatest yards that I ever saw at most any time of the year. I saw one place where I think there was at least fifty orange trees aroung the house. The country is more broken about Tallahassa than it is here, though there is a goodeal of of flat sandy land between here and there.

Capt Tiller [came] here yesterday to go to Atlanta after equipage for our other guns that we are to get. Genl Cobb ordered two more guns for us and they have started from Atlanta. Col Sander,[2] one of Genl Beaurgard staff, told the Capt when he was here that he would take the guns we had and give us a fine battery of six guns, but I dont know that we will get them.

Well Sallie, I did [not] get through with this letter yesterday so I will finish this morning. I went out to church night before last. I never was as much at a loss to know what to do. it was the Episcopalian church. The preacher come in, went to the pulpit, and went through a short secret prayer. then got up to a table before the pulpit and commenced reading. the members with books in their hands followed suit. Which I thought from the reading was their prayer. then they got on their [knees] for prayer again, and [went] through the same movements the second time with singing by the choir and the malodian. he then went into the pulpit and read out his surmon of about 18 or 20 pages, then sung a hymn, went to prayer again, and dismissed [the members] while they were on their knees.

Last night I went to a Tableaux given by the ladies of Quincy. There was quite a crowd out and some very well acted pieces. I will not have time to tell you any thing about it. James Barrow was one of the actors and several others of Genl Cobbs staff. Sallie I wish I had more time to write. I have not eat breakfast and will have to drill before I have time to write any more.

I am sorry to say to you that we have to leave Quincy and take up our abode at some other place. We will go to a place called alum bluff[3] on the Appalachacola river the last of this week or the first of next. Lieut Gibson is in command of the Company. he has told us we will go.

The prospects for peace are still brightening, there is no telling what a month will bring forth now. Sallie you wanted me to send you some good pens if we had them here. I bought what I have used at Griffin before we left there. I do not know what sort they have here or what they are worth. I must close Direct your letters to this place and I reckon I will get it sometime. George Martin got a letter from home yesterday written Saturday, they did not say anything about bringing Frank home.

Give my love to all. I remain your affectionate brother James

1 Dr. Glenn was James Mallory Glenn, listed in the 1860 Georgia census as a 27-year-old physician residing in the household of Clarinda Davenport, a 22-year-old farmer in the Glade District of Oglethorpe County. Glenn apparently was boarding there along with Dr. David A. Matthews and George R.J. Glenn, a clerk. James Glenn enlisted in the Echols Artillery on March 4, 1862, as a Corporal but was later breveted to 2nd Lieutenant.

2 Colonel Sander probably was William J. Saunders who was Assistant Adjutant General to General P.G.T. Beauregard.

3 Alum Bluff was a vantage point on the Apalachicola River, 22 miles below the town of Chattahoochee, Florida. The Confederates had a seven-gun battery of cannons there to help prevent Union boats from penetrating the interior of Florida from the Gulf of Mexico.

QUINCY
GADSDEN CO. FLA.
FEB 22ND/63

Dear Sallie

I received yours and Marys letter to day from the hands of Cousin John and was very glad to see him and hear from you all. he landed here with every thing safe this morning about ten oclock I had started to church and met him with a wagon, so I turned back to camps with him. he came to Columbus [Georgia] and took the steamboat from there to Chattahoochee [Florida], a little town down on the Apalachacola river. there [he] happened to meet with a wagon comeing by here going to the coast after salt and brought his things along.

Sallie we have been expecting for several days to leave here to morrow for a place called Allums bluff but from some cause or other I think it has been put off   I reckon we will know soon. I will find out if I can before I close this letter when we will start. There was quite a crowd of ladies out last thursday evening to see us drill. Lieut Gibson told some of them the day before that [this] would be the last time they would have an opportunity of seeing us drill here.

Sallie, As I had been out some time writing I thought I would go to the tent and rest a while and who do you reckon I found there. Frank Pope and Pope Barrow, and in a few minute Lieut Lumpkin came in.[1] We had a pleasant time for an hour or two. Pope Barrow has just come here. he went home and started back here and was taken with the mumps and had [to] stop awhile. They told us that we would not leave here before the last of the week or the first of the next. I must stop writing as I have concluded to go out to church to night and the boys are waiting for me now and some of them have gone. I will write in the morning.

Dear Sallie, I went to church last night and heard a very good sermon preached. the text was [taken from] St John, 1st chap, 29th verse. Behold the lamb of God which taketh away the sin of the world. I felt a little more at home than I did at the Episcopalian church where the men [and] women all sit together any where they chose. We have been here nearly six weeks and Jim Barrow has never come around to talk with any of us yet. he has been on the drill ground a good many times with the ladies and has rode through camps here more than a dozen time and he has never spoke to me yet. Pope came down here saturday and the next evening, which was yesterday, he was here wallowing in our tent like he was at home. I did not think there was that difference between them. Pope is a little fellow yet. Brig Genl Cobb heard of the death of one of his wifes brothers and went home yesterday morning.[2] Why cant I or any one else go when any of our friends are sick or die as well as the officers.

Sallie [I] dont know hardly what to write as there is nothin of much importance taken place since i wrote to you. I was glad to see the brandy sent to me. it is the first that I have seen since christmas. I went to town saturday to get some tobacco and writing paper. the tobacco is selling at two dollars and a half a pound and it was so sorry that I would not buy any and paper like this is $1.50 a quire. I bought a half a quire and I saw a poor man have a common pair of cotton cards that he said he paid thirty dollars for. how can poor people live at such rates as that. Sallie tell Pa to send me a pair of shoestrings if [he] pleases. it is difficult to get any such things here as there is no shoe shop in town. you can put them in a letter and send them.

Sallie I reckon this will be an answer to yours and Marys letter. you can send it to her if she is at home or send her all the news and may be I will write again before long. We have got to go out to drilling again this morning and the mail will leave before we get back and if I dont send it this morning I will have to wait till wednesday.

I hate to wast paper as this is done but I have been writing in a hurry to get through. I have not tried on any of my clothes yet. I think my pants will be very warm for this climate. my hat is little too small but I can wear it tolerable well. You must write often. I have received two letters from you and only two from Eliza since I left Atlanta. You all must write oftener. I must close. Give my love to all the relations and enquiring friends. I remain your affectionate brother James

---

1   Middleton Pope Barrow, older brother of James Barrow (already cited), was a 2nd Lieutenant in the Troup Artillery along with A. Franklin Pope (already cited). Edward P. Lumpkin, another 2nd Lieutenant in Captain Stanley's Company, was the son of Joseph Henry Lumpkin, Chief Justice of Georgia's Supreme Court and the brother of Mrs. T.R.R. Cobb.

2   This was not true. Cobb's wife, Mary Ann Lamar Cobb, had one brother killed in the war. This was Colonel John Basil Lamar, killed at Crampton's Gap, Maryland, in September 1862. Most likely, General Cobb had gone home to be with his wife during the final illness of their youngest child, 2-year-old Thomas Reade Rootes Cobb, Jr., who died March 14, 1863.

QUINCY
GADSDEN CO. FLA
MARCH 7TH 1863

Dear Sallie

I received your letter last tuesday dated the 24th of Feb but have postponed answering it because I had written a few lines to you the day before. therefore I hope you will excuse me for not writing sooner as I received one from Eliza the same day that I had to answer. She said they were all well but she had not heard from you all in some time. At one time I began to think that she had quit writing to me entirely. it was at one time more than three weeks that I did not hear from her at all. in fact, I did not receive but two letters from her after we left Atlanta till about the first of this month and about three from you. I reckon you may guess how I felt. I reckon there was some mistake in backing them since that time I received three in five days, one of them was written before Cousin John left home and I did not get it in a week after he got here.

Well I went with a crowd about four miles to take a fishing [trip] this morning at a millpond. but we met with such poor luck some of them concluded to go a little farther to the river, but Mat Norton and I rather chose to come back a little before we got back to camps we saw a black cloud nearly north of us that indicated rain a goodeal and very soon it began to thunder and in a few minutes after we got into camps it commence one of the hardest rains that I ever saw in Florida (but I have seen harder in Georgia). it is still raining and looks like it might last some time and some of us is poorly prepared for it at this time.

Wednesday Genl Cobb sent an order here for twelve men with one bagage wagon to take a load of our bagage and start immediately for Alumns bluff to haul forage that is to be shipped down the river for us. so we had to send a part of the tents and ours was among those that was sent. we kept the fly and stretched it over a pole with both ends open and put a blanket up at one end to keep the rain from blowing in. We are keeping dry so far. it looks like I am very near out in the weather, but there is many a poor soldier that has to lay down to sleep without anything to keep the rain off of him, so of course I ought to be satisfied so long as I can keep dry. It is thundering and lightning like summertime. I expect we will have cold weather after this. As it is raining so much and my paper is getting damp I will stop writing till to morrow.

March 8th   Dear Sallie, I received a letter from you written last monday. I was glad to hear from you all and hear that you were well. I saw the order from Governer Brown Calling out the Malitia officers. I also saw an account in the newspaper last night of Col W.M. Nichols[1] passing through Augusta a few days ago with his Regt of officers. it said he not only had furnished a substitute sometime last year, but had now readily responded to the call to aid Savannah. I dont blame any one for responding readily when they know they will be obliged to comply with the order. I see that congress has pass a bill repealing all the exemptions bills and not leaving quite so many out. I think that all men that have substitutes under forty five will have to go and also no more substitutes to be received. so all those that have been trying to get them so long and have failed are at the end of their row now.

Cousin John seems to enjoy himself very well with the ladies down here. he goes over to town nearly every day and some times he goes over after supper and sits till bedtime. there is several of the company that seems to be taking on considerably with the ladies. I dont know whether they are in earnest or not but I think some of them are.

I dont know of any thing that Cousin John got from Griffin but a nice cake presented to him by Miss Martha Dunn.[2] it was nicely fix up and it was very good, I eat some of it. I saw a nice needle in [his] trunk but I did not ask him who gave it to him. I thought Sallie [Stevens] made it for him. You wanted to know if we could see the yankeys. I have not seen any wild ones yet. I think there is a few tame ones about here like there is in Oglethorpe, but I dont think there is as many here as there is there. it is too far from the coast for us to see the Yanks here. it may be that we may see some when we get on the Appalachacola river. there is men a long ways below where we will be blockading the river. We are expecting orders every day and as soon as one of those men that went down to Alumn bluff come back to let Genl Cobb know that the forage is there, we will receive orders. so we may stay here several days yet. I will let you know if we hear any thing before I send this letter tomorrow morning. you will direct your letters to this place untill further orders. I received a letter from John Colclough yesterday. he said his Pas folks were all well. Write as often as you can. Give my love to all. I remain your affectionate brother James

P.S. tell Pa I am very much obliged to him for the shoestrings he sent me

---

1　William N. Nichols is listed in the 1860 Georgia census as a 30-year-old farmer in the Bowling Green District of Oglethorpe County. Also in the household were his wife, Marion, age 24, and his mother-in-law, Anna R. Lumpkin, age 69. Mrs. Lumpkin was the widow of Reverend Jack L. Lumpkin. Nichols was a Justice of the Peace and was disabled; thus he was exempt from regular service in the Confederate Army but served as Colonel of the 22nd Reg. of the Georgia State Militia..

2　Martha E. Dunn was listed in the 1860 Georgia census as a 28-year-old "Common School Teacher" in the household of Mary P. Dunn in Spalding County (already cited).

CAMP LEON
LEON COUNTY FLA
MARCH 22 1863

Dear Sallie

I have taken a seat to write you a few lines in answer to yours sent to me by Oliver Cooper.[1] I am very comfortably situated in a house by a stove, though I feel rather dull this morning.

There has been quite a change in the weather yesterday and this morning, it is cooler than it has been for some time. I wrote to Mary and told her to send you the letter so that you could hear from me. [That] is one reason that I did not write to you sooner, because I thought that would be enough for both of you to read awhile and immuse your selves with. I reckson you think I might have written to you before I left Quincy, but I will tell you how it was. I received your letter friday evening withe the other two just as we were fixing to go out to drill. so the next morning I put off writing for a while thinking I would have ample time to write to you all before the next mail would leave, which was monday morning. but about the time I commenced writing, we received marching orders and then I only had time to write a few lines to Eliza before we had to commence fixing up to start. So I wrote to her to let you all know that we were going to leave Quincy.

I received a letter from Eliza yesterday evening and one from James Davison[2] of Woodville[3] asking me about the chance of getting salt, sugar and syrup from here. Salt is selling from two to five dollars per bushel and I think it woud be rather a difficult matter to ship much of it at a time. Sugar and Syrup is getting scarce and more than that Genl Cobb will not allow it to be shipped from the state. I guess Jim wants to get something to speculate on, but I guess he will [not do] it this time, for I dont think he can get sugar enough from down here to make much of a fortune on soon. Eliza says they are all well except John. he has been in the bed for a week at Woodville. It seems that you all dont visit much. most every time she writes she says she has not heard from you all in a long time, or such as I call a long time, and be as close together as you all are.

Well Sallie if you have seen the letter that I wrote to Mary it would not be worth while for me to undertake to tell you about our trip from Quincy down here, or even to tell you any thing about the situation of Capt Gambles Company. more than to say they have not come back yet. one of the men here received a letter from the Capt yesterday from Jacksons Ville [Florida] ordering him to keep all the furloughed men that come into camps here. heretofore the orders had been for him to send them to the company immediately if they were able to go. We are just lieing here doing nothing awaiting some orders. So none of us knows one day where we will be the next. the orders have been given by the Capt again to keep a days rations cooked ahead for fear that we might be ordered off immediately and not have time to cook. but I dont think there is many that obeys the order, for it is a little more than we can do to make our rations hold out any how, and if we were to keep it cooked a head I am confident it would give out sooner.

We get but very little bacon. about a pound to the man for ten days and about half rations of beef. So there is nine in our mess and I think we got ten or twelve pounds and by the slight of hand we have lost every bit of ours, so we will have to depend on our beef or bye some thing to make out on. If I was at home I would not eat as much meat as we get in camps because we generally have something else, but when it is nothing but meat and bread it takes a goodeal to do us. We have always made out very well some how and I hope we will. I know there is many a one in the army and even at home that does not have as good a chance as we do here, so when I think of them I feel ashamed of my self for grumbling at what we have. As the mail will not go out till to morrow evening and it getting late, so I will postpone writing till tomorrow morning.

1   Winston Oliver Cooper was 2nd Bugler in the Echols Artillery. He is listed in the 1860 Georgia census as a 26-year-old farmer living with his wife Permelia and two daughters in the Bowling Green District of Oglethorpe County.

2   James Davison was the father of William Davison (already cited).

3   Woodville is a small community in Greene County on the Georgia Railroad, about 10 miles south of Antioch and 4 miles east of Penfield.

CAMP LEON
LEON COUNTY FLA
MARCH 23RD
MONDAY MORNING

Dear Sallie,

I have eat breakfast and concluded to write a little more this morning, though I hardly know what to write. It is cloudy this morning and looks very much like rain. I would not be surprised if we had rain a plenty this spring as it has been a very dry winter in this country.

There is a new fashion telegraph from Tallahassee to St Marks from any thing that I have ever seen before. the news is carried by sentinels or watch man posted along the rail road in little houses and some of them have tents as far a part as they can see each other and they have flags of different kinds and by the wave of the flag they under stand each other. At night they use lights in the same way. So they can operate at any time except foggy or rainy weather. they all have spyglasses to look through. Such a thing as that would be expensive in our country as it is so hilly. they could not see [as] far. here they are near two miles apart.

I heard some bad news about McKinnebrew day before yesterday. he was one of the guards that was left at Quincy to guard the ordinance stores and was found asleep on his post. he was put under arrest. it was said that F Pope went there with a wagon and took out some powder without his knowing of it. Frank Pope has the management of that department. I expect he will have to stand a court martial.[1] I dont wonder at it much, for he visited the ladies so much and lost so much sleep that he could not stay awake. I talked to him and Cousin John before we left there about going to see the ladies so often and losing so much sleep. I am glad that Cousin John did not stay there since I heard of that scrape.

Well Sallie I will tell you my dream last night. I thought I was at home and Mattie could talk to me. I thought she was glad to see me and said this is Papa. I thought I took her in my arms and she was nearly as much as I could carry well, but I awoke and found it was all a dream. Cousin Johns trunk was sent down from Quincy this morning. there is as nice a bouquet [in it] as I have seen in a long time with some ripe strawberries in it. Two gentlemen passed down on the train this morning and told Cousin John they heard Genl Cobb say that we would go back to Quincy as soon as Capt Gambles[2] company come back from Jacksonville. It has been my notion that we would [go] back there but I dont know that it will ever be so. I had rather stay there than here, though we may have to go to a much worse place than this before the war ends. the reason I dont like this place [is that] it is too poor for any body to live at and consequently it is lonesome.

Well I really dont know what to tell you about directing your letter, but if you will write immediately and direct your letter to Tallahassee I reckon I will get it. I dont like the idea of having to pay ten cents for forwarding letters from Quincy. I dont think it is right for us to have it to do. I have always thought that soldiers letters were forwarded free of charge before we came here. Twenty cents is high to pay on a letter for a poor soldier. I believe it is the post masters doing to fill his own pockets. Well I must close.

Give my love to al. I hope the time will soon come when I will see you all again, though everything is rather gloomy in that respect now. Write soon. I remain your affectionate brother James

1   There is no record that Marcus B. Kinnebrew was court-martialed during his service in the Confederate Army.

2   Gamble's Artillery was organized in the spring of 1862 with Captain Robert H. Gamble in command. The unit saw service at Johns Island near Charleston, South Carolina, Natural Bridge, Florida, and various other places in Florida. Gamble retired from service in 1863. The 1860 Florida census lists Gamble as a 44-year-old Virginia-born planter in Leon County, living in Tallahassee. His 25-year-old wife, Martha C., and 4 month-old daughter, Jane S., were born in Florida.

[This letter is in the collection of the
Robert W. Woodruff Library at Emory University]

CAMP LEON
FLORIDA
MARCH 26TH 1863

Dear Sallie

I received your Welcome letter yesterday evening written the 18th. I was glad to hear that you were all well. As [I] wrote to you about four days ago and consequently I have but little news of importance to write. I am still enjoying as good health as I could wish for. The health of the company has been very good and is still so yet. there [is] not a man in camps sick at this time. there was one sick for two or three days but he has got out again. Cousin John is well. he has the blues occasionally because he wants to go back to Quincy or to see Sallie one. He seemed to get along finely while he was there but since we came here where he cannot as much as see a lady let alone talk with them he seems to be lonesome and I dont know who could blame him. I feel so myself because we have all been stationed where [there] has been a great many people and now we are where there is very few to be seen. I have not been to Tallahassee since we came through there and by the by I dont recollect whether I told you where Camp Leon is situated when I wrote to you. If I did you must pardon me for I forgot.

We are six miles below Tallahassee near the railroad that leads to St. Marks and about fourteen miles from that place. Well Sallie I will tell you about the battle at Ochlockony bay. I think it is quite likely you will have heard of it from the newspapers before this reaches you and also tell you how near I come of being in it. I will commence at the first and give you as good a history of it as I am able at the present time.

Day befor yesterday which was tuesday, about eleven oclock, a curier [courier] came galloping up with orders for us to go to the Ochlockony bay as quick as we could get there. there was some yankeys that had gone up the river and stold an old boat and got off about ten miles down the [river] and run aground. Capt Scott Cavelry was not far off but they thought they could not do much with them on the water at the distance they were from the shore but before the curier got out of the camps another one rode up and countermanded the order. After dinner the capt. started to town but before he got there he met a curier and had to turn back with him and fix off one section with two guns to go there so they got ready and left camps about an hour by sun to go thirty miles. but as it happened I did not belong to that section and I stayed here, so I was in thirty miles of the yankeys that time. So they traveled on till half past one oclock that night when they landed at Capt Scotts camp where they found that the Yanks had skedalled so they spent the ballance of the night. The Cavelry watched them till they become impatient and thought the tide would rise and float them off before our men got there so they pitched into them with their little guns and the Yankes throwed a few grape shot in return with two cannon that was on board but they found that the rebels were most too close to them and getting to hot for them so they concluded there was some better place for them. they quit the deck and went down in the boat and cut a hole on the opposite side got into their little tug boat and left after setting the boat on fire. The Cavelry succeeded in getting their flag which has been sent to Genl Cobb at Quincy. It is thought that there was only about twenty or twenty five on board though some reports say there was as many as fifty. It is not certain that there was any of them was killed though some say they thought there was at least four or five fell overboard. one man on our side was slightly wounded under the chin from a piece of bark shot off of a pine tree. so the battle was ended and the Cavelry returned to their camps Seven miles before our men got to their camps. So this ended the battle of Ochlockony bay and our boys come back the next evening about the same time they left here without seeing any of the fun as some of them called it. The most of them was as keen to go as you ever saw a crowd to go any where, but as for myself I was not anxious at all. to tell you the truth I was glad that I belonged to the right section, for if I had been called on to go I should have hated to have backed out. Our section would have gone instead of the other had it not been that commander Lieut Gibson has been detailed by Genl Cobb at Tallahassee for the purpose of holding court martials. he has been attending there regularly nearly every day since we have been here and he says he will have to go there for some time yet as there is a good many cases to be tried.

Well Sallie I was sitting in one of the houses a few minutes ago when I heard Jack Edwards commence blowing the horn and it is at least two hundred yards from our camps so I had to drop every thing and put out to get there to answer to my name if it was called. I thought it was more orders come for some of us to go some where as it was at an unusual time for him to blow but it was only to have some seats fixed for our accomodations at prayer meeting at night. We have a regular prayer meeting every night unless providentially hindered, which is conducted by the Capt, Lieut Gibson, and Frank Collier. Lieut Gibson takes interest in trying to get [the] company to do right and leave off their wicked ways. he takes several numbers of the Christian Index for the benefit of those who want to read them. also some tracts occasionally for us to read.

Sallie I dont know hardly what more to write that would interest you. I have been buying some more paper as you may see by looking at this. I was not quite out but I saw this and I thought it was as cheap as any I could get any where one of the boys bought half of a large book so I got thirteen leaves like this for sixty cents. it is as large as the paper that we get at a dollar and a half and a long site better paper [even] if it was made by the yankeys. Well I must try to fill up this side with something as it will not do to leave it blank. it is about five oclock and Jack is going to blow for dress parade and then I will have to eat supper and water and feed my horses so I will have to put off writing till tomorrow morning and then maybe I can think of something to write.

March 27th Well Sallie I have taken a seat at the same table this morning that I was at yesterday evening but I hope I will not be interupted this morning by the sound of the bugle before I get through writting. today is a day set apart [for prayer and fasting] by the President of the Confederate States. We had a lecture on it last night by Lieut Gibson. He says it is not the [fasting] that will [do] any good but by so doing it will make us think of the things that this day has been set apart for and to pray that God will bless us and make a determination to forsake our sins. It will be kept by a goodmany in camps today. Some of them say it is a matter of necessity with them because they have not got any thing to eat but I dont hardly suppose that is so for I dont think there is any that are entirely out of something to eat. they may be out of meat for anything I know as today is the time for us to draw some beef and [as] it is fast day I reckon it will be put off till tomorrow.

The Capt told us last night that he was sorry that we could not go to preaching today. it is so far to town that it would not do for us to leave that far for we might receive orders to move from here and then we would be out of the way. If we was at Quincy we could all go to preaching that wished to go. He says that we will have some kind of services here in camps today. I am sorry to say that I have never kept the fast days that have been ordered but I have promised myself to try to keep [it] this [time] though. I may be doing wrong by writing but I dont consider it so. If I donot mail this letter to day it will not leave Tallahassee till monday moring. The mail leaves Tallahassee at seven Oclock in the morning and it leaves here the evening before and sunday there is no mail so all the letters that is sent off saturday have to be in the office till monday.

Well Sallie in your letter you wrote that you was sorry to hear that we had to go to Alum Bluff, but that was one time we were all mistaken. we did not go to that place but if that is much worse than this I dont care to go there. It is generally believed by the company that we will go back to Quincy when Capt Gambells company comes back here as there is no doubt but they will come back some time as they left so many of their things here. and more than, that they are under Genl. Cobb, and he has sent then to Genl Finagin to assist him at Jacksonville in case there should be an attack there. There has been a little shirmish there. It is reported that the yankeys have several rigments of negroes there armed but I dont know whether it is true or not.[1] I will close. I hope the time will soon come when I can see you all. I have dreamed several nights here lately about being at home. write as often as you have the opportunity. Give my love to all. Also to brothers family when you see them. I remain as ever your affectionate brother James

1   The rumors were true. In March 1863 Union soldiers, mostly Negro troops, raided and burned Jacksonville and left before Cobb's Confederate reinforcements arrived.

CAMP LEON
MARCH 31ST 1863

Dear Sallie

I have concluded to write you a few lines to let you know that I am still in good health, as I expect to have a chance to send this by hand. Mid Johnson[1] has put in a substitute and expects to leave here tomorrow evening. The weather is disagreeable cool to day withe the wind from the north. It has been so warm here that a little cool spell is very sensibly felt. It commenced raining saturday morning and held on till the next evening most all the time and, in fact, it rained some monday.

Well now I will tell you what a fix [we] were in saturday evening. between two and three Oclock we received orders to go fifteen mile down below here, so the horn was sounded and the company assembled to hear the orders (you will recollect as I told you it was raining and [a] good part of the time as hard as it could come down). so the Capt said that every thing must be ready to move off by four Oclock. So we had but little time to do any thing, even if the weather had been good. we could not get any supper but we let loose to work to get ready. So jus as the last tent was put in the wagon the orders was countermanded and then if it had not been for the houses of this other company here, I dont know what we would have done for the tents was as wet as they could be and the ground where we had them was wet and the most of the men just as wet as if they had waded a river.

I did not get wet myself. I have not had my clothes wet on me since I have been in the war. The most of them [have] got houses to stay in. Our mess got in the same house that we were in when we first came here and we have been staying here ever since. We did not have our tent to stay so we had an excuse for staying here, as it was so much more comfortable in a house by a fire.

Well the boys have come from Alumn bluff with our tents and mess box, so I reckon we can get along now. if we can get anything to put in the box may be we can keep it. we had a little box with out any top to it and last week somebody or something else stold all our bacon the first night after we drew it. It was but little, but it would have helped out some with the beef we had, and night before last the dogs got the last of our beef. We will draw this evening and it will be a jubilee with a good many. This a very poor country around here. We cant buy anything when our rations does not hold out. several of the boys went out yesterday to see what they could get, but come back with a few eggs [for which] they payed about forty cents a dozen.

I would not be surprised [if] the next you hear from us if we are not at some other camp. there is some talk of our going down near St Marke. I reckon you have heard the news from Jacksonsville by this time. the news came here yesterday that the Yankeys had burnt the town and left there. Capt Gamble will be back here in a few days with his company, or at least they are looking for them. Three or four of the company started from here yesterday with some things for the company and were turned back from Tallahassee. The Col. told them that it was not worth while for them to go down there with any thing for the boys as they would be here in a day or two.

I forgot to tell you how that false alarm got here the other day. it was done by that new fashion telegraph that I wrote to you about. they said there was seven yankey vessels in sight of St Marks, and swore that it was so after being asked about it several times. I thought they would not be allowed to give false alarms that way without having to be dealt with, but I suppose they can tell as big lies as the other telegraph operators. I dont see what good it can do any of them to tell as many lies as they do. I am getting a little tired, I will stop writing for a while until I see Mid Johnson.

Well Sallie I have eat supper and taken a seat to write a little more. We had a better supper to night than we have had in several [days], but it was not the best that I ever eat. We had some good old coffee. We thought we would save it so we put it in the mess box and it went to the bluff and we got hold of it again and concluded to try it again.

We received Marching orders again this evening so we are to leave here in the morning at nine oclock. The Capt did not tell us wich way we would go, but we have heard from other sources that we will go to Camp Broker[2] about three miles this side of St Marks. Lieut Gibson says that we will not stay there long. Capt Gambles Company is going to get two more guns and divide the company with four guns each. they have raised their company to about two hundred so they will have about one hundred [men] to four guns. We have got two more pieces at Chattahoochee, but I dont know when we will get them from there.

Well Sallie I must close. I hope to hear from you all soon. It has been over two weeks since the last letter I got from Eliza was written.

I am looking for a letter from her. Give my love to all. I remain your affectionate brother James

P.S. Direct your letters to Tallahassee Florida

1   Middleton Witt Johnson joined the Gilmer Blues as 1st Sergeant May 28, 1861. He transferred to the Echols Artillery as a Private June 12, 1862. He was discharged April 1, 1863, by furnishing W.L. Padgett as a substitute but reenlisted in the Echols Artillery January 3, 1864. The 1860 Georgia census lists him as a 24-year-old farmer in the Bowling Green District of Oglethorpe County. Also in the household were W.W. Johnson, age 22, also a farmer, Mid's mother Lucy Lumpkin, 58, and Julia Johnson, 3. Mid Johnson's tombstone in the Lumpkin family cemetery in Oglethorpe County states that he was born August 13, 1834, and died March 29, 1885.

2   Camp Brokaw (not Broker) no doubt was named for Perez B. Brokaw, Captain of the Leon Cavalry.

CHAPTER IV

At Camp Brokaw

*"There is a considerable difference between being here and
at home if you have anything to eat there"*

Dear Sister

I received your letter yesterday written the 29th. I was very glad
to hear from you all. I thought that the mumps had left you all and
you would not be troubled with them any more. I reckon they will
go through the family now before they stop.

I received a letter from Eliza thursday, it had been written about
ten days. she was complaining and she wrote a very short letter.
Well you said we left Quincy and you did not know it. The reason
of that was I did not have time to write after I heard that we were
going to leave there, and more than that, I did not know where we
would stop at as it was thought by some that we would not stop at
Tallahassee, but go on to Jacksonville. And so we have moved again
without my letting you know any thing about it.

We left camp Leon last wednesday and came down the railroad
about 12 miles to this place which is about three miles from St.
Marks and about two miles west of Newport. I have not learned
how the name of the camp is spelt. some say it is broker, some
others brockawe, [and] others say brochall. I will try and find out
how to spell it before I finish this letter. but I dont know that it
will make any difference, for we all will have our letters directed to
Tallahassee, for a while at any rate. Lieut Gibson is still there at their
courtmartials and he told us the day we left camp Leon that it was
very likely he would be there as long as we would remain down here

and he would send the mail to us as long as he stayed there without its costing us any thing. he said some of Cobbs staff told him that we would not stay here long, for they were going to divide Capt Gambles company and move them down this way and we would go back to Quincy or to Alumns bluff. I have been thinking that we would go back to Quincy but if we go much lower down the country I will get out of that notion. I want to go to see the Gulf one time, but I dont want to stay there. Some of the boys say they have seen where the tidewaters come up the rivers close by here but I have not been to the river.

Well Sallie I thought I had seen some level country before We come to Tallahassee, but it is so level here that I dont think it ever rains enough for the water to run. there is a little branch about a mile from here that seems to be running, but I think it is about as much as it will do. there is no more hill about it than there is in the middle of Pas bottoms if the creek just had a little to run in. It is a limestone country and water is not good. the people all use well water as a matter of course. When we got here the first thing was to see about getting water so the Capt order a well dug immediately. I thought I had seen some shallow wells before, but two men set in to dig one and dug to the enormous depth of four feet when the water rushed in so [that] they had to quit diging. so with two or thre such wells as that, our company is furnished with water. we have neither winlesses nor poles but have steps to go down and dip the water up. I can dig a well here about as quick as I could fix to put up a gate post there about home.

The greatest curiosity that I have seen down here is the palmetto tree. there is one close by here that some of the boys cut down the other day. it was at least sixty feet high and about twelve inches in diameter at the ground and at least eight at the top. it has no limbs at all on it. the leaves were all near the top and the stems of the grown one are about as long [big around?] as my wrist and from four to six feet long with the leaves about as large as a peafowls tail spread. all the leaves of that one were in about three feet of the bud of the tree. it looked like a post that had been turned in a turning laythe. the wood is as much like the pith of a green corn stalk as any thing you ever saw. The small one resemble a nicely plated whip with the stems of the leaves split and cross each other, which is caused by the growing of the tree. the bottom leaves die and shed off like the under limbs of a pine tree. I can give you but a very poor description of them at best. I wish you all could see them. The small palm leaf grows all over the woods here like broom straw in our old fields. I wish I had some way to send you all some fans as they are more plentiful here than oak leaves a long site. I have started to plat me a permeta [palmetto] hat like that piece that I sent to you. The women make them and sell them from three to five dollars after they whiten them a little. They get the bud before it opens which is folded up like one of this paper fans and is white and tender. after it opens it turns green and is more brittle. If I was sure I could send it, I would get a box full of it and send up for you all to make hats and bonets of. but it would be very uncertain whether it would ever get there if I was to start it, as there is no railroad from Quincy to Albany. I will let you know in a week or two how I get along with my hat. I dont expect to make one because I need it, but for amusement.

The paymaster came down yesterday to pay us off but the pay roll was not exactly right and he did not pay us. he is to come back tuesday to pay us four months wages. The Capt has made out a new payroll, so I reckon it is right now. It looks to me like if i had seen as many as he has I could make out one right by this time. but this is not the first time that he has failed to have it made out right. I cannot tell you any thing about how the people are getting along farming in this country, for I have not seen a farm since we came two mile this side of Tallahassee, which was the fifteenth of last month. I saw some houses as we came down here, but no plantations that I could see more than a little patch or two around the house about large enough for a potatoe patch. I reckon they eat fish as they are plentiful about here. They think as much of their fisheries down here as a man up the country does of his cottoncrop. The cattle looks better than any I have seen before since I have been in Florida. I heard Capt Tiller say there was a man told him he would let him have milk and butter a plenty in a week or two. [He said] they would have about a hundred cows to milk. they don't milk through the winter season at all and some of them say they have not commence milking yet. The woods is as green with grass now as a wheat patch and I reckon it has been so for some time. The weather is very cool for this climate. I saw frost the morning we left

Camp Leon and it has been cool ever since. we pile the cover on us here at night like we were in a cold climate. The wind blows gently from the south which keeps the air so cool. There is one thing I forgot to tell you, the people here say they never have any march winds, there has not been any this year. Well sallie as I am getting tired of writing I will put it of till another time to finish. so goodbye.

Well Sallie I eat dinner and lay down and took a nap and I feel dull. I slept too long. I have taken cold and it keeps my nose running. Cousin John is complaining to day with a sore throat and aching of his joint, which is no pleasant feeling I know by experience. the health of the company is not as good as it has been a week or [two] back. some of them have been troubled with their bowels. I reckon it is the water that does not agree with them. I dont like the water here, it dont wash clean. the soap dont do any good scarcely at all. [When I] put [it] on my hands they feel like they were greased and the best of soap wont make any suds at all. I saw the first rocks comeing down here that I have seen in the State. the people dont have rock to build chimneys like we do. they build wooden chimneys and just daub them up with mud in the back and when they have hot fires they will take fire if they are not particular. but they do not need hot fires much like we do up the country.

Some of the boys went out to the Wakulla river and got a lot of fish and six of them have gone to St Marks now to get some. Some of the fishermen have been out to day and caught a boat load and carried them down to town. One of the company bought a fish to day for $1 dollar that weighed 25 pounds. I have forgotten the name of it. its mouth was about as long as my hand, and at the nose about the size of my thumb. it looked like it mouth was made to catch something out of holes in the bank of the river or like the pictures of the ant eaters you have seen.

Well Sallie I slept so late this evening I have not time to write much. as the boys are now watering and feeding I will have to close. I will write a few lines in the morning if any thing of any importance takes place, so I will close for the present. I hope this war will close before long and we all get home, but it dont look much like it now.

Monday morning   Dear Sallie I feel better with my cold this morning than I did yesterday. Cousin John is better this morning.

he took some pepper tea and some kind of powders last night by the Dr Mapps[1] directions.

Sallie the mail is about to leave and I must close. Direct your letters to Tallahassee. Give my love to all. Cousin John sends his love to you all. I remain your affectionate brother James

1   Dr. J. Lawson Mapp, Staff Assistant Surgeon.

CAMP BROKAW
NEAR ST MARKS
APRIL 14TH 1863

Dear Sallie

I received your letter this morning dated the 8th. I was glad to hear that you all were well, and to hear the health of the neighbors was good. This leaves me in good [health]. I have been troubled with cold since I have been at this place, which I took about the first night after we got here. I am nearly well of it now   Cousin John is well. I think he is getting a little better with the blues, but I heard him say that he would give fifty dolars to go back to Quincy to stay three months. It looks by that like he is anxious to be there.

Our Quincy Guards[1] came down last week, all but a few of them. John Kinnebrew was taken sick at camp Leon and when we left there he went up to Quincy and Mc [Kinnebrew] stayed there to wait on him. Mc came down today, he said John is up again and knocking about.

Well Sallie I don't think I can hardly make out a letter that would [be] very interesting as I have not been out to see any thing and we never hear any news here. I will try and interest you for a while by telling you some few things. I heard of a man in the neighboorhood whose wife had been dead three weeks when he was married to the widow of a soldier. at the time he was not able to stand up to be married and his child was a corps in the house, which died the day before. did you or any one else ever hear of such a case before in your life. I dont suppose that Pa, as old as he is, ever heard of just such a one. the times are so now that I am not much supprised at anything I hear or see.

I have not had an opportunity of going to the Gulf yet. Some of the boys go down there every day. They bring up some curiosities occasionally You have often heard the expression as flat as a flounder. Well I never knew the origin of it till the other day I saw a fish by that name resembling a perch, but it was as flat as a pancake and both of its eyes on the same side of its head, and one side black or dark brown and the other white. the eyes were on the brown side and I suppose from the looks of it, it floated about on its side. I also have seen the sea crabs. they have a little resemlance of our common crawfish.

Well Sallie, I and Jack Edwards and George Whitehead[2] went out to Newport last saturday morning to see what discoveries we could make. it is a small town with very few people living in it. the most of them have left since the war commence. There is two large sulphur springs there which used to make it a notable place. The water has the strongest smell of any that I ever saw. it smells like the wipings of an old nasty shotgun. at each of those springs there is a bathing house for the benefit of the visitors. the town is on St. Marks river.

Well I promised you when I wrote to you last to let you know how I got along with my hat. I made it, but when I finished it, it was to small for my big head, so the next one I make I will try and have my head along with me. I let Oliver Cooper have it for thread enough to make two more. I made it in a very good shape. it was not as much trouble to sew as I thought it would be for me. I have enough platted to make another one, which I think I will try tomorrow of seven plat, like our common straw hats.

I received a letter from Eliza saturday. she said that Martha had been quite sick and had got about again and before she got through writing she heard that she was bad off again. I dont know why it is that Bud will not write to me. he has not written to me in five or six months. I have been waiting for him to write a long time. Sallie I want you to send me some bees wax. if you will, take a knife and cut a thin slice. make it as thin as you can get it. there will be no difficulty in sending it in a letter. you can send a little at the time till I get enough for my use. I think I will learn how to make sleighs before I leave here as there is an old fellow at work close by here. he sells them at four dollars a piece. I think I can make one without much trouble.

Well Sallie I will stop writing for this evening. I hope you will excuse me as I feel rather dull. Direct your letters to Tallahassee till further orders.

---

1   The Quincy Guards was a local unit formed before the War Between the States. Early in the war, under the command of a Colonel Duryea, the Guards seized the U.S. Arsenal at Chattahoochee and confiscated 500,000 musket cartridges, 300,000 rifle cartridges, and 50,000 pounds of gunpowder. Later the Quincy Guards, commanded by Samuel B. Stevens, became a home guard company composed of citizens of the Quincy area who were under 16 or over 50 and were therefore ineligible to join the regular army.

2   Cpl George W. Whitehead was an original member of the Echols Artillery, having joined March 4, 1862. In the 1860 census he is listed as a 28-year-old county surveyor, living in the home with his mother, 61-year-old Polly C. Whitehead, in the Pleasant Hill District of Oglethorpe County.

WEDNESDAY MORNING
APR 15TH

Dear Sallie

According to promise I will write a few more lines this morning to let you know that I am well. There is nothing of importance taken place since yesterday. Our Quartermaster went up to Tallahassee Monday to get our rations for this week, but he came back yesterday without anything at all. the excuse was, the Quartermasters wife was sick and he would not attend to giving out our rations. There is at least four [other] companies that draw rations there the same day with ours and if they are like ours, they were out of something to eat. So we shelled some corn yesterday and sent to the mill and got a little meal. I reckon we will have to live on dry bread till the Quartermasters wife gets well or steal some hogs. he promised to send our rations down today. I think it very hard that four or five hundred men should be put off in such a manner as that through the carelessness of one good for nothing scamp, for he is not worthy of a home in the confederacy, let alone an office in the army. All that kind of officers are very independent. if they can get to manage the comissary department, they are the most independent of any body that can be started. Well I reckon I had just as well stop writing such as this for fear I will make you think we are suffering for something to eat. I have got so I love cornbred and can eat it without any thing else and it is very sorry at that. the corn is half eat up with the weavils.

There is a boat load of cotton down at St. Marks of 110 bales fixed up to run the blockad for Cuba. They say that when the wind suits they will start out. there is a bloackading vessel lying out about eight miles from the coast. They came up in four miles last week and then ran off again about twenty. I have no doubt but they will find out that cotton is there before it leaves and be ready for it. I would not be supprised in the least if it is for them anyway.

Well Sallie you must excuse this short letter and I will try to do better the next time. Lieut Jarrell is at home and [will] start back about the 25th of this month. he has promised to bring some things for cousin John. I wrote to Eliza to send me some cotton socks if she coud get them there. Cousin John wrote to his Pa to send the box to the depot by the 28th, but he wants you to send him word to have it there by the 23rd or 24th, as his furlough is out the 28 and he will have to be here by that time, or soon after. If you get this in time be sure to let Uncle Billie [know] if there is any chance. if he dont [know], he will not have the box there in time. Give my love to all. I remain your affectionate brother James

APR 16TH

Dear Sallie,

I did not get this letter off yesterday morning, for the mail boy started before I knew it.

Well I reckon the Quartermasters wife has got well, or at least she must be better, for he sent our rations down yesterday as we had some meat for supper and breakfast this morning. Well Sallie, Capt Tiller told us last night that he had clothes for us at Tallahassee and we must let him [know] to day whether we would [take] them or not. We have to take the clothes or wait twelve months to get their value in money. Coat & pants (Yarn) 18 dollars, 1 pair drawers $1.25, Shirt $1.25, Shoes $5.00, Cap $2.00. I dont know what to do about taking them. I dont need them, but I think it will be the best for us to take them and sell them, or some that we have, where we have more than we want. I think we can sell them at government prices very easy. I will try it this time and I will find out something maybe.

I received a letter from John Colclough yesterday from Woodville.[1] They were all well the 8th when he left home. Well Sallie I made another hat yesterday evening, liking a few rounds on the brim. I think I can sell it for two dollars and half. I have several applications for hats but I dont think I will [make] many. I must close or else I will be too late again.

Give my love to all. I remain as ever your affectionate brother James

P.S. Why dont Mary Crowley write. tell it must take her a long time to read that long letter that I wrote at Camp Leon the fifteenth of March.

---

1   Woodville, Florida, is a small town south of Tallahassee. John Colclough worked for the railroad in the area.

CAMP BROKAW
APR 23RD 1863

Dear Sallie

I have received a letter of Yours this morning bearing date 14th. I was very glad to hear from you all. I received a letter from Mary Crowley and one from Eliza the same day. I received one from John Colclough last monday night. Billingsly[1] went to Tallahassee to get our rations and went up horse back and come back after I had gone to sleep, but as soon as I heard there was a letter for me, I was wide awake in a minute and got a light to read it.

Well Sallie I am still enjoying good health. Cousin John is well. he received a letter from Cousin George[2] today. We lost one of our company last sunday evening. it was Shemi Tiller,[3] a substitute for Andrew Goolsby.[4] he come to the company at the same time that I did. He was taken sick sunday evening with the headache and in a day or two he was delirious and was in his right mind but very little of the time he was sick. he died just a week after he was taken. the Dr said that it was the pneumonia. I have but very little confidence in our physician. he is a young up start in his 22nd year. he says he has been in service two years. he was in virginia a while. he came from there to a hospital in Atlanta and there he stayed untill he got the appoint ment of a physician in our company. he is too young for my use, though he may do as well as some others. his request to the company was not to visit Mr. Tiller, only those that were to wait on him. I, for one, did not go to his tent but one time during the week, and he was not in his right mind at that time. I went to see him again sunday while he was in the act of dieing. he got up from the bed not more than hour before he died as though he was not satisfied about some thing. he has left behind a poor wife and children to mourn after him. he never made any profession[5] at all, nor did he say any thing about dieing, more than he told his brotherinlaw that he must carry him home if he died.

I will now tell you how the corpse was sent home. we sent to Tallahassee sunday evening after a coffin and there was but one there and that would not suit so they had to make one here monday, and the corpse ought by all means [to have] been ready to be sent off that day. after making the coffin, they washed the inside with tar and then diped a blanket in tar and put in it for the winding sheet. then the coffin was packed as tight with sawdust as could be and that put in a large case with some charcoal in [it]. so it was not moved from here till tuesday at eleven oclock, and I have no idea that if his brother gets home with it all, that it will be a week from the time he died before he is buried. The capt would not agree to let any one go to carry the corpse home till Lieut Wade[6] went to Quincy to see Genl Cobb. Col Smith[7] the commander of the post at Tallahassee told him to send it a long with some one with it, but he said that he would not take the responsibility on him self and the corpse never would have been [sent except] for the company urging it so much. there is no place here to bury anyone, for it is getting dry now and in the most of places there is [still] a plenty of water by diging about four feet. When we dig our wells we strike veins of water which boils up like a spring. I should not feel satisfied to see one of our company buried in any such a place as this.

Well Sallie, Hopson Tiller[8] left here tuesday the 21th on a fifteen days furlough, so he will return about the seventh of May. but he will have to start from home about the third or fourth to get here in time. Lieut Jarrell will be here in a few days. Cousin George wrote that he had seen Jarrell and he [Jarrell] told him that he would bring a box for Cousin John if they would have it fixed up for him.

Well Sallie, I am going to draw some of the government clothes, not that I need clothes at all, but there has been a different arrangement about paying us comutation money. we have to take clothes or wait untill next march to draw the money, which some say will be $40. I thought I would try some of them and if I dont like them I can sell them at cost. I dont recollect whether I wrote you any thing about them, so I will give you the prices of what I have sent for. Coat $9.00, pants 9.00, shoes 5.00, Shirt 1.25, drawers 1.25. some of the boys say they have seen some that a company here has drawed. they [say] the coat & pants are sorry, a little wool mixed in with the cotton. the other articles are said to be cheap, but I will let you know after I see them what I think of them.

Well I have often heard of sandflies, but they are very different from what I thought they was. they are nothing more than gnats about the color of the sand. You know how the black gnats bite some times about night before it rains. the sand flies are as bad every evening here. Yesterday and day before it was a little cloudy most all day and I tell you they were not scarry at all. when one lights on you any where, you will have to stop every thing till you kill it. they get in my wiskers and in the edge of my hair. they bite so bad now I can hardly write a line at a time without stoping to knock them off. It is droping rain now and thundering a little but I dont think it will rain much.

Well Sallie, we get enough to eat to make out very well on for two weeks back. I heard last saturday that Hayes and Mrs George Landrum[9] was married but it may be like Bill Moores wedding. I have made two hats. I sold the last one for two dollars and have got about forty yards platted now. I exspect to make one for myself and one for George Martin, there is at least a dozen of the boys hat making. T.R. Watkins[10] will put in a substitute and leave here about the first of next month. You must excuse all mistakes and this short letter. if any thing of interest happens by morning I will let you know. Give my love to all.

I remain your affectionate brother James   write often

Apr 24th   nothing of importance has taken place. I am well, Cousin John is also well. this morning when I went out I found a pig in our well swimming about. I must close Give my love to all. I remain your affectionate brother James Jewel

1   William A. Billingslea was the Quartermaster Sergeant for the Echols Artillery. He joined the service on March 1, 1862, and served until the end of the war. Billingslea is listed in the 1860 Georgia census as a 26-year-old grocer in Lexington.

2   Cousin George was George Hughey Jewel, Cousin John's older brother and the oldest son of William Jewel, I.

3   The Tiller family Bible, as recorded in Florrie Smith's *History of Oglethorpe County, Georgia,* names Shimmie Tiller as one of the eight sons of Randall and Jane Tiller. Shimmie is listed as born January 26, 1818, and married to Nancy Jane Crook. Tiller is identified in the 1860 Georgia census as Chemmie or Chermid and was a farmer in the Goose Pond District of Oglethorpe County. His name is listed in the Confederate Records both as Shimer and Shimmie. He died of pneumonia April 19, 1863.

4   Andrew J. Goolsby is listed in the 1860 Georgia census as a 24-year-old farmer in the Goose Pond District of Oglethorpe County.

5   Jewel meant that Tiller did not profess any religious belief.

6   James Bolton Wade is listed in the 1850 Georgia census as an 11-year-old in Oglethorpe County in the home of Mariah Bolton, age 59. Also in the household were Elizabeth, 68, and Elisha Norman, a 25-year-old overseer. By the time of the 1860 census, Wade had removed to Mississippi and was listed in the census as a 21-year-old planter on a large plantation in Yazoo County. Wade apparently returned to Oglethorpe County when the war began and enlisted in the Echols Artillery as a Private on March 15, 1862. He was eventually promoted to 3rd Lieutenant and served until the end of the war.

7   Colonel Carraway Smith was in command of the second Florida Cavalry. The 1860 Florida census lists Smith as a 40-year-old planter in Madison County. Smith was born in South Carolina. Others in the household were Sarah R., 31, and five children.

8   See footnote 3 above. Hopson Tiller is entered in the family Bible as born December 8, 1829, and married to Elizabeth Sorrow. Hopson Tiller was a Private in the Echols Artillery. He is listed in the 1860 Georgia census as a farmer in the Simston District of Oglethorpe County, along with wife Elizabeth and two small children.

9   Howard A. Hayes and Susan Clarke Landrum were married July 6, 1863. Susan Clarke Landrum was the daughter of Zachariah H. Clarke and previously was married to George T. Landrum. She and Howard Hayes had three children. Hayes had first married Sarah A.V. Walker of Greene County on April 19, 1853, and had four children by her. Sarah Walker Hayes was the daughter of Henry and Mary Walker. She died August 29, 1862, at age 26.

10   Thaddeus Reese Watkins is listed in the 1860 Georgia census as a 37-year-old farmer in the Simston District of Oglethorpe County, along with his wife Mary and four children. Watkins joined the Echols Artillery in March 1862 as 2nd Sergeant. He was discharged May 1, 1863, by furnishing T.A. Glines as a substitute.

CAMP BROKAW
NEAR ST. MARKS
MAY 3RD 1863

Dear Brother

I received your letter day before yesterday dated the 23rd of April. I was very glad to receive a letter from you. I did not know why you did not write to me. I [used to] could hear from you once and a while and I wrote to know why it was that you did not write to me. I was glad to hear that Martha[1] was getting better. I heard that she was sick some time ago. Well this leaves me well. Cousin John is also in good health. It is cloudy this morning and thundering in the south. I think it will rain today.

I dont know that it would be worth while for me to undertake to give you a description of this country as I recon you have heard what I had to say about it. When we first came here there was water nearly every where. the Country is too level for the water to run off fast. we crossed a stream a little before we got here which I thought was about as large as the creek there at your house. it is now dry and has been for more than a week. we could then get water by diging but very little. The first wells we dug was about three feet to the water, but as the weather gets dry we have to dig down deeper. Our mess have about the deepest one in camps and it is about nine or ten feet deep. I recon you have heard of the sand fly. what sort of things do you think they are. I thought before I came down here that they were something like a house fly, but they are nothing more than a gnat. You have no idea how bad they bite. they were worse here yesterday evening and last night than I have ever seen before, and in fact they were so bad this morning that any one could hardly write, but it is raining now and they dont bite. you may think when the black gnats bite they hurt, but these are the worst. I have often thought of the fellow that was asked if the mosquetoes were bad and was knocking as hard as he could to keep them off but sayed just below here they are pretty bad.   that is the way here, if you say the sand flies are bad here some body will say that they are worse down below here. The mosquitoes are also making their appearance [and] they are large enough to hurt when they bite.

I think you are mistaken about the legislature putting you under the conscript law. there was a bill to that effect, but my understanding of it was it did not pass. I recon you know whether it is so or not by this time. You have a better chance to know anything of that sort than I do, for we hardly ever hear any news at all, only what we get by letters from home. If you do have to go off, I dont think there is any difficulty in your getting in this company. George Martin asked Capt Tiller if he would take Tom. he sayed he would if he come. There has been a goodeal of talk about dividing our company. if that is done we will need about fifty recruits. Gen Beaureguard has ordered that all companies that had more than four pieces [cannons] and over one hundred men shall be divided. we have two 12 pound howitzers at Chattahoochee that have been there a good while but it is a very hard mater to get horses. we would have had the guns here before this time if we had horses for them.

There is some talk of going back to Quincy yet, but I dont know what will [be] done. I dont think there is any use for us here. I have no idea that the yankeys will attempt to come out here. There is a boat load of cotton, 110 bales, at St Marks to run the blockade. they have been waiting for some time for a favorable wind. the blockaders are watching them I think, from what I can hear. There is three small companies of infantry close by here, and at a little town called Newport there is one cavelry company and one of infantry. There is very few troops in this country. Genl Cobb has not got more than two Regt of soldiers under his command all together [2]

Salt is six dollars a bushel and on the decline. When we first come here it took [a] start up and was twelve dollars in a few days, so it has fallen 6 dollars in about a week. I think if it gets down to 4 dollars it would be a good time for you all to buy. it will not cost more than two dollars [freight] on the bushel to get it home. I dont know whether any one could ship a quantity at the time or not. some of the salt makers will deliver it at Albany. Ips Ragan[3] is down here at work making salt he lives about four miles from here. I saw him day before yesterday. Watkins has put in a substitute and will leave here for home tomorrow. I will send some letters by him as postage stamps are getting scarce. You must excuse this short letter as it has been raining and it is almost impossible for anyone to write and [with] so many in the tent. I will write a little more this evening.

1   William Jewel, II, married Martha B. Taylor in Oglethorpe County on November 17, 1857. It is thought that she was the daughter of John Taylor and Frances Taylor, listed in the 1860 Georgia census as farmers in the Falling Creek District of Oglethorpe County. Apparently, Martha Taylor Jewel died sometime during or soon after the war. Another daughter of John and Frances Taylor, Sarah F. Taylor, was married to Jewel's brother-in-law Thomas F. Colclough.

2   A similar report dated January 31, 1863, disclosed "...there are presently on duty in the Confederate District of East Florida, 810 officers and men, and in the District of Middle Florida, 715 men." A report dated December 3, 1862, stated, "There are presently five infantry companies, one cavalry, one partisan ranger, and one artillery battery, in all approximately 700 men protecting middle Florida."

3   Ips Ragan was Ibzan H. Ragan, listed in the 1850 Georgia census as a resident of Oglethorpe County. By the time of the 1860 census, Ragan was listed as a 38-year-old farmer in the Starkville District of Lee County, Georgia, along with his wife, Caroline R., 38, and seven children, ranging in age from 1 to 16 years old.

MAY 4TH

Dear Brother

As I made such poor speed yesterday writing I thought I would try to write a few lines this morning. Cousin John sent some money to Ragg[1] and put the letter in care of you about five weeks [ago] and he has not heard whether he got it or not.

Capt Tiller appointed Cobb Davis 5th sargt friday in Watkins place. he has been corp. and I thought he had the swell head bad enough, but I reckon he will get too big for his breeches now. The Capt has appointed about a half a dozen noncommissioned officers and the most of them ran for office sometime ago but could not [get elected] by a long ways. We could elect all of our officers before we come to Florida, but since we have come here we cannot elect any but the commissioned officers. the others are appointed by the capt.

I like to have forgot to tell you about our hatmaking we have here. I reckon there is at least thirty of the company that have been platting and making hats of palmetto. I have made four and have enough platted to make another one. I have sold them at two dollars a piece and one at two and [a] quarter. I think the company will all have hats now soon and then I reckon the demand will not be so great. I intended sending some of the palmetto home by Watkins but he says he will have so many things to carry that he cannot carry it for me. Cousin John, George Martin, and I will fix up a box in a few day of it to send home, if we do not have to leave here before get it off. I dont know whether it will go or not, but we will not pay the freight on it so if it is lost it will not cost anything, only our labor.

I will close for this time. I hope you will write again soon. Joseph Armstrong says tell Dr Landrums folks that he is well. our company are all in very good health. If you do have to go to the war, come here, but my advice to you is to keep out as long as you can, there is a considerable difference between being here and at home if you have anything to eat there. Give my love to Martha. I remain your affectionate Brother James

1   Ragg is probably Ibzan H. Ragan (previously cited).

CAMP BROKAW
MAY 6TH 1863

Dear Sallie

I received you kind letter last monday from the hands of Lieut Jarrell. I also got the two pair of socks. I wish they had not been quite so fine. I hope you will excuse me for not writing sooner as I have been hindered by some duty here in camps. And the worst of all, I have felt but little like writing. it has not been over two weeks since the last letter I got from Eliza was written and in that she said

Mattie was quite sick, but she got some better before she finished the letter and Beck was very sick also her mother was sick, and I received a letter from Bud last week. he said that Mattie was still sick and I also heard from John [Colclough] the same day that bud wrote. John said that he had heard that Dr. Harris[1] & Dr. Durham[2] was to meet in consultation at his Pas. he did not know who was sick they both promised to write to me again in a day or two, and I know if they wrote I ought to have heard from them before this time. I dont want you to think that I am at all unwell. I have very good health, but I have been very anxious to hear from home. I do not feel at all like writing, but I thought I would to keep you from being uneasy about me. Cousin John is well. The health of the company is very good.

I have no news of importance to write. I heard to day that there was a big fight going on at Fredricksburg [and we had] taken 25,000 prisoners. Stone wall Jackson [was] badly wounded and Hill[3] slightly. that is [the] telegraf news here. I reckon you all have heard all the particulars before this time. I went out to the sulphur springs to bathe this evening. I saw some large Oleander bushes all in full bloom. they looked very nice. there is some of them in most every yard in this country. I have seen some a goodeal larger than Pas orange tree. I have not seen any farms but I heard some of the boys say they saw some corn about six feet high. I have not seen any more than wast high and that was in a lot in Newport. I cant tell any thing about the farming interest about here. some of the gardens look very nice in Newport. I saw some bean vines full of blooms last week. I reckon they have english peas a plenty to eat by this time.

Well Sallie, I had some palmetto to send you by Sargt Watkins as he went home. he put in his substitute last friday and left here monday but he could not take it for me. I & Cousin John & George Martin gathered up some and have concluded to send a box full of it if we can get a box. We have to split it up and then dip it in boling water and then put it out in the sun to whiten but from some caus I am not able to tell, it has not turned white. I reckon we will have to try again. I will let you know when we send it. I have a gage to strip up [the leaves] to plat. we generally split it out ready for platting while it is green and then let it dry, but if I send any, [I will] not split it so you all can make it any width you want it. I have finished a hat for George Martin at last I thought I had a big head, but his is enough the largest.

Well Sallie, I am writing by fire light to night, so I will stop writing till morning. I do hope I will hear from Eliza by tomorrow. so good bye.

Well Sallie, I have made my breakfes of corn bread this morning without any meat at all. We get a little poor beef and enough bacon to last us about two days in seven. We will draw today. the quartermaster told some of the boys yesterday that he would let us have flour this week. It was very warm yesterday and this morning it is cool enough to stand about the fire. I think the weather is more changeabl here than it [is] any where that I have ever been. early of a morning, or rather in the latter part of night, it is, and then about nine oclock it is warm enough for summer. then about twelve, the sea breeze rises and then it is pleasent in the shade.

I think from what I have heard you all are mistaken about Bud being subject to the conscript. I dont think that law passed in the Legislature.

Cousin John received your letter last week. I reckon he will answer it after a while. Well Sallie, I will close for the present. you must excuse this short letter and I will try to do better the next time. Cousin John sends his love to all. Give my love to all and to brothers folks. I remain as ever your affection brother James

---

1   Dr. W.L.M. Harris is listed in the 1860 Georgia census as a 30-year-old physician in the Penfield District of Greene County, along with his wife, Sarah F., 26, and two small children.

2   Dr. A. Frank Durham, age 28, and his wife Sarah, age 21, are listed in the 1860 Georgia census as residents in the home of the James Armstrong family, merchants in the Penfield District of Greene County.

3   Lieutenant General Thomas J. "Stonewall" Jackson was accidentally shot by his own men May 2, 1863, during the Battle of Chancellorsville and died 8 days later. General Ambrose Powell Hill, second in command to Jackson, was felled in the firing and cannonading that followed the shooting of Jackson. He recovered but was killed at Petersburg, Virginia, April 2, 1865, just a week before the end of the war.

CAMP BROKAW
NEAR ST MARKS
MAY 14TH 1863

Dear Sallie

I received your kind letter yesterday with one from Mary, also one from John Colclough. I was glad to hear that you were all well at that time. I have heard nothing but bad news from home in some time. John said he did not know [how] they all were at home. I received a letter from Eliza last sunday which was the first of my hearing of the death of Rebecca.[1] Eliza wrote to me that they were all well one day and the next day in the same letter she wrote that Mattie, Beck, Susan,[2] and her Mother[3] was all sick. the next letter brought the sad news to me she said that Mattie was still very sick but Susan and her Mother was able to be up. Several of the Negroes was very sick.

Sallie I have felt very little like writing in sometime. We are here where we hear no news that is reliable. I suppose from the newspaper accounts, there has been a great slaughter at Fredrickburg. I was very sorry to hear of the death of [General Stonewall] Jackson, he was one of our ablest Generals. the newspapers report the Yankey loss at forty thousand and ours four in killed, wounded, and missing. sometimes the papers are several day behine the times. I am getting tired of this war. I can get along tolerable well when I know that you all at home are well, but when I hear of my sweet little babe being sick I want to be there to see her. I tried hard to get a furlough but it was all to no purpose. Capt Tiller would not let me go.

I heard this morning that Wile Young[4] and John Paul[5] have got furloughs to go home next monday, and Lieut Gibson expects to start home to morrow. we looked for him down to day. he has been attending the Courtmartials nearly ever day since we left Quincy. He said some time ago that he was getting tired of that place. I think they carry on business like they do at some of the legislatures [and] stay there to kill time. Gibson says he only get one dollar a day and his board cost him four. I would think they would all be anxious to leave.

Sallie, I and Cousin John intend fixing up our box of palmetto and start it tomorrow. we have got the box made. we will send it by freight as there is no express this side of Savanah and Albany, so I reckon it will be sometime on the road. If you get it you will have to soak it untill it is perfectly wet before splitting it and wash it off   it has got smutty here. we burn so much pine that smut gets on every thing near here. get Pa to make you a gage to split it up. get a thick piece of leather and drive some tacks in enough to split a leaf at the time. when plating have it just wet enough to keep from breaking. if you have it too wet it will shrink when it dries and leave the plat open. I would have split it up for you but I thought you all could split it according to the size you wish the plat. I will stop writing till morning as I will [not] have time write any more this evening.

Friday Morning 15th. Sallie, I will finish this this morning and will have but little time. John sent me a lot of paper of this kind the other [day]. it was old U.S. Mail paper. I have got enough of it to write on [for] some times. it only cost .10 ct postage.

We had twelve more horses brought from Tallahassee. I reckon we will get our other two guns from Chattahoochee soon. Sallie I thought I would tie up the palmetto in bundles for you and Eliza but it will suit better to put it all together and then you all can divide it. I will close this short letter but I hope you will excuse me this time as I cannot write any more.

Give my love to all. I remain your affectionate brother James Jewel

P.S. Sallie I forgot to tell you we drew some flour last week and we had some biscuits. What we drew yesterday looks like shorts.[6]

---

1   Rebecca D. Colclough was one of Eliza's younger, unmarried sisters. Her tombstone in the Colclough family cemetery in Greene County gives her birth date as September 9, 1840, and her death as April 26, 1863.

2   Sue was another of Eliza's younger unmarried sisters, Susan E. Colclough (already cited). Her tombstone in the Colclough family cemetery in Greene County gives her birth date as September 8, 1842, and her death as November 8, 1879.

3   Eliza's mother was Nancy Nelms Colclough. Her tombstone in the Colclough family cemetery in Greene County gives her birth date as February 14, 1812, and her death as February 14, 1892.

4   Wiley Young [not Wile, but seen as Wyley] joined the Echols Artillery on May 3, 1862, as a Private and served until the end of the war. He is listed in the 1860 Georgia census as a 34-year-old farmer in the Bowling Green District of Oglethorpe County, along with Sarah, 31, and five children, ranging in age from 1 to 10 years old.

5   This was John William Paul who joined the Echols Artillery in March 1862 and died of fever in 1864.

6   Shorts is wheat bran resulting as a by-product of processing wheat for flour and is normally used as livestock feed.

MAY

Well Sallie,

this is saturday morning and I have not got my letter off yet. Gibson came down yesterday and will start home today, so I reckon I will [send it by him] I have put the palmetto in a box to send. it is raining this morning too much to be out. it rained a little yesterday. I thought I would get some fruit to send you all but I could not find any hardly worth sending. I have put in a few [pieces of fruit] of the small order. I expect they will be dry by the time you get them. I got some last week that I thought I would send but they dried up so small I hated to send them. I put my palmetto in the bottom of the box and then put a bundle on top of Cousin Johns. I wanted to send some walking sticks. I did not have a chance of getting nice ones so I got up some dry ones here at the camps. I have also put in two of the leaves like we get to work for you all to look at. I am afraid the box will get wet as I have it under the fly of a tent. there is not room in our tent to keep it. if the palmetto gets wet I will have to take it out and dry it again. it will not do for it to remain packed up wet, it will mildew. it is still raining. There has been very little rain here since the last of March. there has been one shower enough to lay the dust.

I lost my other front tooth one day this week. It got so loose that it come out and I did not know it. Cousin John has been complaining with the bowel affliction several days. I have not done much at hat making this week. we [have to] to drill every morning and carry our horses out to graze an hour or two in the evening. Tom Martin has not got here yet. we are looking for him every day. if he started here last saturday he ought to have been here before this time. I will close hoping to hear from you soon. Give My love to all. I remain your affectionate brother James

PS   Sallie, I dont mean by writing to you about the palmetto that it [is] any more intended for you than Mary and Maggie. I did not know but what they would think from the way I wrote that it was for you but that is not my intention. You all must let Eliza have a part of it for herself and the other girls. I think I have said enough about it for I think it very doubtful whether it will go through or not.

Yours truly JJ

CAMP BROKAW
MAY 18TH 1863

Dear Sallie

I received your letter from the hands of E.T. Martin last saturday morning. I had sent one off for you the day before, and [thought I] would have a chance to send you one by hand to day or tomorrow. Wiley Young and John Paul are expecting to start home tomorrow. Wile says he will try to get off this evening if he gets his furlough to day from Genl Cobb.   This leaves me well   Cousin John is still complaining with his bowels. I think he is some better. I started the box of palmetto saturday by Lieut Gibson. he said he would carry it up to Quincy and then I wrote to one of our company up there to send it to Chattahoochee. there is three of the boys that have been detailed there to drive wagons. Isham Cheatham is one of the wagoners. I would like very well to see cheatham, he was in our mess while we were at Quincy.

Well Sallie, I have no news of any importance to write. We were ordered saturday evening to be ready the next morning for a review and inspection at nine oclock, but I was glad it did not come from some cause or other. it was put off untill tomorrow so we have been cleaning out our camps this morning. Tom Martin brought a large trunk with him. he will have to put it on the cars when we move from here. Cousin John brought his from Quincy on the cars and if we have to leave the railroad they cant be carried. Tom came dress up in his cloth suit, and linen bosom shirt. he will not get it white again while we stay here.

We had a very pretty rain saturday morning and also a shower in the evening   it has been dry here for some time. our wells dried up and we have to keep diging down after it. it is tolerable warm today. The weather has not been as warm down here as I expected it would be. Ipson Ragan was here today. he had a little boy and girl with him on their way to Greensboro to go to school. his little boy is about twelve years old and the girl is less. he is going with them up to Tallahassee. I think they will get lost if they dont mind, or have some body to take care of them. Some people you know send their little children most any where.

Ragan says that salt is selling at seven dollars a bushel. they ask ten for it but will take seven. Tom Martin says it is worth fifty cents a pound in oglethorpe. I think it is very uncertain about it getting much cheaper than it is now, though it may. Cousin John told me that the farmers were drawing salt, a bushel a month, but he did not know why it was or how much they paid for it. he said his Pa sent up to Lexington depot[1] twice while he was at home and got a bushel each time and [so did] every body else in the neighborhood. I never heard any thing of it before.   I want to know how it was and if Pa has ever got any that way.

Sallie, You must excuse this short letter as it has been but a short time since I wrote to you. You must write soon and often. Lieut Gibson is gone after recruits   he sayed he would take fifty if they could be found. Bud wrote to me to know if he could come to the company. You can tell him if he is obliged to leave, there is plenty room for him here. I will send this letter by Wiley Young.

Give my love to all. I remain your affectionate brother James

P.S. There was a letter found in the mail box a few days since backed to Mrs Huff and with this written on the back of it. Direct Your letters to St Marks now darling, home sweet home. I think I would have put that much inside of my letter. J. Jewel

1   Lexington Depot was the early name for Crawford, Georgia, and is located on the railroad line three miles west of Lexington.

Camp Brokaw
May 26th 1863

Dear Sallie

I have taken a seat to write you a few lines to let you know that I am well, as Cousin John has written. I did not know that he had wrote till a few minutes ago, so I will not have time to write much.

I have no news of any importance to write as I have written to you before. we cannot hear much news here and unless we go out from camps we never see any thing. I, with a good many of the boys, went out to a Quarterly meeting about two miles from here. there was about twenty women out there and but few men except the soldiers from the different camps. there was four or five nice looking ladies. they were better looking ladies than I had any idea was in this country. We have seen very few of the fair sex since we left Quincy.

Well Sallie, We drew our clothes last week. I think I have given you a very good description of the coat and pants before. the cloth is wove plain and a little wool mixed in it. the coats are little short sacks like you all make for the negroes some times and some of the seams are sewed so slack the stitches show on the out side. I think the cloth will last tolerable well. The shirts are made of good nice shirting and the drawers of nice cotton jeans, which are nice enough for any body to wear at home and they are all made large enough. the caps are not much and the shoes only tolerable. some of them are good and some others are worth very little. I drew a pair that was too small for me and swoped them off and got a good pair with the exception of one of the vamps being rather thin. My pants are most too small but I think I can fix them so they will do.

Well Sallie I must close. I am looking every day for a letter from you. It was a week last Saturday since I have heard from you and Eliza and then her letter had been written about a week. Give My love to all the family. I remain your affectionate brother James

CAMP BROKAW
MAY 27TH 1863

Dear Sallie

I have taken a seat to write you a few lines though I have no news of much importance to write. We have received orders to report at Quincy and to start tomorrow morning. So it will take us at least two days to go. it is forty odd miles and we will not travel more than twenty miles a day. Sallie I am really glad that we are going back there but I have no idea that we will fare as well as we did when we was there because there is 7 companies of infantry there and there [has been] a good many soldiers there since we was there.

We will have better water when we get there if nothing else. Well Sallie, I am getting very anxious to hear from home. Tom Martin brought the last letter I received from you and I received one from Eliza the same day. I do hope I will hear from you all in a few days. I [do not] have time to write [more] before the mail will [leave], therefore you must excuse me this time. Cousin John is well.

Give my love to all. I remain your affectionate brother James

CHAPTER V

Back to Quincy

"I thought sometime ago the war would close before a great while but all such hope as that have vanished"

Dear Sallie

I received your welcome letter yesterday written the 21st & 22nd. I thought you had forgotten me as far as writing was concerned. the last letter I received from you before that was brought by Tom Martin three weeks ago. I received a letter from Eliza day before yesterday. They were all well except two of the negroes.

Well Sallie we have got back to Quincy once more. We had an unpleasant day to travel thursday. it rained the most of the day and a part of the time very hard but I believe the thought of comeing back to Quincy was enough to make them come cheerfully. the canoneers had to walk nearly all the way and every thing being so wet caused them to have blistered feet. We got here at the same camping grounnd.

Sallie, I would be glad to write you a long letter but I have not time to write, and besides, I feel a little sleepy. Last night about the time we were going to bed the Capt had the horn sounded to assemble the company. he had received orders that they were expecting the yankeys to land on the Appalachachola river and wanted a part of our company to go. there was four guns here at the depot that had to go out to Chattahoochee so he took out four detachments and drivers enough to carry the guns. The drivers are going to come back when they get to Chattahoochee with the horses, and the cannoneers will take the guns on a boat down the river some 50 or 60 miles. as it happened, Collier was all the one that went from our mess. they had [to] cook three days rations to take with them and start this morning about sunrise.

I expect it will be like that scrape we had soon after we left here when the yankeys had stolen that boat. We have had some very warm weather for several days. The last night we stayed at camp Brokaw we had a considerable storm. the tide from the gulf destroyed all the salt and about twenty-five of the hands were drowned about seven miles from our camp. the wind blew very hard. the corn was badly torn to pieces and blown down. it was not so bad here, there was a good many trees across the road. There is but little cotton planted along the road. The people have vegetables a plenty to eat. they had some fine large squashes two weeks ago. We had a mess of snaps yesterday for dinner.

I went out to preaching sunday. there is quite a change in the looks of the ladies. When we was here before they dress in winter clothing and the most of it black, but now they have come out in their fine summer fixing. Mr. Anderson preached a very good sermon. I had the pleasure of seeing Genl Beauregard[1] yesterday. he and General [Howell] Cobb, Maj Stanley[2] and capt [Frank] Pope came over yesterday morning about nine Oclock and stayed a few minute. Beauregard is quite a nice looking fellow. Genl Cobb represented our company very highly to him.

We drew our wages day before yesterday for six months, which was seventy two dollars. Genl Beauregard says if the yankeys ever got persession of Vicksburg they would have to do some hard fighting. they have been trying it but they met with poor encouragement.

I am about out of envelops and some of the boys have been buying some here at fifty cents a pack and they made of sorry brown paper. that I think is very high. I brought a supply with me from Atlanta that I gave 10 cents for, much better ones than we can get here.

Well Sallie, I must close. this leaves me enjoying good health. Cousin John is well. Give my love to all. I remain your affectionate brother James

1   General Pierre Gustave Toutant Beauregard, a native of Louisiana, was Commanding Officer of the Department of South Carolina and Georgia for the Confederacy. On November 4, 1862, the Departments of East and Middle Florida also were placed under his command.

2   Marcellus Stanley had resigned as commander of the Troup Artillery and was on the administrative staff of Major General Howell Cobb, now in charge of the Middle Florida District. Before the war Stanley had taught at the University of Georgia, Randolph-Macon College in Virginia, and Wesleyan College in Macon, Georgia. He also had spent a year in Europe as secretary to U.S. Ambassador Henry Hilliard.

QUINCY FLORIDA
JUNE 15TH 1863

Dear Sallie,

I have taken my seat to try to answer your letters written June 4th at Uncle Billies and the one you and Eliza wrot from Pa's, sent by Wiley Young.   both come to hand the same day, which was last thursday with three others; one from Mary [Jewel], Sis Jane [Edwards], and John Colclough. So I had a real time of reading letters, but answering them is not such an easy task. This leaves me and cousin John in very good health.

Capt Tiller was ordered to take four guns and men enough for them, last friday was a week ago, and go down on the Appalachachola river where they thought the Yankeys were trying to land in small boats or barges. One of the boys come back from there saturday sick. he was with Lieut Wade. The Capt took two of the guns and went about thirty miles lower down the river to Fort Gaddens.[1] Five companies of the first Ga Regulars went with them. one company remained with Lieut Wade and the others went with the Capt. There was some troops down there before but I have no idea how many there was. The boys have been at work throwing up breast works, for the first time the Echols Arty ever had any of that sort of work to [do]. There is about fifty of the company down there and the rest of us here in camps under Command of Lieuts Jarrell and

Glenn. They did not carry our battery. the guns they carried were some that was sent here to be carried to Chattahoochee, so the Capt took them. We have got six guns now and one hundred and three horses and ten mules. We got twenty five [horses] from Tallahassee saturday that cost upon an average $460, and very common horses at that. but they are like every thing else, very high.

Well Sallie I went out in the country saturday about twelve miles with the boys after a load of corn. The corn crop looks very good. it is rather low on the thin land but it has a beautiful color. all the forward corn is silking and tassleing out, a great deal of it with two silks to the stalk. The prospect for the crop of oranges is promising. the tree are very full [of oranges] about the size of a hickory nut. I wish you could see the large magnolia tree with its pretty white blooms on it. they are very much like the cape jesamine only they are so much larger. They are about as large as a large saucer when opened. The Cape Jesamine and and Oleander are very common in this country. the bushes grow some eight or ten feet high.

Jim Freeman [2] landed here safe with Wiley Young. he seems to be much better satisfied than I expected he would be. Cousin John has got Frank Pope to promise to help him get him [Jim Freeman] in. Pope talked to Genl Cobb about it but he cannot succeed untill Tiller comes back and we dont know how long that may be. it may be a month. Freeman wants Cousin John to pay him half of money if he stays here fifteen days and does not get in the company. I think that would be a great Sallery for about twenty days (seventeen hundred and fifty dollars). I think myself he will do very well to get his expenses paid and a negro to work in his place while he is gone. it is worth something for a man to come this far just to see the country, if nothing else. It has got to be about as hard to get in a substitute as it used to be to get a regular discharge. I thought I would try to get one if Cousin John got one. I hate for him to go home and leave me here, but I know I am not able to pay the present prices myself if I could get one in. Pope told Cousin John that it would be very necessary for him to have a certificate from a phisician or several of the neighbors [confirming] that his Pa is not able to attend to his business and his presence at home was actually necessary. [the] certifficate [is] to go with the application, which is to be signed by the Genls. Cousin John says he will try to keep

Freeman here this week and if [he] dont get him in he will send him home.[3]

Well Sallie I heard the other day that one company of the Reg. here was all taken off but four because they had deserted from Braggs army. I [don't know] that it is true, but it is nothing but common chat here. There is some that deserted and come here [for] sure, because there is a good many in these companies here that belonged to the Battallion in Atlanta. One of Dr. Smiths company that was in the Bat. when we was in Atlanta says about two hundred of them deserted.

Well Sallie, you must excuse all [the] mistakes as this has been written in a great hurry. I expect to send it by one of the boys going home on a sick furlough. six of the boys went home last week on a fifteen days furlough. if they keep giving furloughs I reckon I will come in sometime between this and christmas. I must close. Write soon.

Give my love to all the friends and connections.

I remain your affectionate brother James

1   Fort Gadsden [not Gaddens] was built in March 1818 on the former site of Negro Fort (cited elsewhere) at Prospect Bluff on the Apalachicola River. Lieutenant James Gadsden, engineer and aide-de-camp to Andrew Jackson, was directed by Jackson to erect the fort during his campaign against the Seminole Indians in the Florida panhandle.

2   James S. Freeman was in the 1860 Georgia census as the 17-year-old son of Zachariah and Margaret Freeman, farmers in the Scull Shoals District of Greene County, Georgia.

3   John Jewel attempted to hire James S. Freeman as a substitute but was unsuccessful. There is no record that Freeman served in the Echols Artillery.

QUINCY FLORIDA
JUNE 18TH 1863

Dear Brother

I received your letter day before yesterday written the 9th   it had just been a week on the way. I was glad to hear from you all, I had [not] heard from you in sometime. This leaves me well except a slight cold. Cousin John is well. There is a goodeal of complaint of bad colds. I reckon caused by the changes of the weather.

I recon you have heard by this time that a part of the company has left here. Two weeks ago the Capt was ordered to take four guns that had been here from Tallahassee on their way to Chattahoochee, and take men enough to manage them [and] go down on the Appalachachola river. it had been reported that the Yankeys were slipping up the river trying to get the obstruction out of the river. They placed two of the guns on the bank of the river at one place and carried the other two lower down the river with horses. The Capt has sent up for more men to relieve those there. they will leave here early saturday morning. those that went down there did not expect to stay and they did not carry any thing with them, not even tents to stay in. I reckon they will be glad to get back here. I would not be surprised if I have to go, but I reckon I will know by morning and I will let you know before I close this letter. I do not like to go. The water is sorry. some of the boys say they have to drink river water. that you know is not good at this season of the year. it is the best in the winter season.

The corn crop is very good, the old land corn is small but it all looks finely. but the seasons have been as good as any body could wish. We had a very heavy rain this morning. some of the corn will make fine crops if it does not rain any more. There is a fine crop of Oranges comeing on. they are about the size of common hickory nuts. I am a little surprised at the way the people farm here. in the spring they bed up their corn land with large turning ploughs and plant their corn in the middle of [the] furrow and then plough all the time with the same ploughs when it is layed by it is bedded up like bottom land. I think a good many of them have not ploughed their corn but twice. There is some cotton planted but not a great deal. I saw a large field as we came up from Tallahassee.

You wrote to know about the storm down on the Coast. We felt the effects of it some but I dont know that I can give you a correct history of it. but one thing certain, it is not half so bad as it is represented in the papers. We were ordered to leave Camp Brokaw thursday morning. wednesday about two oclock it commenced raining from the east, and continued about twenty four hours. about dark the wind began to blow from the south and blowed hard all night. several of the tents blowed down and a goodeal of timber. In the morning we had to fix up to leave there. it rained so hard that the most of the boys did not get any breakfast. So I did not hear the effect of the storm down on the coast. But after we come here I heard that there was twenty or twenty five lives lost at the salt works on Goose creek bay[1] and all the salt that was there, about eight hundred bushels [was lost], but that was not more than two or three days work to make that much. the works were on a little rise some two or three hundred yards from high tide. So the water got around them and then covered the place all over. I reckon it damaged the works a goodeal, but that works is a small affair to what is on the coast. I dont think that ought to affect the price of salt.

Friday morning. Dear Brother, I put off till this morning, thinking I would have time to write, but I have delayed to go after a load of corn and will not have time to write any more. I am not going down the river but Cousin John will. Tell Martha I would be very glad to have the chance to eat some of her turkeys but I dont know that I will get the chance to eat any turkey at home, though I hope I may. Write soon. Give my love to all. I remain your affectionate brother James

1   Goose Creek Bay is located in the Gulf of Mexico south of Tallahassee.

QUINCY FLA
JUNE 28TH 1863

Dear Sallie

I have been looking for a letter from you several days. I reckon you will be supprised When I tell you that Wilie Young brought the last letter that I received from you. I received a letter from Eliza yesterday. they were all well. I am still in very good health. There is several of the company have got the chills. There is about two thirds of the company here now. I wrote to you about part of them going down on the river. We had to send down and relieve them last satturday. I will try to tell you so you all can under stand it. A part of them are near the Obstructions in the river at the narrows, as it is called, because the river is so narrow there.[1] the others are some distance below there at fort Gadsden, where there was a fort blown up by Genl Jackson with the British in it.[2]

Cousin John, George [Martin], and Tom Martin had to go to the narrows with the other boys. I thought they would get me any how, but I got out of it. I would not be supprised if I have to [go] the next trip. I got a letter from Cousin John this evening. he says he is well but he is too much confined there.

Those that are at fort Gadsden have good water to drink, while the others have to drink out of the river. in going from here to there they had to walk to Cattahoochee, 22 miles. then go down on the boat to Riccoes bluff,[3] and then take it afoot again about thirty or forty miles through a country almost covered entirely with water from the wet weather. Those that came from there the first of the week say they had to wade through the water about fifteen miles from shoemouth [deep] to waist deep, but I suppose those deep places were branches and creeks. some of the creeks were deep enough to swim the wagons and mules. I have no doubt but it is bad, but I reckon some of them make us think it is worse than it really is. I think the cause of the boys being so weried was they walked too fast at the first start and they could not hold out. They never looked like soldiers before. I thought I would have to go any how this time, but I got out of it and I am in hopes by the time those that are there now have to come away, they will get in the notion to let our company stay away from there.

Genl Cobb was down there about two weeks ago. he told Capt Tiller to have the men that was there relieved, but as he was commanding the post he would have to remain there. he said, well I had just as soon stay here as any where. Some of boys had just heard him say he did not want to stay there and was very anxious to leave there, but he thought it would not do for him to complain to the Genl. He had been very familliar with the boys before that but quit eating with them and would not speak to one of them unless on some business. in a few days after the boys come off he wrote to Cobb to let Lieut Gibson come down to relieve him. So Gibson went down this morning. One of the boys got bit by a ratlesnake last sunday on the foot as he was going down there. he has got back this evening. he has to go on a crutch.

Well Sallie, I did not finish this letter yesterday. I thought I would finish it. I have been busy today making a hat for one of the boys to send home, so I had to put of writing till tonight. I have no news of much importance to write. the most of the boys are mending with their chills. I am in hopes they will get over them in a few more days. I have made a ring for you and one for some of the other girls, who ever it will fit. I am afraid they will not be large enough. I will [make] you all one if can get the gurtapercha to make them of. I made thes out of a piece of a walking stick that one of the [boys] bought for that purpose. There has been lots of buttons of this kind made into rings by the boys and sent home. I had one to send to Eliza and wrote to her that I would send [it] [but] sealed up the letter and forgot to put the ring in it.

Well Sallie, I am out under a brush arbor and it is raining so I reckon I will have to move from here or quit writing one, as my paper is gitting wet. It rains here every day more or less and has done for a long time. The corn crops are very fine here as far as I have seen they have not suffered a day for rain since we have been up here. I am in hopes there will be a large crop made. Three of the boys are going home to morrow. they will get back by the fifteenth if they come according to the time. I expect to try to get off about that time, but you all need not look for me for [me]. it is just as uncertain as the wind whether I come or not.

There is one going tomorrow that [has] been [home] since I have. I hope to see you all before a great while any how. I must close. Give my love to all. Cousin John wrote to me to let you all know that he was well. I remain your affectionate brother untill death James Jewel

1   The Narrows is a 5-mile-long section of the Apalachicola River, 55 miles below Chattahoochee, Florida, and 36 miles above Apalachicola, Florida. This was one of the sites where obstructions were placed in the river to prevent Union boats from gaining access to the interior of the Florida panhandle and subsequently southern Alabama and Georgia. The obstructions consisted of two parallel rows 30 feet apart of square wooden cribs 12 feet apart. In addition, a heavy chain was stretched across the river to catch floating debris and create further blockage.

2   Jewel's story about Andrew Jackson was in error. During the War of 1812, British Major Edward Nicolls built a fort at Prospect Bluff on the Apalachicola River as part of his military operations against the United States. At the end of the war in 1815 he abandoned the fort and left a supply of military stores there, including a large amount of gunpowder. The fort was soon occupied by 300 blacks, mostly escaped slaves. Now known as Negro Fort, the structure was destroyed in 1816 by an American gunboat when a red-hot cannon ball landed in the powder magazine. Two hundred seventy-five were killed by the explosion. Andrew Jackson built Fort Gadsden on the site in 1818 (cited elsewhere).

3   Ricco's Bluff, a few miles upstream from the Narrows, was the site of the second obstructions placed in the river to foil Union boats attempting to invade the South by that route. Earthworks were constructed on the Bluffs and 10 cannons were mounted there to guard the barricade.

QUINCY FLORIDA
JULY 1ST, 1863

Dear Sister

I received your letter yesterday evening written the 22nd. I was very glad to hear from you all. I did not [know] what to think about not getting a letter from you. This leaves me well. The health of the company is considerable better than it was a few day ago. There was one or two had chills today. I think they will all be well in a few more days if they improve as fast as they have done for the last three or four days.

I am a little surprised at some things that has taken place. Our third Lieut (Wade) is in command and he give three furloughs yester and two today, so there is eleven of the company at home on furloughs now. all went home since Capt Tiller went off. he would not give more than two at the time and put all the blame on Genl Cobb. Is it reasonable to suppose that Cobb would sign a furlough written by one of the Lieuts and refuse him? it is becaus he dont want to trouble himself with furloughs, only when he wants to go himself.

Well Sallie, I reckon I ought not to complain so much. I know that our company has had more furloughs than any other that went from our neighborhood, but we are here where there is nothing to hinder some of us from going home and if there was ten of the company to go every month it would take a year and a half for all of us to go.

Well Sallie, I have no news of importance to write as it has only been two days since I wrote to you, but I thought as two of the [company] would start home in the morning I would write to let you know that I had received yours. Capt Tiller has [not] got back yet, I reckon he will be here to morrow. I have not heard from Cousin John since I wrote you.

You wrote that it rained every two or three days. it rains here every day. it did [not] rain any of any consequence to day but there [was] a little sprinkle. I have not eat any rosenears [yet] but from the way some of the boys eat they seem to be plentiful. Corn is ninety cents a bushel [and] it is so badly weavel eaten that the bread is not good. you have no idea how the weavels eat the corn here. I dont think our corn would get so bad in two or three years.

I forgot to write to you about Jim Freeman going home. I had to go off early the day he started, and when I got back he and Cousin John was gone, so I dont know anything about the arrangements made between them. I heard from some of the boys that he said cousin John would have to pay him a hundred dollars more if he come back again. Cousin J. says that he would not near give him that much if it was not for his Pa being so anxious for him to come home. I reckon he gave him money to pay his way. he got a ticket to Albany [Georgia] that morning before he started. I have no idea that he will ever see Florida again. he was very fearful he would get sick before he left here.

I have not had the chance to plat any since we came up here. I had enough to make four hats on hand and I have been sewing them for the boys. I have made two this week and have three more to make as soon as I can get them done, at .50 a piece. it keeps me pretty busy to make one in the day and do everything else I have to do. I have to cook since Simon left us. I have improved some at the business, but I cant say I love to cook yet. You must let me know what that box cost, for I might want to send another one some time or other. I wish I could get some more [palmetto] to send you but there is none about here, but I reckon you all will get tired by the time you get through with that if you dont understand how to work it. Lieut Gibson had a hat one of the boys made here when he went home he said he was offered ten dollars for it. I mad one for Willie Young [and] he swoped it to his brother Jim for a tolerable good old hat and five dollars to boot. I expect you have seen it before this time.

I reckon you have heard as much of the war news as I have or more. it seems that our armies have been very successful. The Va army is reported in Penna but I reckon they wont stay there long. There is some little talk of peace but not much. I hope it will soon come, for I tell you I am getting very tired of war as well as some other.

I must close. You mus write as often as you can. You must not let that palmetto keep you from writing. if you do I will be sure not to send you any more if I know it. Give my love to all, and Brothers family. I remain your affectionate brother James

QUINCY FLA,
JULY 6TH 1863

Dear Sallie

I have taken my seat to write you a few lines as I have a good opportunity of sending it. I am still enjoying [as] good health as I could wish, which is more than every body can say here at this time. some few of the boys are having chills, but there is only a few cases. There is six more to start home tomorrow on twenty five days furlough. I think if they keep on going the six will get home before long.

Oliver Cooper had bad luck last saturday. he went with [undecipherable] after corn and just before he got back to camps he attempted getting in the wagon and missed his step and fell. the hind wheel of the wagon run over his left arm and broke one bone about half way between his elbow and hand. He is one that is going home. Jos. Armstrong and Ches Daniel[1] the others, are from the other side of the county. there is alredy fourteen at home on furlough besides three that went before we come to Fla [and] one soon after we got here. I have not heard from Cousin John since I wrote to you last week. Capt Tiller got back last friday. he say [letter torn and parts missing] have been sent from the Narrows to Fort Gadsden where he was since he left [letter torn and parts missing] there. I reckon they will all be better satisfied. they do not have a chance to get their letters only if there is somebody passing from here [to] there and [it] is very seldom there is anyone passing.

Well Sallie, I have just received a letter from Eliza. I was very glad to hear that they were all well. She wrote that you had been sick but had got better. she has made Mattie a hat and she was the proudest little thing of it. I have made a little ring for her with the initials of her name on it. she writes that Jim Freeman had got home [and] he [told her] that I was as fat as a bear. I am [now] as heavy as I ever was, but I dont think I look so in the face. I weighed 155 1/2 pounds to day.

We have received news this evening that our Army had gained a glorious victory in Maryland and I hope it is so, but the news has not been confirmed. Well sallie, you must excuse this short letter. I have not time to write much and nothing of importance to write [about]. Jos Armstrong says he will get to Antioch the next third sunday. Give my love to all. I remain your affectionate brother James

1   This was John Chesley Daniel, a Private in the Echols Artillery. Daniel is listed in the 1860 Georgia census as a 22-year-old farmer in the Grove Creek District of Oglethorpe County, along with Lou A., 20, and two children.

QUINCY FLA
JULY 14TH [1863]

Dear Sallie

I received your kind letter last saturday evening and I was sorry that I did [not] have the opportunity of answering it sooner. I was fixing up to go out to Chattahoochee sunday morning. Apart of the boys had to go down on the river to relieve those down there and I, with some of the others, had to go to bring back some ammunition from Chattahoochee. so we got back yesterday a little after twelve oclock. I received a letter from Eliza and one from John C. [Colclough], they were all well. I was very sorry to hear that Aunt Sallie [Parris] was so sick. What can be the cause of so much sickness in that country. I dont wonder at sickness in such a country as the most of this is, though here where we are now looks like it might be healthy, and I suppose it is the healthiest part of the state.

I wrote to you that those boys at the narrows had been ordered to Fort Gadsden, but they did not get the orders. Lieut Jarrell came up from there saturday sick and said they were all sick but one and his [Jarrell's] negro boy   Cousin John sent Simon up from there the first of last week sick with chills. he is able to be about some, but has a chill everyday. Cousin John was taken sick the day before he left. George and Tom Martin were also sick. We look for them here this evening or tomorrow. I will write to you again in a few days so as to let you all know how they are getting along. Lieut Gibson did not stay there but two or three days before he was taken sick. Lieut Wade[1] has gone to Miss. to bring his negroes away if he can get them. if the Yankeys have taken Vicksburg as has been reported here it is doubtful whether he will get them or not. There is but few men of his wealth that ever went into the army as a Private. if you was to see him you would not think about his being an officer.

Well Sallie, I have been thinking I would get the chance to come home about the last of this month but I think it very doubtful now. Lieut Glenn is in command now. I told him I wanted to go home [but] he says it will be a very hard matter for a well man to get a furlough as there is so many sick. I would be more anxious to come than I am, but I know if I go home and [then] get sick after I come back, there would be no chance for me to go then. so I will try to be as well satisfied as I can as long as I keep well and while there is so many sick. the chance will be better when all those get back from home that have gone now.

I wrote to you about my trip to Chattahoochee some time ago but this time we went another rout so I saw the old U.S. Arsnal. it is now occupied by the first Ga Regulars. it is a nice place. There is about an acre of groung inclosed by a nice brick wall about ten feet high and several nice buildings around, forming a part of the wall. one of them is quite a large building three storries high with a steeple five stories. there is two large gates through which all have to pass in and out. We had to go through with our wagons to get amunition which is out side of the wall it is more like a penatentiary than any thing else from the idea I have of them, only it is grown over with grass and nice shade trees in side of it. You know it has been thought the 1st Ga reg were terrible. a part of [them] were with our boys down on the river some time ago and they say they are as good hearted soldiers as can be found. They are very wicked but they are far superior to the Floridians that have been there since in every way.

Well Sallie if the news from the wars be true that we have received here for several days last week, there is not much hopes of peace soon. It is said that Vicksburg has fallen but there is some hopes withe the people here that it is not so. also Genl Lee badly whipped in Maryland and Bragg fallen back to Chatanoogga, and all the bateries taken on Moris Island near Charleston. these [stories] have all been telegraped here and we have not yet found out the truth of the matter, but I recon we will in a day or two.

I will close for this time hoping to hear from you again soon   I recon your ring has come to hand by this time. Give my love to all. I remain as ever your affectionate brother James

1   James Bolton Wade is listed in the 1860 Mississippi Slave Schedule as the owner of 45 slaves and 7 slave houses. The value of his Yazoo County real estate was placed at $54,400, and his personal property (mostly slaves) was appraised at $53,890.

WEDNESDAY MORNING
JULY 15TH

Dear Sallie,

Lieut Jarrells negro boy came in from Chattahoochee early this morning. he says he left the boys about nine oclock last night. he says the most of the boys are able to be up. Cousin John has been having chills but he missed having one yesterday. They will get here about one or two oclock today, but I will have to close this letter before they get here   this leaves me well and I hope may find you all well

Give my love to all. I remain your affectionate Brother James

QUINCY, FLA
JULY 17TH [1863]

Dear Sallie

According to promis, I have taken my seat to write you a few line. I am still in tolerable good health. The boys all came up the evening of the day I wrote to you. the most of them was sick, but the most of them [were] able to creep about a little. Cousin John is getting along tolerable well since he got here, he has not had a chill since tuesday. I think he will be able for duty in a few more days.

Tom [Martin] looked badly worsted when he come. he is improved considerably. his foot has been swollen so that he cannot wear his shoe since he took the march down on the river. George [Martin] is getting along tolerable well. Well Sallie, I have no news of any importance. it was reported yesterday that the Yankeys had taken the light house near St Marks, but there was so much difference in the statements that I dont know whether any of it is true or not. Sallie I have but very little time to write and I reccon it is very well, for I have nothing of importance to write.

The corn is doing as well as it can. The people will commence pulling fodder before long. I think if there is not better weather than [there] has been there will be but little saved. but there has not been quite as much rain for about a week as [there] has been heretofore which the people say when the rains cease then the chills and fever will increase, but I hope it will not be so with us for there has been so much already. I am very glad that I have never had any of the chills yet, but I dont know how soon I may have one. I received a letter from John Colclough which informed me that aunt Sallie was dead.

Dear Sallie, I have just received a letter from Bud. they are all up. he also wrote of the death of Aunt Sallie and Cousin sarah still being very sick. Well Sallie, I must close as the mail is about to leave. Give my love to all, I remain as ever your affectionate brother James Write Soon

QUINCY FLA.
JULY 24TH 1863

Dear Sallie

I received a letter from you last friday but I had just written the day before, so I put off writting longer than I should have, expecting to hear from you again. I am still in very good health. Cousin John is not quite well yet. George Martin and Frank Collier are sick yet. George has been having hard chills, but he miss yesterday for the first time in several days. he is not able to be up. I think Frank is more troubled about going home than any thing else. he exspected to go home this week, but he has found out he can not get a furlough and was taken sick. Tom Martin is hobling about with his foot. he has not been well, he is working to get a discharge again. John Edwards stayed with us night before last. he was on his way to the salt works. he brought us a nice shoulder of meat and some butter. Mr. Cheatham come back yesterday. he brought me some Irish potatoes that Sis Jane sent to me.

Well Sallie, it rains every day here yet. I am in hopes it will get a little drier than it has been. I believe I wrote to you about the Regiment that was here being ordered to St Marks. Two companies remained here to do gard duty here in town. There is a great difference in the people about letting us have anything. There is so many mean men in that Regiment, the people dont want the soldiers to know that they have any fruit or Watermelons or any thing of that sort. I think there is a great difference in them some way.

I received a letter from Sis Jane. They were all well. she says Brother Marshal will have to leave for the war.[1] I was sorry to hear that he will have to go. he will come to this company if he can get in. I heard that Berry B.[2] was wounded and Ben Gilham[3] and Trav Maxey was killed.[4] I have not heard how Berry was wounded. I thought some time ago the war would close before a great while but all such hope as that have vanished. The times are very dark and gloomy now, but I hope it will not be long before there will be a chance. You must excuse this short letter. Write soon. Give my love to all the family. I remain your affection brother James

1   Marshall W. Edwards joined Co. H, 9th Georgia Volunteer Infantry (State Guards) on August 19, 1863, and served until the end of the war. The unit was part of Mell's Battalion, Lipscomb's Volunteers, and was commanded by Captain Flournoy W. Adams.

2   Thornbury J. Bowling (already cited) was wounded at the Battle of Gettysburg July 2, 1863.

3   Benjamin F. Gilham enlisted in the Oglethorpe Rifles as a Private May 15, 1861, and was soon appointed Sergeant. He was elected 2nd Lieutenant September 4, 1862, and was killed at the Battle of Gettysburg, July 2, 1863.

4   Trav R. Maxey is listed in the 1860 Georgia census as a 34-year-old merchant in the Falling Creek District of Oglethorpe County, along with his wife Martha. He was among the first volunteers to join the Oglethorpe Rifles when it was formed May 15, 1861. He was killed at the Battle of Gettysburg July 2, 1863.

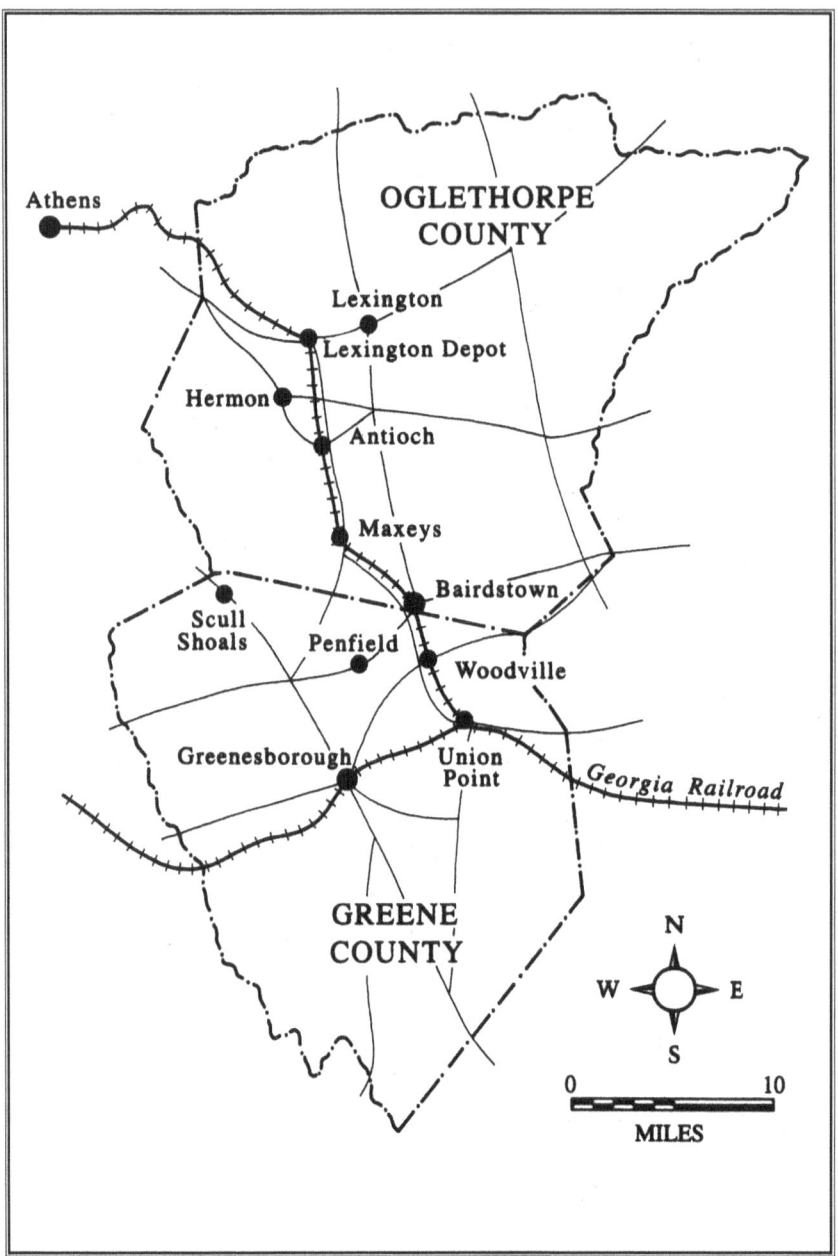

Map of Greene and Oglethorpe counties in northeast Georgia in 1860, showing the railroad, major public roads, and the communities that comprised Jewel's environs before the war. Drawn by Gisela Gresham.

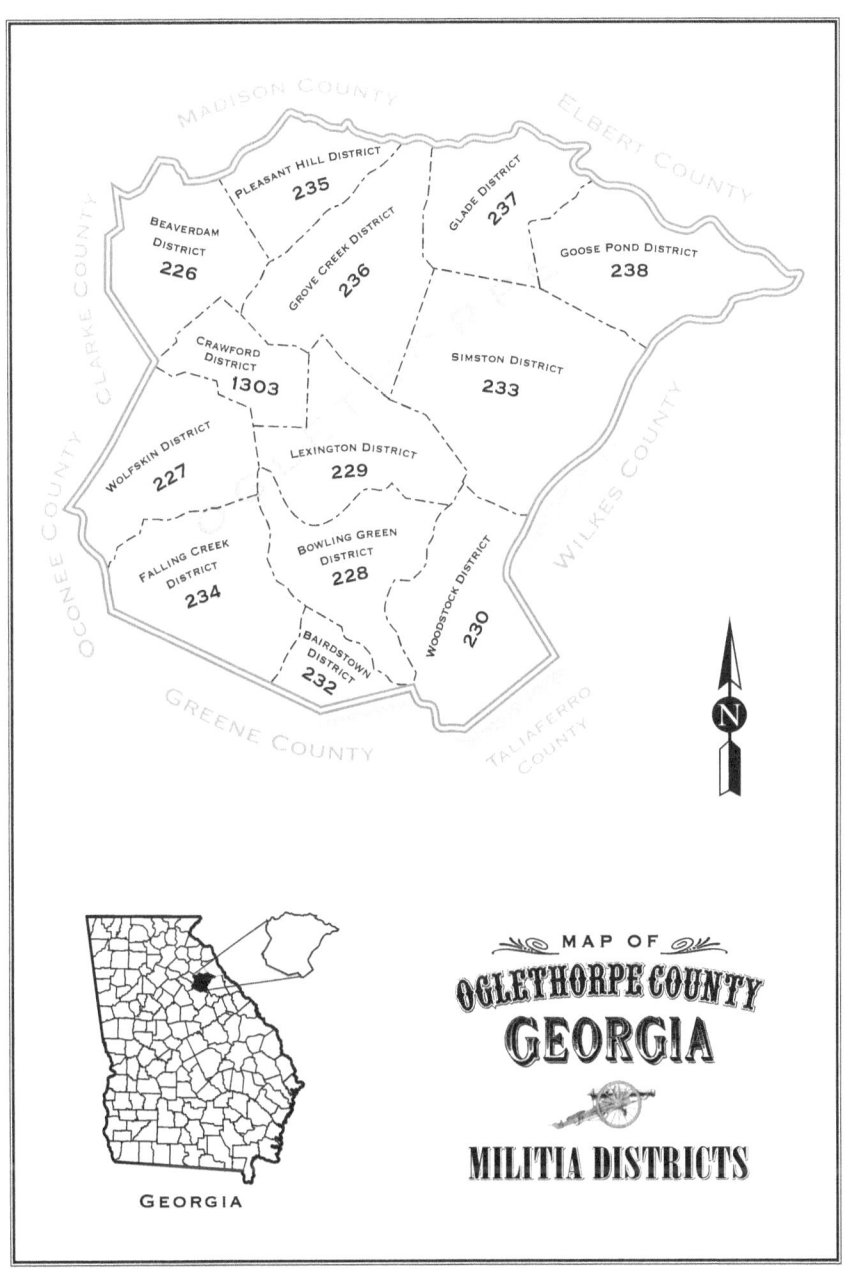

A map showing the approximate boundary lines of the Georgia Militia Districts in Oglethorpe County, Georgia, in the late 19th century. Adapted from a *Map of Oglethorpe County, Georgia, Surveyed and Drawn by Thos. B. Moss, May 1894.* Drawn by William Reeves.

NORTH CAROLINA

• Raleigh
• Smithfield
Averasboro • • Bentonville
• Fayetteville
• Rockingham

Cheraw •

SOUTH CAROLINA

Athens •
Atlanta •
OGLETHORPE COUNTY
Kingstree •
Moncks Corner

Griffin •
GREENE COUNTY

Pocataligo • James Island

GEORGIA
Hardeeville •
Savannah •

ATLANTIC OCEAN

Albany •

Quincy •
Chattahoochee • •
Tallahassee •
Madison •
Baldwin
• • Jacksonville
St. Marks • • Newport
Darby Station (Macclenny)
Lake City

FLORIDA

N
W ◆ E
S

GULF
OF
MEXICO

0 ————— 100
MILES

Major locations of activities of the Echols Artillery during the war. Drawn by Gisela Gresham.

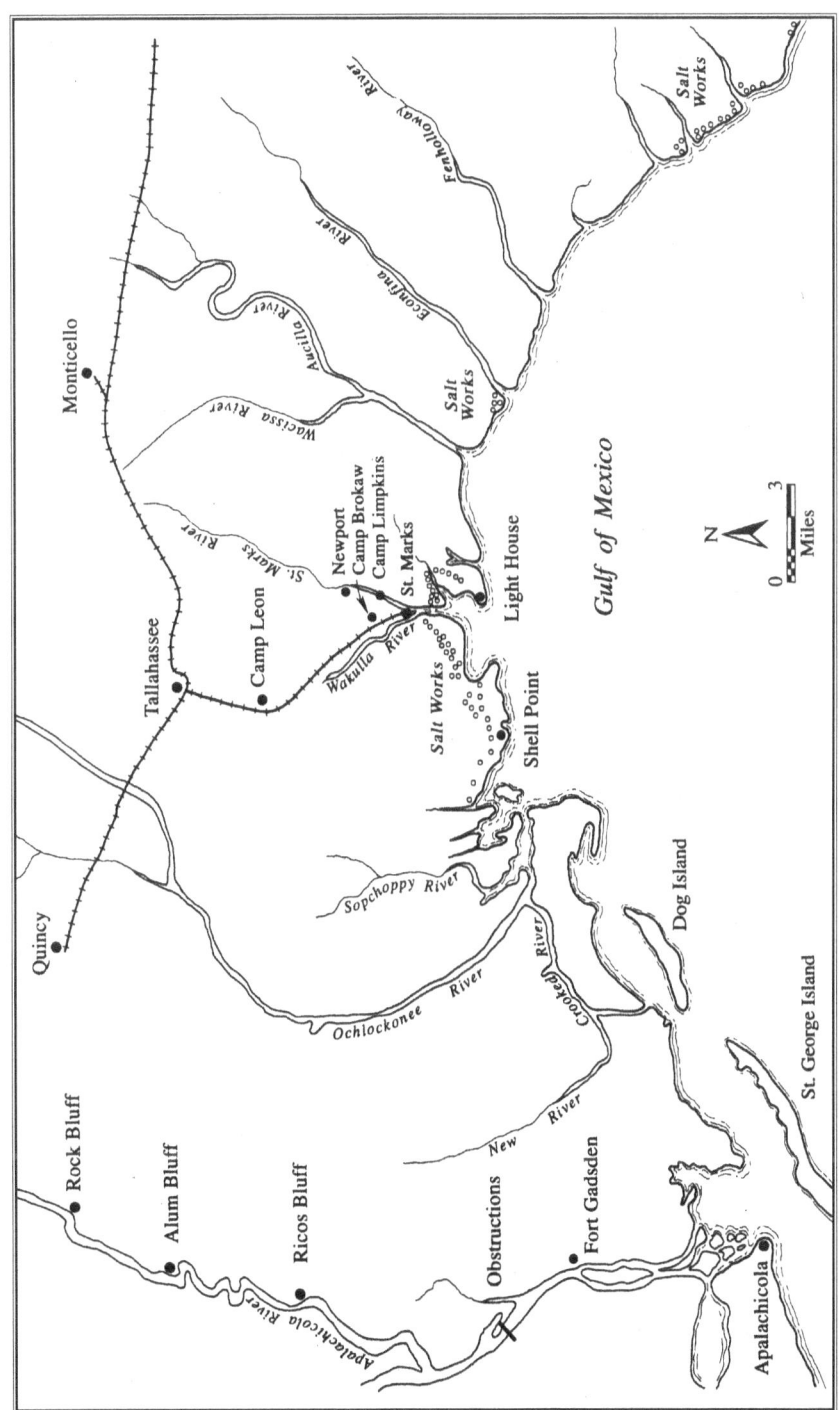

Locations of Confederate camps and other important points of interest in the Florida Panhandle. Original map is in the George Washington Scott Papers in the Florida State Archives, M-87-22. Redrawn by Gisela Gresham.

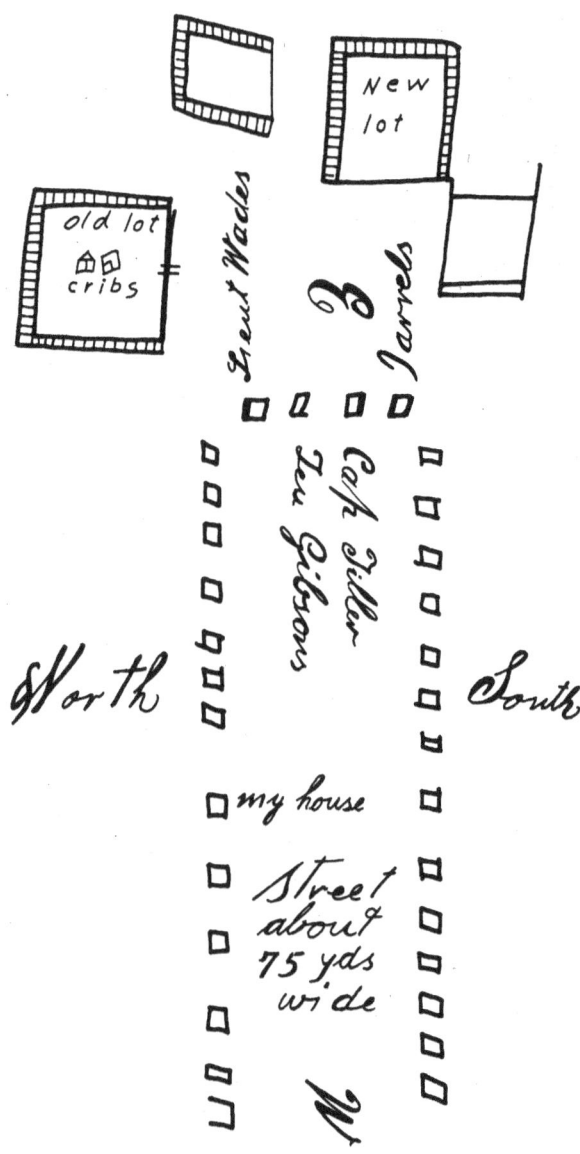

Jewel's sketch of Camp Leon, located six miles south of Tallahassee. In James Jewel's words: "This is sorter of [a] sketch of our camps. The railroad and public roads pas at the west end of the encampment."

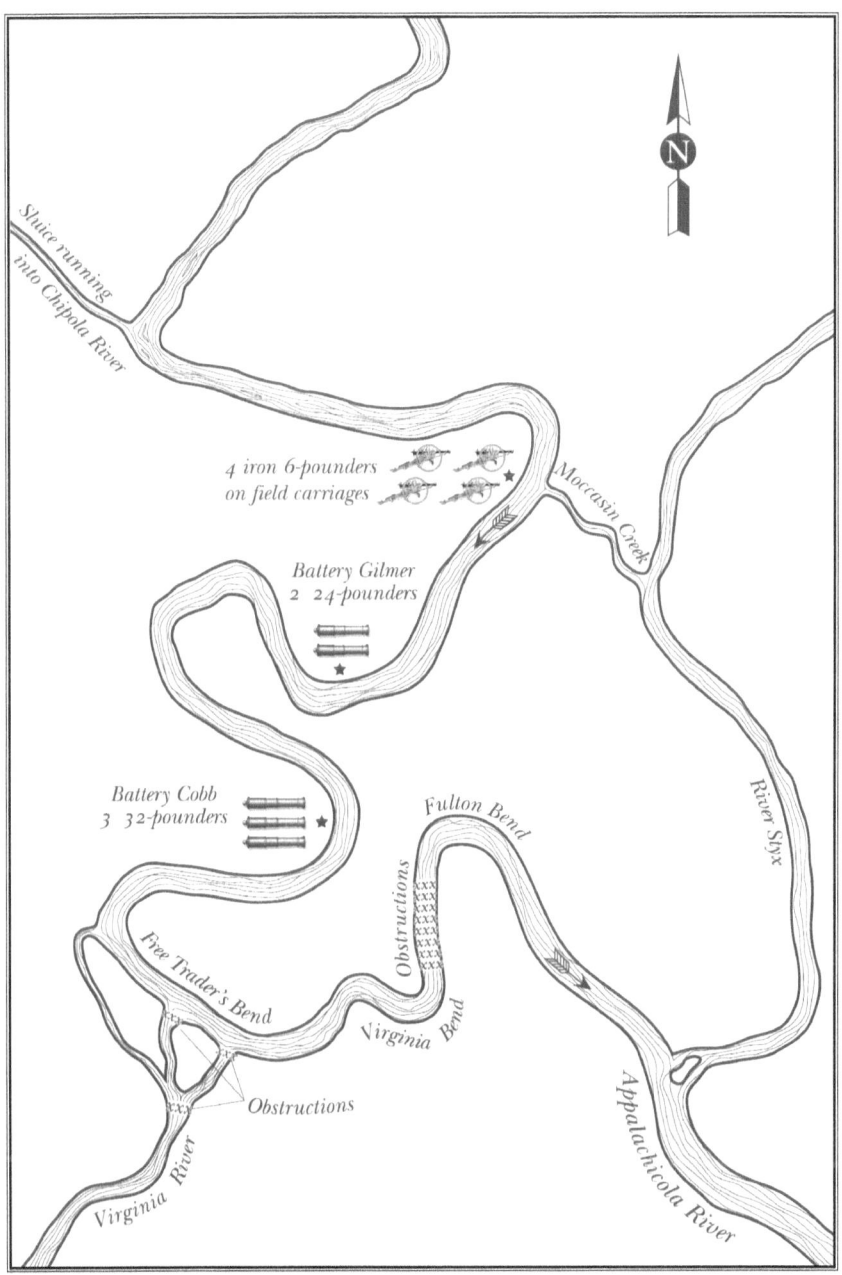

The obstructions and locations of Confederate cannon emplacements at "The Narrows" on the Apalachicola River. The original map was published in *The War of the Rebellion: A Compilation of the Official Records of the Union and Confederate Armies.* Series I, Volume 28, Part 2, page 245. Redrawn by William Reeves.

Camp Sidney Johnson Aug 10th 1863

Dear Sallie I reckon you will be a little surprised to hear that we have left Quincy and gone in the direction that we have. About thirty of us left there saturday about two oclock with two guns and come within 8 miles of Tallahassee where we camped for the night we then come through the town about ten oclock and stoped one mile this side untill four in the evening. I don't think I ever felt any hotter weather in my life. we then left there and traveled till nearly nine at night. We landed here about ten today, we are now about ten miles from St Marks, at Capt Pitipigos camp he has gone to Savanah we met him yesterday in Tallahassee he was very much opposed to going there. but the most of our boys was very anxious to go there so we would be in Georgia again but we had orders to be ready to go there but some of the boys was down at Fort Gadsden and so many sick that Gael Cobb wouldnot send us there and there he ordered one of the Fla companies there, and us to come

Copy of a letter written by James Jewel to Sallie Jewel

~ 148 ~

My Dear Brother

Feb. 7th. 1863.

I received your dear letter this morning and was so glad to hear from you. You spoke of having snow we have had real white hard snow. I will commence at last Sunday and give you a short sketch of the event of this week. Eliza and Sue came to Antioch Saturday and stayed here. John Christopher and Cousin Becky and Bird came also. Sunday it rained in the morning but stopped time enough for us to go to Antioch the sun shone out and we thought we would have a good day so off we went to church and found quite a large congregation and in a few moments it was raining hard. Brother [illegible] Jane and the children. Mrs [illegible] and Sue came down on the cars I was sorry it was such a disagreeable day. William funeral was preached. Mr. Bell preached more of a funeral sermon than he generally does. his text was the 28th verse 14th chap. of Johns gospel. Monday was a clear beautiful day first rate weather for work. I [illegible] as fast as I could all day and was out getting supper when Aunt Sallie Cousin Lizzie and Babe came. Tuesday it blew up cold weather Aunt Sallie and Babe went home and Cousin Lizzie staid with us. Wednesday we went over to Brothers it was cloudy and cold that night it commenced sleeting and by morning the ground was covered it was white round snow. Thursday we had to stay in the house it was so slick we could not walk well. and you can just imagine how we spent our time sitting around the fire pitying the poor soldiers slipping out once and awhile to get some ice to eat. The children had quite a jubilee over the snow. Mary has been quite sick since Christmas that abscess has stopped running and her body has broken out in red rough spots what it is time alone can prove. It has been reported all over the country that she had the consumption and was not expected to live but she is not that bad off yet. She looks better now and does not cough. We were all uneasy about her because she had such a cough and that [illegible] is thought to have come from her lungs. She has been very low spirited. I think if she will only take care of herself during this cold weather she will get over it at least I am in hopes so. I have heard of [illegible] deaths this week and the last. old Mr. [illegible] Mrs [illegible] Mrs Gibson and Alvin Robinson

Copy of a letter written by Sallie Jewel to James Jewel

Grave of Sara R. (Sallie) Jewell, located in family cemetery near the old Jewel homeplace in the Wolfskin Militia District of Oglethorpe County, Georgia. Photo by Tom Gresham.

One of two chimneys that mark the old Jewel homeplace in the Wolfskin Militia District of Oglethorpe County, Georgia. Photo by Tom Gresham.

Dear Sallie

I have taken a seat to write you a few lines to let you know that I am well and I exspect to send it by Tom Martin if [he] gets chance to start tomorrow. he has not got a furlough yet, but the sergeon of our company has gone over to the hospital to try to get him a furlough. George [Martin] left here saturday evening. Cousin John is well again. The health of the company is about the same as when I wrote to you last. I have just been over to the hospital to see some of the sick boys. Frank Collier was taken very severely last saturday with what the Dr. call hemorage of the bowels, which left him in a very critical situation. he is a good deal better to day. the Dr told him he thought he would be well enough to go home the last of the week.

Capt Tiller has sent a telegraph dispatch for a wagon to meet him and two other at Chattahoochee as they were there sick. Drue Dunn[1] come down saturday evening to join our company. he has been overseeing in Miss and he had to run the negroes to georgia. the owner lives in Wilkes County. he come to his mothers[2] in Griffin, but he could not stay there because the enrolling officer was talking about taking him up. he had to be very sligh to get through Macon, they are taking up every one that passes without some showing of exemption from the service.

Well Sallie, I wrote to you about John Edwards coming down to see us, but there was one thing I for got to tell you. You dont know any thing about the family, but the rest of them do. Old Mr Wade that use to live there at Hermon was killed by his son Thomas[3] and one of his daughters. John said it happened about two weeks before he was here. there is no proof to do any thing with them.   Tom acknowledged killing him, but [said] it was in self defense, but it is the general opinion of the people that the cause was this: he [Mr. Wade] was flying around a young woman and they were opposed to his marring again. John says the old man always seemed to think more of Tom than any of his other children and had managed to keep him out of the war up to that time, but he has gone into the war since that time. He worked twenty five or thirty hands and had a very valuable plantation and owned nearly a thousand head of cattle, which are very valuable nowaday. There is no counting for people nowaday.

Well Sallie, I will stop writing untill I find out whether Tom will go or not. if [he] dont go, I will have to wait till wednesday before I can send this.

Tell Pa salt is worth 12 dollars per bushel here and can be shipped for a dollar and half or two dollars to Lexington depot, which will be 11 dollar cheaper than it is there. several of the boys have sent some home and some have gone down now to buy and will be back this evening.

1   Drue T. Dunn served as a Private in the Echols Artillery for a time and transferred to another unit.

2   Drue Dunn's mother was Mary P. Dunn (already cited).

3   Mr. Wade and Thomas Wade are unidentified.

WEDNESDAY
AUGUST 5TH [1863]

Dear Sallie

I have just got back from the hospital. I went there this morning see the boys. they are mending some, but slowly. Tom Martin has got a furlough this morning and I will send this letter by him, for it will go as soon as if I send it by mail. I received your letter yesterday evening written the 27th of June. You all did have company sure enough   it must have been a great time for visiting. I would have been so glad to have been there, but some other time will do as well I recon, if I can come.

Capt Tiller came up yest. quite sick and two of the boys with him. We have very warm weather now there has been several days clear weather. it is a splendid time on the fodder. it ripenes as fast as I ever saw it, I think. all that is not gathered in a few days will not be worth saving. I have nothing more of importance to write.

Why did you put so many postage stamps on that letter. there was one ten cents on the face that was crossed and two five cts one on the back, not marked, so I will save them to send another letter. one of them might have been put on at the post office. What has become of Mary, the reason she dont write. Tell her she must have forgotten me or she is waiting to get a lot of news to write so that I will have a long letter to read. I am fond of reading long letters, but I had rather read [a] short one than to wait allways for a long one.

Sallie, you said you thought it would soon be my time to come home. I think it would if it was taken in regular rotation, but that is not so. for there is several at home now the third time since I was there and there is some here that has been from home longer than I have. so you can see how it goes. some of them have very urging business but go and come back without attending to it.

I will close for this time. Cousin J sends his love to you all.

Give my love to all. I remain as ever your affectionate brother James

QUINCY FLA
AUGUST [1863]

Dear Sallie

I have taken my seat to write you a few lines to let you know that I am well. George Martin has got a furlough to go home and exspects to start this evening, if he can get a horse and buggy to go to Bainbridge, where he can take the stage to Albany. The stage only goes from here to Bainbridge every other day, and that is Mondays, Wednesdays, and fridays. He has got [a furlough] upon the grounds of his fathers being very bad off and not likely to live long.[1] They wrote for him and Tom both to come as quick as they could get off. Tom is at the hospital. he went there the first of the week. he was over here yesterday evening and said the doctor had promise to give him a furlough and he would exspect to start home Monday. He has never had his shoe on his foot since he went to the Narrows. it is a little strange that walking when he went there would hurt him so much worse than dancing all night would. But I reckon I have said enough about this for the present. one thing certain, if he goes home now he will not come back here soon, I think. Georges furlough is for only fiften day, but I have no idea of seeing him by that time again.

Tell Pa to send me a bottle of bitters of wild cherry and dogwood bark, or the brandy to make it, if he has it to spare. I had rather have it fixed up because I think I could keep it better than I could the brandy. I can get the barks here if you dont have the chance to get them. I told cousin John to write for some by Jos Armstrong. if he brings it I will fix it up immediately. I want to keep from having the chills if I can. Cousin John and I went out about five miles this morning and bought ten pounds of butter at fifty cents a pound. that is what I call a high price for butter. Once and awhile we can get some at fifty cents but not often. We have quit our old mess. some of them became dissatisfied about Simon and Cousin John concluded to quit them and let them cook for themselves awhile. so there is John Kinnebrew, Jim Hurt, Cousin John, and Myself in a mess together for a while.

Sis Jane wrote to me that Brother Marshal thought he would have to go to the war and if he did he would come to this company if he could.

Well Sallie, george Martin has come back from town and says he cant go unless he can get two passengers to go with him in a hack. so I reckon he will have to wait till monday. I have no news of importance to write to you. this is the third day now we have had without rain. the people are pulling fodder rapidly, some of them must have lost a gooddeal of it from the wet weather. I saw some burnt up on the stalks today.

O how I do want to come home to see you all but I dont know when I will get there. I dont see any chance now for me to come unless some of them comes back [from] home. There is not but one come yet that went on sick furloughs and about a dozen of their furloughs are out. two of the substitutes started from here last week sick. one of them lived in Jackson County [Georgia]. He got to the Union Point last thursday and was speechless. One of the comp, Mr Broach,[2] came by there monday and he was lieing there and had never spoken a word to any one.

Well Sallie, I will close for this time. write soon as you can. Give my love to all the family. I remain your affectionate brother James

1   According to the inscription on his tombstone in the family cemetery in the Wolfskin District of Oglethorpe County, John Martin, father of George, Frank, and Tom Martin, died October 26, 1863.

2   There were two members of the Echols Artillery named Broach. Charles Willis B. Broach was a Corporal and James Alexander Broach was a Private.

QUINCY FLORIDA
AUG 7TH/63

Dear Sallie

Joseph Armstrong landed here yesterday evenin by way of Albany [Georgia]. I was very glad to see him. he brought all the things safe to me. I have not cut my cake yet nor opened the brandy. he also brought yours and Marys letter, which I was very proud to receive them.

Sallie, I have no news of any importance to write as it has only been two days since I wrote to you. I am still enjoying good health. Cousin John is complaining a little but he is about. The health of the company is about as usual, it dont seem to improve very fast. Capt Tiller is quite [sick], but he is better than he was when he first came up from fort gadsden. I have not been to the hospital since day before yesterday. there is seven of the boys there. the most of them seem to be mending slowly.

The weather is a good deal dryer than it has been and very warm during the day, but it is very pleasant at night and the latter part [of the night] a blanket feels very comfortable. it looks strange to see people wrapped up in three or four blankets and the [temperature] ranging about a hundred. I dont know how high it has been, but it looks to me like it was hot enough to run the mercury to a hundred severall days. the hottest part of the day is generally about nine Oclock, after which time the breeze begins to rise from the south. Sallie, Joe [Armstrong] said he did not know you. he says you dont favor me much and he says that Mattie is a heap better looking than I ever was. he dont think she favors me at all. he says there was so many women at church that he did not begin to know them and spoke to a many a one that he did not know. I was surprised to hear of Billie youngs marrying Miss Asbury.[1] I thought he would set his cap for some biger fish than she was, but any body need not be surprised at any thing that happens now a days, there is so many strange things happening.

Well Sallie, I wrote to you that some of the boys had gone down to St Marks to get Salt. They have got back. They bought Salt at ten dollars a bushel and then it cost them fifty cents to get it delivered at the depot. It will cost them 13. or 14. dollars by the time they get it to Lexington depot. They are going to put it up in barrells here at the depot today, as that is much the safest way to ship it so far. If Pa and Brother wants any and will let me know, I will try to get it for them. I dont know whether I could get barrells to put it in or not but I can try.

Sallie, tell Mary I will try to answer her letter before long, a little sooner than she answered my last. I exspect to have to go to the war next week or before long. I reckon you will wonder what I ment by going to the [war]. We have been thinking that the boys would be relieved by some other company, but I reckon we will have to try it before long. So you need not be uneasy if you dont hear from me very often about that time.

Sallie, it is getting late and will soon be time for the mail to go out so I will have to close. I am so sorry that I could not be there to go with you all to meeting and to see Sis Jane and Brother M., but I am affraid it will be some time before I will see you all there yet. those that have gone home on furloughs look like they will never come back again. Some of the boys said there would be preaching here at nine Oclock and I thought there would not be any thing of it as it was past ten, but I see two men have come in to the capts tent I supose are preachers. I will close. Give my love to all the family also all of brothers family. I remain your affectionate brother untill death. James Jewel

Write as often as you can, at least once a week.

1   William T. Young and Henrietta Asbury were married July 29, 1863.

CHAPTER VI

Camp Sidney Johnston

"The yankey don't care any thing about Fla no how.
if they did they would have taken it long ago"

CAMP SIDNEY JOHNSON[1]
AUG 10TH 1863

Dear Sallie

I reckon you will be a little surprised to hear that we have left Quincy and gone in the direction that we have. About thirty of us left there saturday about two oclock with two guns and come within 8 miles of Tallahassee, where we camped for the night. we then come through the town about ten Oclock and stoped one mile this side untill four in the evening. I dont think I ever felt any hotter weather in my life. We then left there and traveled till nearly nine at night. We landed here about ten today. we are now about ten miles from St Marks at Capt Vilipiges[2] camp. he has gone to Savanah, we met him yesterday in Tallahassee. he was very much opposed to going there, but the most of our boys was very anxious to go there so we would be in Georgia again. we had orders to be ready to go there, but some of the boys was down at Fort Gadsden and so many sick, that Genl Cobb would not send us there then he ordered one of the Fla companies [to go] there and us to come here and take their place. It is a part of the company that was at camp Leon that I wrote to you about being fixed up so well. They divided the company and Old Capt Gamble was sent to Camp Brokaw and the other one here.

There is two infantry companies and one cavelry here. This a pleasent looking place, but I tell you it felt like burning a fellow up here this evening untill a cloud come up and rained a shower and it is quite pleasant now. it has set in like it might be dry weather for a while. I have no idea how long we will stay here, but I would not be supprised if we were here some time, if the flies dont take us away. I thought I had seen some flies before, but I never saw them half so bad in my life. We traveled over twenty five miles of as sandy a road as can be found any where. there is not a firm place I dont think in the whole rout, and a part of the way looked like there never was anybody seen, only traveling the road. but this morning we come to a plantation where there looked like somebody lived. he had two very large cornfields. the corn is plenty ripe enough to gather. in fact I saw where some had been gathered.

Well Sallie, I will have to write you a short letter this time. You must excuse all mistake, as I have been writing in the tent where [there] was five or six talking and moveing about so I could hardly write at all. I wrote a few lines to Eliza from Tallahassee yester. I got a small bottle and put a part of the brandy in [it] that Pa sent me so that I could put it in my knap sack and brought [it] along with me and I think if brandy ever did do me any good, this was one of the times, for the watter along the road is so sorry it is not fit for a horse to drink harly. we travel yesterday evening till nearly sundown when we come to a well where the [water] farely stunk and [had] wigeltail[3] aplenty in it. I have no doubt from my feelings [that] I would have been sick by this time if I had not had that along with me.

Cousin John is still at Quincy. as I before said, you must excuse me this time and I will try to write a long letter to you and Mary in a few days. I am afraid that we will be troubled some about getting our mail here, but you all must write and maybe I will get a letter once and a while. Give my love to all the family. I remain your affectionate brother James

Direct your letters to St Marks

1   Camp Sidney Johnson was named for Albert Sidney Johnston, one of only eight Confederates to attain the rank of full general. Jewel erroneously spelled his name Johnson, as did many of his contemporaries, and, indeed, as many do today. General Johnston was killed in battle at Shiloh, Tennessee, April 6, 1862.

2   Camp Villepigue (not Vilipige) was undoubtedly named for Fred L. Villepigue, who served as Florida's Secretary of State from 1853 to January 1863. When Gamble's Artillery

was organized in the spring of 1862, Villepigue entered service as its 1st Lieutenant. In November 1862, the Battery was divided and he was promoted to Captain in command of one of the new units which was known as both the Kilcrease Artillery and the Villepigue Artillery. Villepigue resigned from the Confederate Army January 12, 1865.

3   Jewel was referring to mosquito larva.

CAMP SIDNEY JOHNSON
SEPT 3RD [1863]

Dear Sallie,

I received yours and Mary's [letter] sent by Ches Daniel. also one that you had [written] a few days before. I was glad to get them. I tell you it took me agood while to get through reading and [I] do wish I could return the same compliment, but it is out of my power to do so now. I have written to you that I was sick. I am still a little under the weather. it seems like it [is] hard for me to mend much, or at least like I thought I would by this time, but there is one thing I like and that is something good to eat to strength me. something that I could eat like I could get at home. that is what a many a poor soldier needs while he is sick. We have a little chicken soup once and a while, but you know that [it] is not fixed up like we would have it at home.

I dont know how it will be about Pa's and Uncles Billies salt sent by express. I have always understood there was no express line to Quincy at all, it gives out at Albany. I reckon it will be forwarded by the stage line. I have no news from the salt works lately, nor no other part of the world.

Well Sallie, I said to you in the first start I would have to write a short letter. it pesters me to think of any thing to write, and you know it is very annoying for any one to be trying to write and [a] fly trying to get in each eye [and] two or three on your nose, and just as soon as I raise my hand and scare them off they come back again. Out of our squad of thirty men, twenty of them are complaining. There is an other company of the regement come here to take the place of Capt Thomas[1] company, but I think myself we all had better be some where else for all the good we could do if the Yankeys were to come. I will stop writin till morning when I will have a better time.

Well Sallie, I have taken my seat to write a few more lines but I have nothing of importance. I feel a goodeal better this morning than I have done in several days. it is a very pretty morning. it does not rain as often here lately as it did some time ago. I reckon I had just [as well] quit trying to write, for I cant make any [thing] out at all. Give My love to all the family. I remain your affect brother James

1   Captain Thomas is unidentified.

SEPT. 25TH 1863

Dear Sallie

I received your letter written the 15th, also one from Eliza of the same date. I was very glad to hear from you all and hear that you all was well, which found me getting along very well. I was very much Surprised to hear that Brother M. had gone to the Wars. I thought from what I had heard he would not have to go, and I was glad to hear that he would stay, for I thought he could do as much good in that neighbor hood as any body and men was very scarce there any how. I will have to excuse you for not writing sooner than you did in such a case, but I have been thinking for some time that your letters come sorter scattering and now you will have to write to Bud and you will not have so much time. You must tell him to write to me as often as he has time and give me all the news about Atlanta. I heard this morning that there had been a big fight up towards Chattanooga and our forces were in persuit of the yankeys.

Well Sallie, I wrote to you the first of the week that I would ship Pas salt in a few days, but I went to the railroad day before yesterday and there is a very poor little scaffold and it is [as] full of salt as it can be. But the plan that some of us adopt is to take it there and put it in the cars when they leave there with corn and fodder for us and when they are emptied. so we are now hawling fodder from there and I will take the salt over [in] time enough to get it in. I sent a barrel for Uncle Billie this morning with five bushels. I have put in six bushels and a half in the three sacks and marked it as good as I could, but I am afraid that the sacks will get so dirty that it may be difficult to see the marks. I have heard from good authority that the river is too low for boating and there is a lot of salt there to be shiped. Tell Pa if he dont want it all to sell 1 1/2 bushels and pay the money to eliza. I dont know what the exspenses will be to Chattahoochee [Florida,] but I will find out long before it gets home. Some people ship it by Savannah, but there is a stage line between here and [there and] it would have to be carried 20 miles in wagons and the shipper has to pay for hauling and also have a Com. Merchant to pay the freight there before it will go any further, which I cannot do you know.

Sallie, you wrote to know what had become of Cousin John. I wrot to him on some business sometime ago but I never heard a word from him till yesterday. Drue Dunn wrote to me that he had gone home and left last saturday evening and was very weak and feeble. He says the boys are mendin very fast since this cool spell. but I dont see much diffirence with them here. We drew a quart of whiskey yesterday to the man. that was some thing I did not think we would get. it is not the best, but it will do to drink where there is no better. it is as good as they buy at $30 a gallon here, so they say. I never bought any.

Well Sallie, you wrote about a wedding down there and we heard that one of our [girls] there and [one of the] boys at home on furlough was married a few days ago. Well, I will tell you a little circumstance that took place here yesterday   One of Capt Blockers[1] men went up six miles this side of Tallahassee and was married and Col. James Barrow met with him and ordered him back to camps yesterday evening, about 30 miles.

Well Sallie, it now time for me to begin to help about getting supper so I will close till morning, so good bye.

Saturday morning   Well Sallie, I have just eat breakfast and taken my seat to finish this letter but I dont know whether any one will go to the [post] office or not today, but I think it doubtful. We had some potatoe buiscuit for breakfast. I hid two large ones and a half. I have no news of any importance to write this morning. If the weather has been as cool in proportion up there as it has [been] here for a week, I think it must have been cold enough to kill everything. It felt nearly cold enough for frost several morning the first of this week. There was a gentle man came down from the neighborhood of Talla. this week, he says there was frost at his house. Well sallie, I learned that Cousin John got a furlough to go home to get married, but I think that was just an excuse with him.[2] I will close for this time. I dont know when I will get home. it looks like a bad chance. Give my love to all the family. You must write often. I remain your affectionate brother James

1   Captain Haley T. Blocker was commanding officer of Co. E, 2nd Florida Cavalry (Beauregard Rangers). The 1860 Florida census lists Blocker as a 42-year-old surveyor, born in South Carolina.

2   John Jewel did not marry Sarah F. Stevens until March 3, 1864.

CAMP SIDNEY JOHNSON
OCT 4TH [1863]

Dear Sallie,

I have no doubt you will be looking for one be fore you get this. I received your letter friday the 2 inst written the 26th ult, but I was not well enough to write. I also received one from Sis Jane and Eliza. I have had about three chills with some fever after them. I miss yesterday and I will miss this evening. it [is] near about time for them. I got the box that Pa sent me all right. I am very proud of such a present. I have some whiskey bitters, but I think I will give them away and fix some of the brandy. Well Sallie, I will have [to stop] writing till tomorrow, it take me a long time to write a short letter. I am in hopes of being [better] in the morn.

Well Sallie, I have been up all the morning [and] it [is] now about ten [o'clock] I dont feel much like [writing] yet, it looks like every thing has a dazzly appearance that I hardly know what I am doing. James Bolton got a nice Cakes, potatoes and apples, but he is not well enough to enjoy it. it is the first box that I have seen brought from home [without] things of that kind mostly [being] spoilt. I think from what I learn, we will go back to Quincy before long. I dont know that it will be so, and if it was I dont know that it would be much better. Sallie, I know you think this a short letter but I cant write when I feel a chill.

give my love all the family. I remain as ever your affectionate Brother James

Hello Sallie, I will write you a few lines this morning. I have just received your letter written the 14th, which afforded me a great deal of pleasure in reading. I am getting a long finely now. Two of the boys went down to the bay yesterday and brought up a lot of fish and we had a mess for breakfast you aught to see me eat them. we have had them ever once and a while. I reckon I will get tired of them before long. they are the [only] thing that is cheap down here. they are worth ten cent apiece at the bay where they are fishing. they are not like our little fish, they are about the size of Macerel. Well Sallie, Jim Hurt is waiting for me and I must close. Give my love to all the family and brothers folks. Tell Mary to write and if I am well I will try to write to her. I remain your brother James

CAMP SIDNEY JOHNSON
OCT 11TH 1863

Dear Sallie,

I received yours of the 29th yest. and was very glad to hear that you were all enjoying good health. As for myself, I am not very well, but I am mending up again, so I think I will be well in a few days. I think I wrote to you that I had been having chills. I had several chills the latter part of last week and one or two the first of this, but I have got them broke on me and I hope not to return any more. but as soon as I am exposed a little too much, I exspect they will come back again. I exspect we will leave here in a few days for Quincy. Lieut Glenn has gone up there to try to get away from here. there is so many of us sick here that there is not enough to do what duty there is to be done. Out of 28 there is not one that is well, but the most of them are able to be up. I reckon if we get back to Quincy we will mend up some. The weather has been very cool here for some time. it looks like it is cold enough for frost here any morning and some of the boys said they saw frost one morning on some fodder at the horse lot.

Well Sallie, I have no news of importance to write but I know you want to hear from me and I feel it my duty to try to write something. Well the Regiment has relieved that company that come down when I was taken sick. they did not let them stay here two weeks. if they stay here a month they nearly all get sick. so they think they will move them often. I believe I wrote to you that I had received my brandy that Pa sent me with the dried fruit. I would not have cared if the box had been filled up with dried peaches instead of cotton, but I am very thankful for it as it was and I hope it may be a benefit to me. James Bolton is in my mess and he got a box with a lot of sweet cakes, a pone of light bread, a cake of butter, some sweet potatoes, apples, and other things. but he has not been well enough to enjoy it it at all. the bread was moulded some. I have seen several boxes brought from home but nearly every thing that was cooked would be spoilt. he had a fried chicken in the box that was good, I reckon the box was not on the road long and the weather being cool kept them good.

Well Sallie, I bought a quire of paper like this the other day at 4 dollars, and a pack of envelopes made in Tallahassee, I reckon of the paper torn off from some of the old walls with the calico side turned in. I dont know how they will do, but I think 75 cents a long price for such things. It is a wonder to me they dont charge fifteen cents for postage stamps, and think they will after a while. It seems that the people are going in for the chine ease [Chinese] syrup sure enough up the country. Syrup is getting scarce down here now, but we draw a little.

They people have not commenced making syrup yet. I dont reckon they will commence till the latter part of next month or the first of december unless the weather is cool enough to kill the cane. it is growing now, but I think the weather has been very dry for that and the potatoe crop. I know it has been too dry for potatoes.

Well Sallie, if we get up to Quincy again [I] hope I will get the chance to come home before long, but I dont know unless a crowd of them would come back that is there. I am going to try any how to see what I can do. I would be glad to see you all and I hope I will be there before a great while. I must close this letter as I want to write to Sis Jane as I have neglected to write to her some time.

You must not forget to write and I will try to write as often as I can. Give my love to all the family and connections. I remain your affectionate brother James

CAMP SIDNEY JOHNSON
OCT 16TH 1863

Dear Sallie,

I received your welcome letter yesterday evening written the 6th. I was truely glad to hear that you all are well, though it is a little more than I can say. I do not feel stout and well like I have done before I came down here I can eat enough for any body, I think, but it looks like it dont strengthe me like I think it would at home. that is something I can not account for. why it is that any one has a good appetite and eats hearty and dont seem to get any stronger.

Well Sallie, I have no news, but perhaps you may want to know what has been the mater with me, as I dont believe I told you. I had the chills, but I never had any very hard ones. I had five or six, but two of them shook me right smartly and then I had fever after them, but I was not sick at the stomache at all. some of the boys get very sick after their chill is over. it has been about a week I believe since

I had one, so I hope I will not have any more soon. I dont think from the way you wrote about cousin John that he is in much plight for marrying, but the boys that come down from Quincy say that those were the terms upon which he got his furlough, and it was so stated in the furlough. McKinnebrew told some of them that it was exspected he would marry soon. so that is all I can tell you about it. I dont know what was his notions about the matter, But if he did not intend to marry he has acted very wrong by getting a furlough in that way.

Well Sallie, I thought we would be relieved from here and go back to Quincy, but in stead of that they sent down ten more men and are talking of moveing the whole company down here some where. there is no more use of our being here at this place than there would be for a parcel of troops at the Union point or some other such place. the yankey dont care any thing about Fla no how. if they did, they would have taken it long ago.

Well Sallie, there is two of the boys here that the Dr sayed last night must go to the hospital at Tallahassee today if they were able to go (they are from below Lexington). but he would come and see them this morning before they started, and it is now past twelve Oclock and he has not come. I thought if they went I would send this letter by the one that goes with them, as some one will have to go. if I dont I will send it to St Marks tomorrow, which will make it one day later.

Tell Ma I did not find any of the old fashions rasins in my box, but there was something near about or quite as good. I have not had any of them cooked yet but I use them to eat raw to keep a good taste in my mouth. I think I will stew some of the rasins in a few days to see whether they are any better that way. I believe I wrote to you that I was sorry that they did not occupy the space of the cotton. but if they had I recon it would have been a very heavy little box, but it was small and would not have been very unhandy to carry. I have fix up me some bitters out of the brandy, or a part of it. as for George Martin comeing, I thought when he went away it would be a long time before he got back and as for Tom, I dont look for him any more till I see him. he will be at home christmas I exspect. I cant tell you any thing about when I will get home. I hope some time between this and christmas.

You must tell Bud to write me a long letter and tell me where he has been and every thing that he can think of since he left home. all about what he has to eat and how he gets along cooking. who he is in a mess with and the commander of the Reg. or Brigade he is in if any. I ought not to write so much nonsense on paper that cost four dollars a quire. Well I must close for this time. you know I told you that you would [have] more letters to write, but I have no right to complain about your writin to me lately. Give my love to all. I remain your affectionate brother James

P.S. I will send you a sample of my envelops that cost 75 cents a pack, made out of old wall paper I think.

CAMP SIDNEY JOHNSON
OCT 23RD 1863

Dear Sallie

I have taken my seat to write you a few lines to let you all know how I am getting along. I would have written to you sooner, but have been waiting exspecting a letter from you every day as I had not received one from you since the first of last week.

I have had another spell of the chills, but I believe I had one or two when I wrote to you last. They commenced on me last week and I had one every other day till I had about five. I had the last one last tuesday. I thought I would be sure to have one yesterday, but I made some pepper tea and put some whiskey in it and lay down about two hours before the time for it to come on and drunk a little of the tea at the time till my chill time had past. then I got up without any fears of the nasty thing. Well, I mentioned about whiskey. We drew another quart the other day of the best that I have seen in a long time. it is nearly equal to brandy. I think the quartermaster must have made a mistake and gave us some that the officers have to drink.

There is still some talk of our being relieved and going to Quincy, but I dont know how it will be. Lieut Wade is looking for Jarrell to come back to Quincy and then one of them will come down here. Well Sallie, I will now say something about the furlough business. I dont exspect now to get one as long as I stay this side of Tallahassee, unless all the company comes down or Old Col. Smith is removed from Tallahassee. Glenn and the Dr wrote two furloughs and then they had to be approved here by Capt Blocker and then to Tal., where Col Smith wrote on one of them, "disapproved - if all the sick was sent home the army would be broke up," and [on] the other one "disapproved." It seems that [he thinks that] his judgment must be better than the surgeon of the post from the way he wrote. and when they went to Quincy they were still disapproved by Col McGill,[1] who now fills Old Genl Cobbs place. Lieut Glenn thought he would try it himself as he has been in bad health, but his come back the same way. but they told him he could not go til some of the other commissioned officers come to take his place. So you see a fellow like me that is able to be up stands but a poor chance to get a furlough. we have to live in hopes, I reckon. I have written enough on the furlough subject for this time but I thought as I had but little else to write about I thought I would give you a full history.

I heard from Eliza a day or two ago that Sis Mary was sick. I would be glad to hear how she is now. I sent Pas salt, and ten bushels for Uncle Billie, to the rail road and had it shiped, but I dont know what has become of it. you will all have to look for it till it comes. I think there is six bushels and a half in the three sacks that Pa sent, but I have most forgotten, and I sent another sack marked the same way way, but to Woodville depot. it may all go to Antioch. if it does, he can sell it at market price. I recon it will get there by hog killing time. it has fallen to twelve at the Salt works, but there has not been any brought here in some time. but I recon it is because there has been no market for it. the money has give out. That part of the comp'y at Quincy drew their money before Cousin J. went home and we never have got ours yet. We are dew six months wages, nearly, and a suit of clothes some time ago, but I dont know when we will get it.

I am in hopes I will get [a letter] from you this evening when the mail comes Jim Hurt will go to the office to morrow. Billie Davis[2] sent word for him to meet him there tomorrow. I am mending very fast since I stoped having chills. I think I will [be] stout in a few more days. I still have a good appetite to eate. The chills never make me very sick. I had to keep my bed the most of one evening out of two days from the chill, and then the headache, while the fever was on me. but they never made me sick at the stomache.

Well Sallie, there has been some enquiry as to what grey jeans is worth. will you all have any for sale. Tell Ma we had a splendid peach stew for dinner yesterday. Tell Ma she must send me some red pepper if has any to spare, or if there is any in the neighborhood, for we have to eat a goodeal of beef and it makes it better and healthier for us. George Martin has got back to camps at last. Well I will close till morning as I have about wrote up my paper. Your brother James

---

1   Colonel William J. McGill was the Commanding Officer of the 1st Georgia Regulars. McGill temporarily replaced General Howell Cobb as commander of the Middle District of Florida until Brigadier General William Montgomery Gardner was placed in command on October 30, 1863.

2   Billie Davis was William Edwin Davis, older brother of Howell Cobb Davis (already cited). Billie Davis had joined Co. K, 8th Georgia Volunteer Infantry (Oglethorpe Rifles) on May 15, 1861. He was discharged with a disability at Richmond, Virginia, July 10, 1862. He rejoined the Confederate Army on April 28, 1864, as a member of Co. H, 29th Battalion, Georgia Cavalry.

Camp Sidney Johnson
Nov 3rd 1863

Dear Sallie

I received your letter written the 25th last sunday morning, which was the 30th, and was very glad to hear from you all. I hope Sister Mary is well by this time. I would be so glad to see you all, but I cant tell when that will be.

CHAPTER VI

You will want to know why I have not written after receiving your letter. Well I am sorry to tell you that I have had another [spell] of the chills for six days, but I have not had but two that mad me shake this time. one day before yesterday and one to day. my appetite has not been quite as good as it was [during] the other spell I had, but they have not weakened me much. When the fevers are very high, that is the time for any one to be sick, but I never have fevers to last very long, nor make me sick at the stomach yet.

Sallie, [I] have no news of any importance to write. Capt Blocker and his two compy of infantry have moved up to punch bowl[1] and left us alone. I am very glad of it if he will let us stay here, but he wanted to move us when he moved. but Glenn beg him to let us stay here as we had sorry tents and not enough of them, and had two houses to stay in. he finally agred to let us stay a while. Some of them say there is a spring of good water down inside of the pond and when the tide rises it gets over it, so if they dont get it while the tide is down they have to drink the pond water. I guess is rather warm as the [weather] has been tolerable warm for several days. I thought from what I had heard that every thing was killed dead enough in Oglethorpe. I have heard so many talking of frost and cold weather there.

Well Sallie, [I] will put off writing any more till morning, as it is getting late. I will help get supper. all the mess but Jim Hurt are complaining.

Wednes. Morn. I dont know that any one will go to the office today, but I hardly ever know untill it is too late to write. I feel tolerable well this morning. Quinine is so scarce we cant get but very little and the Dr is so sparing with it, he mixes it up with red peper and camphor. It does but little good. There is all sorts of remedies for the chills down here, all sorts of teas that can be thought of. Old Uncle davie Patman[2] is at Quincy, or was there a few days ago. he come down after his son Will Tom. he was very [sick] and the Old man concluded to stay with him till he got well ennough to go home. The boys are mending up very fast. Several of those that come here last are sick. I exspect we will stay some where in this region this winter. It is a good deal cooler this morning than it has [been] there was a change in the night.

Well Sallie, there was nobody that went to the post office this morning. I will write a line or two. I have passed my chill time about three hours, so I dont think I am in much danger of it this evening. I will close for the present. Give my love to all.

I remain Your affectionate brother James

1   Punch Bowl is unidentified.

2   Uncle Davie Patman was David W. Patman, listed in the 1860 Georgia census as a 50-year-old minister in the Simston District of Oglethorpe County, along with Eliza B., 46, and five children, and the oldest was 27-year-old William T. Patman.

CAMP SIDNEY JOHNSON
NOV 16TH 1863

Dear Sallie.

I have taken a seat to write you a few lines, but will have to be in a great hurry. I feel very well this morning, but I had a chill yesterday and one friday. It has been more than two weeks since I have received a letter from you. I would be glad to hear from you all. I receive a letter from Eliza [that] she wrote while she was there.

Genl. Gardner[1] was here last wednesday, and seem to pitty us a greatdeal. he sayed there was not a well man in the crowd, he thought, from our look and then turned to the other officers and said, these men must be moved from here, they will do no good here. so he then ordered us to move to Camp Leon, the place where [we] went to from last spring where Gambles Comp was so well fixed up. He said he would send the other part of the company there and get us all together. We are not able to go, or there is not enough men to drive the battery that does not have chills. the most of us are anxious to go, but Lieut Glenn says he dont want to start till he thinks we can go. Jos. Armstrong is quite sick. he is getting very weak and having hard chills every day. Genl Gardner is a lame man. he can not walk but very little from the wound he received at the first battle at Manassas.

Well Sallie, I will be very short this time. You must direct your letter to Tallahassee. I exspect we will start from here tomorrow. we can go up there in one day. we will be six miles below Tall. Give my love to all. I remain your affectionat brother James

We have come to the conclusion to go tomorrow.

1   Brigadier General William Montgomery Gardner was placed in command of the District of Middle Florida on October 30, 1863. The District was subdivided into three Subdistricts. Colonel Caraway Smith (cited elsewhere) was put in command of the Subdistrict under which the Echols Artillery served.

CHAPTER VII

Back to Camp Leon

*"We may make our calculations for a long war if Lincoln is
not removed at expiration of his term of service"*

*[This letter is in the collection of the
Robert W. Woodruff Library at Emory University]*

CAMP LEON
NOV 22ND 1863

Dear Sallie

I have taken my seat this evening to write you a few line as I have
nothing to do for a little while. I am getting along tolerable well at
this time. I have missed the chills for three days. I had a short spell
this time. I did not have any for about twelve days and since have
had four every other day but there was but [one] hard one. I am
in hopes I will get well now as we have moved a little higher up the
country but there is some that will not get well of them as long as
they are in Florida.

We came up here last tuesday We could hardly get men enough
to drive but we were all so anxious to get away from there. several
of us [that] come with the battery that was having chills, I for one. I
had a chill soon in the morning but it passed off with but little fever
so I got tolerable well much better than I expected. We landed
here about dark where we found apart of the boys that come down
from Quincy on the cars with a part of their baggage and the others
come down the next day with the other part of the battery. so the
company have got together once more. there is several strangers to
me here they are recruits that have come in since we were divided
and some of them I wish had never seen the company from what I
can see of them, though I may be mistaken. Bill Gauldin[1] I think is a

rough customer. he tried along time to get in before he succeeded but finally he got up a swop with a substitute at a cost of four or five hundred dollars.

Well Sallie it is getting late and [I] will have to hurry as to get my letter done for I will [not] have time to write in the morning before the mail leaves. We will have a good deal of work to do here before we get straight. All the floors on most of the houses have been taken out and some of them with all the boards taken off [the outside] and the horse lot torn to piecies. So the houses will [have to] be repair and a lot of boards to get for the lot. but if every man was well it would be but a small job. Jos Armstrong and me and John Kinnebrew Jim Hurt and Drue Dunn are in a house together. We have quit George Martin and Jack Edwards entirely. Jack got so contrary that every one in the mess got out with him and left him but George Martin and I dont think they will get along well so they have gone in with another mess with Oliver Cooper and his brother. so I think they will have a time of [it] now. I have not applied for a furlough since I have been up here. Jarrell is in command and he come down with the company and went back to Quincy the next day and come back yesterday evening. I am going to try him, though I know he would give me a furlough if there is any chance to get it signed up by the higher authorities. but there lies the rub now. Jarrell has come in and I told him I wanted a furlough and he said he would sine one for me, but it was in a sort of a joking way. I must close hoping to see you all before long. Give my love to all. Your brother James

1   William D. Gaulding is listed in the 1860 census as the 24-year-old son of Richard and Mary Gaulding in the Grove Creek District of Oglethorpe County, Georgia, along with five younger brothers and sisters. According to the Compiled Military Service Records and Georgia Confederate Pension Files, William D. Gaulding served in Co. I, 15th Georgia Volunteer Infantry from July 15, 1861, to October 31, 1861, and was discharged due to disability. He later enlisted in Co. E, 66th Regiment, Georgia Volunteer Infantry but subsequently transferred to the Echols Artillery. There is some evidence that Gaulding also served in Co. D, 9th Georgia Volunteer Infantry during the war.

CAMP LEON
NOV 25TH 1863

Dear Sallie

I received your letter this evening written the 18th. I was very glad to hear from you. also one from Eliza and one from Cousin John. I [had] begin to think surely there was something wrong. I could not hear from any of you. I am getting allong tolerable well now. I had one chill the 2nd day after we came here. I am afraid I will have another spell before many days.

I wrote to you a day or two before we left for this place. The company all met here last wednesday that did not get here tuesday. a part of of our crowd got here tuesday and some from Quincy. We are in the houses that we occupied last spring when we came here on our way to camp Brokaw, but they have been torn to piecies a good deal by the regiment that was here last summer, or some other crowd. some of the house have been taken away and all of the floors taken out and scattered about. tops torn off of some of them and the boards off the cracks.

Well Sallie, I recon you will hardly be able to read what I write as I am writing by the light of one of our old fashion tapers, which makes such a poor light that I can hardly see the lines. the reason I am doing so is Lieut Glenn is going to start home on a furlough to morrow and I have written to Cousin John and will send this with his. The officers can get furloughs but the poor Private has to do the best he can. There was a furlough sent up for Mat Pass, but it was disapproved at the same time. I told Lieut Jarrell the other day I wanted a furlough and he said he would sign one for me and if I can get it approved I would come now, but I had rather be at home christmas as it is near at hand. but I think it very doubtful about my getting one now or then either, but I do hope that I may get [one], for I tell you I want to see you all bad enough. Eliza wrote that she had not written to me in two weeks. but you wrote while she was there and she told you to write for her as she was busy. If you did I have not received it, for I did not know that she was there, untill she wrote that she was there, and the next news she had gone home.

We have not drawn our clothes nor money yet, those of us that was down at Punch Bowl, and it is now rumored that we will not get our money till January. He sent up after the clothes last week but they did not have them, but [said they] would get them before long. I am not needing either money or clothes, but then as long as apart of the company have drawn them, the others all want them. for we dont know what may happen and what need we may have for such things, and with a little neglect we may be cut out entirely of the clothes, which are put down to us at about sixty dollars. I would have been out of money before now if I had not sold some of my old government clothes. I sold my coat and pants for 18 dollars after wearing the coat all the summer.

I think it is time we was hearing something from the salt that I bought. The last of it was shiped from Quincy about the first of oct, which was two sacks for Uncl Billie. I hear of some getting home occasionally that has been gone a good while. I am fearful that the sacks will get so dirty that the name will put out, but there is some that goes in sacks. The health of the company does not seem to improve much. Jos Armstrong has been quite sick but is getting better. Jack Edwards went to the hospital monday.

Well Sallie I will close. Give my love to all. write often.

I remain your affectionate brother James.

CAMP LEON
DECEMBER 6TH 1863

Dear Sallie

I received your letter friday evening written the 27th and was very glad to hear from you all, and to hear that you was well. I am getting along very well at this time. I had two chill the first of the week, which was the shortest spell that I ever had. I am in hopes I will not be troubled much more with them. There is some little improvement in the health of the company since we have been here, but not a great deal.

Sallie, I commenced writing this morning but I have no news to write, but maybe I can think of something between now and night to amuse you for a few moments. We have heard here of the fight at Chattanooga, which was a bad lick on our side, but the latest news is that the Yankeys have been whiped back to Chattanoga again. Gen Bragg has resigned and Joseph E Johnston will take command of that army. I am in hopes that the soldiers will have more confidence in Johnston than they have in Bragg. A great many people have been cursing him for a longtime, so I recon they will be satisfied for awhile. but then there was others that was in favor of Bragg and thought he was just the man, but that, you know, is the case with all public men.

Well Sallie, I tell you we had some cold weather for a few days the first of this week, but I have no idea that it was near so cold as it was in Oglethorpe. but the sudden changes make us feel it very sensible here and then a good many of us are poor and have not got flesh enough about us to keep us warm. Today is a beautiful sunny day, but the wind blows cool from the north. I thought I would have been there with you all before this time, but I am here yet and likely to stay here. there is no chance for any one to get a furlough unless given by the sergeon of the Reg or company. I will stop writing till after dinner.

Well Sallie, I have eat a hearty dinner of beef and cornbread and syrup and loll about awhile so I will try to fill out this page, but I dont hardly know what I will write. I could tell you many things that I cannot think of now, but I can not tell any thing about when I will get home. Genl Gardner will not grant any furlough unless they are based upon the certificate of the surgeon. he says that he will not approve a furlough for any one on any business whatever. I dont know what I will do. I recon I will have to get Cousin John to bring my clothes when he comes. I can make out with what I have untill I have the chance to get there, though I need some socks. I thought we were going to draw clothes sometime ago, but we have not drawn them yet. if you recollect, I wrote about a part of the company drawing. We had the requisition made out and sent for the clothes but they did not have them, and now I understand that we will have to take money instead of the clothes and we have not drawn our money. We will draw the first of next month, which will be next year (1864). Genl Gardner sent an order to Lieut Jarrell to have the payroll made out by the 31th of this month. he is one of the military men and makes every body come up to the mark. The officers are all afraid of him. They cant wheedle around him like they did Genl Cobb, he will curse them and quick. we received orders the other day that the inspecting officer would be here, but he has failed to come. two day and tomorrow we look for Genl Beauregards inspecting officer, but he may be like the other. I would not be surprised if we have to go up in Georgia. I hope if we leave here this winter that we will not go higher up than Savanah.

Well Sallie, I will close, hoping to see you all before long. Give my love to all. I remain your affectionate brother James

DEC 14TH 1863

Dear Sallie

I have taken my seat to write you a few lines to let you know that I received your letter written the 9th. I was glad to hear from you all and hear that you was well. I am getting along very well now. I have missed the chills about 14 days and have been mending tolerable fast. I dont fell quite as well today as I have done, which is very often the case on the seventh, fourteenth, and twenty first day after having chill and any one is very apt to have chill on those days, or more so than any other. I am very thankful that I am getting so well now. It looks like it takes me a long time to gain my strength. I am not half as strong, nothing like as I was before I commenced having chills.

I was very much in hopes that when we came up here that I would get the chance to come home about christmas, but I am here yet and no probability of my getting home soon. I believe I wrote to you what would be the chance for me some time ago. There is no talk of furloughs now at all, only with the boys, which dont amount to any thing. You know I would be so glad to spend the christmas with you all. it would be a happy time, but to stay here it will not be any more than any other time. I would not be surprised if we have to be run down on the coast about that time for a frolic, or move some where. I hope we will stay here untill we have to leave this state, and I dont care much how soon that was to be. If we could have our health here in this land of flowers there might be some inducement to stay here, but the flowers is a poor consolation to any one that is always sick with the chill and fever.

Well Sallie, my ink is so pale that I can hardly tell what I am writing sometimes, but it turnes a little darker when it gets dry. it look like writing with water. I received a letter from Eliza friday and one from Cousin John thursday. He dont write much like coming back to camps soon. I think he will have to come back to the land of flowers to get well, as he seems to think they [the chills] are a great deal harder up there than they are in this country. I have been very anxious to get up that way to see if it would not cure me.

Well Sallie, we dont hear much war news down this [way]. We occasionally hear something from Chattanooga. there is no prospect of there ever being any fighting down this way. I reckon the most of the people in Oglethorpe are whiped now and if they were to get to Atlanta they would give up entirely. It is a dark time with us and it has been so for a good while. I dont see any prospect of peace myself. We may make our calculations for a long war if Lincon is not removed at expiration of his term of service, which is very uncertain. One of our company, John Banks,[1] died last wednesday at the hospital in Tall.

Well Sallie, as I cannot be with you all to enjoy christmas, you must let me know how you all enjoy your selves, and let me hear how much meat Pa has for the next year and all such things as that. I want to know whether you have a plenty to live on. not that I can send you any, but so if I would get close enough to get any thing, for I have no doubt we will be scarce of bacon. There is no sugar for sale down here now. syrup is from 4 to 6 dollar a gallon.

Well Sallie, I will close. You must write often. Give my love to all the family and to all enquiring friends. I remain your affectionate brother James

1   John L. Banks and two of his younger brothers, James and Henry D., all served as Privates in the Echols Artillery. The three brothers entered service on March 1, 1862, and James and Henry served until the end of the war. In the 1860 Georgia census they were listed in the household of Thompson and Susan Banks in the Simston District of Oglethorpe County, along with two sisters and another younger brother.

*[This letter is in the collection of the
Robert W. Woodruff Library at Emory University]*

CAMP LEON
DEC 26TH 1863

Dear Sallie

I received a letter from you day before yesterday but I can not say what date for you neglected to date it. I was glad to hear that you were all [well]. I would have written to you yesterday but I was not well enough to write. I have taken another spell of the chills. I have had four this spell. They commenced on me last saturday and I have one every other day. Yesterday was christmas day but I did not enjoy it as such. We had an egg nog early in the morning and I drank tolerable freely of it thinking it would be an advantage in having a chill but I dont know that it done me much good, but that with some other remedies kept my chill from being so hard. Before this spell came on I have missed them about twenty days and during the last week of that time I was mending up fast, fattening like a pig and I felt well. I am in hopes I will not have any more this spell. I sent to town to day to get me some quinine as they have none here and it looks like they wont get any more soon. but the way of it is, we get a months allowance at the time and that will not last much more than a week. Well Sallie I reckon I have said enough about the chills for one time.

I have no news of any importance to write. I received a letter from John Colclough the other day he says he thinks there will be an attact made on Savanah soon. there was sixty vessels at Pt. Royal. he said he had been out and spent one night in camps with Bud. he was well then. I do wish I was there a while. he says their time will be out the first of february but I think it will be like the 12 month volunteers.

Well Sallie I reckon you have seen the order from Ajutant Genl Cooper[1] about furloughs. He has put a stop to all furloughs for more than seven days and that is in extreme cases and when they get home they are required to report to the enrolling officer the length of their furlough. and all those that are at home are to report at the Genl hospital or be sent to the conscript camp.

One of our company (Hardman)[2] from Madison Co, has been at home for a good while and I understand has been sent to the hospital in Augusta. There is seven or eight of those at home that are now reported absent without leave. they have not sent in their certificates and there has to be a report made out every month of the condition of the company, the number sick in camps and at home on furlough etc., and sent to the Genl. Those that are not here in three days after their time is out are reported absent without leave. Cousin John is one of that number.   I expect they will send him to the Augusta hospital.

Sallie it looks like there is no chance for me to come home now and I dont know when there will be but I hope there will be a chance after a while. if I could get a furlough for seven day it would do no good for it takes about eight days to go home and back now adays from here. I will postpone writing for a while as I can not send this letter off till monday morning, and I may hear some news by that time.

Well Sallie I have taken my seat to finish this letter. This was the day for me to have a chill but I lay abed till after one oclock and have missed it thus far, so I dont apprehend any danger in about a week now. I forgot to tell you that there was 11 recruits joined our company the first of [the] week. some from Green, Oglethorpe; and Madison counties, and [it is] reported [that] Capt. T. will bring more soon. I will close for this time. Give my best love to all. Your affectionate brother James

1   This was Samuel Cooper, the highest ranking general in the Confederacy. He served as Adjutant General and Inspector General throughout the war. Cooper was born in New Jersey in 1798 and served as Adjutant General of the U.S. Army during much of the 1850s, before resigning his commission in March 1861.

2   This was Ezekiah F. Hardman (also Hardeman) identified in the 1860 census as a 24-year-old wagon maker in Madison County, Georgia. Hardman was among the first volunteers who formed the Echols Artillery March 1, 1862.

CAMP LEON
JANUARY 5TH 1864

Dear Sallie

I received your welcome letter yesterday evening of the 29th inst. and was very glad to hear from you all. I am getting along very well now. I have missed the chills for a week and am begining to mend up again.

We did not have any christmas here, or at least I did not. there was some parties in the neighborhood. I believe I wrote to you about a wedding that was to come of wednesday night in the christmas. It happened sure enough. the man has a wife and five children at home (in Oglethorpe), and I exspect a good wife from what I can learn. They first talked of having a sham wedding and there was a good many of the boys went exspecting to see the marriage and pay a doller for their supper. but when they got there the marriage was over. the ceremony was performed by the Esqr with lawful licens. I think he has got himself in a bad scrape if the law was pushed on him.

Well Sallie, it has been cloudy and cool for three or four days and raining occasionally. in fact, the most of the time we have all been thinking there must be bad weather up the country. I would not be surprised to hear of a big snow up in the mountains. We are looking for Capt Tiller this week, but I dont know whether he will come or not when he hears of the order that has been issued. Lieut Jarrell received orders the other day that every man that was not here by the seventh of this month must be taken from the muster roll and published as [a] deserter, or, if he did not send a certifficat from the board at some Genl hospital. no other kind of a certificate would be received. You know there has been Army surgeons, as they were called, about at diferent places who had the power to extend furloughs, but that is all done away with. The object of their having to report at the general hospital, I think, is to get them there and then they will be kept there. If that order is carried out there is ten or twelve of this company that will be sent to the conscript camp unless they report in two more days. And Jarrell also received orders that fifteen of the last recruits would have to leave the company or get some of the others to go in their places as there was that many too many in the company. if that is so there will be some men in trouble. I know some of those at home [will] have to to be conscripted and sent to some other company. I hope Cousin John will not be treated that way. There has been so many men in the confederacy at home on furlough that Ajutant Genl Cooper has taken this method to get them in ranks again.

Well Sallie, I am in hopes that there will be some chang after awhile so that I can get to come home, but we cant tell any thing about what will be. Col Ivens'es[1] Reg (64th) left for Savanah yesterday evening. I recon they are exspecting an attact there. I have thought that we might go there, and we may yet for any thing we can tell. Sometimes I get anxious to go there and then I think I had better be satisfied here where we are, if we do have the chills. There is one thing certain, we will not fare as well in many respects as we do here, but we would be so much nearer home and where we can get anything from home so much easier than we can here. I have no doubt but what we will stay in Fla another year.

Lieut Gibson is to be here by the fourteenth. he will leave home about the 10th or 11th. I recon that will [be] the only chance for you all to send me anything before Cousin John comes. I would like to have some flannel shirts and socks. I can make out very well as for anything else. I dont need my shoes now. I dont exspect Gibson will bring any thing for me, or not much at least. I will close. You must write all about the affairs at home, what is going on.

Give my love to all. I remain your affectionat brother James

1   This was Colonel John W. Evans [not Ivens], commander of the 64th Regiment Georgia Infantry. Evans entered service in the Confederate Army March 18, 1861, as Captain of Co. G, 1st Regiment Georgia Volunteer Infantry. He mustered out at Augusta in March 1862 but rejoined May 26, 1862, as Colonel of the 64th. Colonel Evans was killed near Petersburg, Virginia, July 30, 1864.

CAMP LEON
JANUARY 13TH 1864

Dear Sallie

I have taken my seat this rainy evening to write you a few lines as I am at leasure and think it is time for me to write. I have had one light chill since I wrote to you, which was last sunday. I thought I would have one yesterday so I kept my bed from nine in the morning till about three in the evening and did not leave it.

The health of the company is improveing some. One of the Tillers[1] died in the hospital night before last. There is one or two more of the boys there quite sick. Wilie Young went there having the chills and a very bad rising on his right hand. I heard a day or two ago the Dr said that would not be surprised if his hand had to be taken off. it will bad for him to loose it. he makes as good a soldier as we have and will not be worth much at home unless he does better than he used to.

The law that was passed to conscript every [one] that did not report by the 7th of January brought in a good many of our boys. Capt Tiller and Gibson came down last week and some eight or ten with them. They did not wait to get well before they come. They did not like the idea of having their names taken from the muster roll. I dont know what will become of those at home yet. there is five besides Cousin John. Capt Tiller says their [names] will have to be taken from the muster roll and they [will be] reported to the enrolling officer according to the law. he is a great man for trying to carry out the law, but I dont know what he will do in that case.

I thought last week that our company was to be cut down to 150 men. Genl Gardner told Jarrell that it would, so I understood, which would take off about fifteen of the last recruits. but Tiller went to Quincy to see him saturday and he says that Gardner told him he might raise the company to 200. So that is the way it goes. we cant tell what will be done by what we hear. Gibson is going on a crutch. he has not got well from the fall he got from the cars sometime ago and the Capt is still having chills.

Well Sallie, I thought last week there would be a chance for me to get a furlough soon. Jarrell received orders as soon as we had 120 men for duty he could give three furloughs and the understanding was that forty men for duty would entitle us to one on furlough. so Jarrell wrote two and carried them up to Tall. and Col. Smith would not approve them. so that was the last that I have heard from them. Genl Gardner has left us and gone to Charleston to have his leg operated on. it is a gooddeal shorter than the other one and I have understood he exspects to have it broken over again. it pains him so much that he cannot rest with it. It is from the wound received in the first Manassas fight. I recon he thinks it will never get well.

Miss Lieu [Lou] Pass[2] came down with the boys last friday. she could not wait till Cousin John come. I dont know how long she will stay. I dont know what is the reason.

I have never heard from any of that salt that I sent home. the most of the boys heard from theirs, but some have been like myself. There was one that got five bushels more than he sent home. I hate for that to be lost, but I cant help it. I marked it as plain as I could and I know a great deal better than some sent from there that went home. What I bought was worth about $200 dollars down here. I dont know how [much] it would have been worth up there. I will close hoping to hear from you all soon. I have no idea when I will see you.

Give my love to all. I remain your affectionate brother James

1   Private Woodson Tiller died in the hospital in Tallahassee, Florida, January 11, 1864.

2   Lou was Ludie Pass, sister of M.J.H. Pass (cited elsewhere).

CHAPTER VII

CAMP LEON
FEB 4TH 1864

Dear Sallie

I received your letter day before yesterday and was very glad to hear from you all and hear that you were all well. I was very sorry and surprised to hear of cousin Joes[1] death, but life is very uncertain no one knows how long they will have to stay here on this troublesome earth. I intended writing to you yesterday evening, but there was a sudden change in the weather and I felt so chilly that I concluded to put it of till this morning. this is a beautiful morning, but it was rather cool before sunrise with a big white frost.

Well sallie, I had a light chill last week. I was fearful of having another spell, but I am glad to say I did not have but one and that was very light. I am getting along finely now. I would be so glad to come home to see you all, but I have no idea when I will get home. I received a letter from Eliza yesterday. I received one from Bud last week. he wrote for me to direct my letters to Maxeys, but as the postoffice is broken up there I thought I would direct it to Scull Shoals. he wanted to know what was the chance to get in this company. Tiller has refused some of the boys that wanted to get some of their friends here, but has taken in some since that time and now [is] looking for several more to come from Oglethorpe, Doc. & Mid Johnson,[2] and Arch Griffith[3] from Ala. it may be that a good many that are already here will have to leave for some other command. I think Capt Tiller will receive all that come untill he gets some other orders. tell Bud he can come if he has to go in service again, but I dont know whether he can stay here or not. I want to be with him if there is any chance. I do hope we will not have to spend another summer down here. we might have tolerable good health here or at Quincy, but if we have to to be lieing about on these lands down on the coast, I have no doubt but we will suffer. It is generally believe that the most of the troops will leave Fla. this spring. we would have been at Savanah sometime ago, I think, if our horses had been in a good plight for moving about, but they are improving very fast now and we will be apt to have to move some where. but there is no telling about what we will have to do.

Well Sallie, We have not drawn any money since last may, or at least a part of us, and I am now out of Envelopes, stamps, and nearly out of paper, and would have been out of money if I had not borrowed 10 dollars, and also nearly out of tobacca. We have been exspecting to draw money for sometime but have not got it yet. Capt Tiller says he will draw clothes for us again soon as he can make out the requisition. I will have to close for this time as I have nothing more of interest to write. Give my love to all the family. I remain your affectionate brother.

I wish I could come to see you all. James

1   Cousin Joe was Joseph Benjamin Smith, the son of Paschal Smith and Polly Jewel Smith. Polly was a sister of James Jewel, Sr.

2   Mid Johnson had been discharged from service April 1, 1863, but reenlisted in the Echols Artillery January 3, 1864.

3   Archer Griffith, his wife Sara K., and their four children were listed in the 1850 Georgia census as living near the Jewels in Oglethorpe County; however, by the time of the 1860 census they had moved to Barbour County, Alabama.

[This letter is in the collection of the Robert W. Woodruff Library at Emory University]

CAMP LEON
FEB 28TH 1864

Dear Sister

I have been looking for a letter from you several days but have failed to get one and I though I would write to you. I am in tolerable good health now and have been for some time. I have no news to write, only about the fight that come off yesterday was a week ago which I recon you have heard of before this time, besides what I wrote to you.[1] We cant get a correct account of it here. our loss is estimated at 800 killed, wounded and taken prisoners.[2] there was but very few taken from us. The wounded are scattered about in every town where they could be carried. There is about three hundred of the wounded prisoners in Tall., and some of them down the railroad at Madison, and a good many at Lake City. John Pace went there to see George. he was shot in the knee and had his leg amputated. John says every house that would do for a hospital is in use. There was six of the Gilmer Blues wounded and killed on the field. Capt Harris and Lieut Dozier[3] was wounded. The 6th Ga says it was the hardest fought battle they have ever been in and they have been in several. I wrote you that James Barrow was killed. he was in front of his Regt urging them on when he fell early in the engagement. his corps was carried up to Quincy monday evening lyeing out on an open car. I recon it was sent home [but] I dont know.[4]

I have not seen any of the prisoners myself but we have to furnish 20 from our company every day to gard those that are in town and the boys say the most of them say they are tired of the war but cant help themselves. I guess the negros that was wounded will not want to go into another fight. I dont think they are treated the best in the world. There was three regiments [of Negro soldiers] in the fight and the most of them was killed and wounded.[5] They were in the front of the battle with a few of the whites to lead them on and the others behind to drive. They say if they attempted to run they were shot by their own men in the rear. We captured all their artillery. Some of the Florridians took a battery and was about to let them retake it had it not been for some of Genl Colquits Brigade getting to it. They had no idea of meeting with the Ga Reg. and Colquits Brig. down here. They thought they would have nothing but the Florridians to contend with and they were going on to Tall. Genl. Finagan has been cashiered and Genl. Gardner appointed commander of all the forces of this state. It is thought by some there will [be] another trial made there soon. Genl. Gardner passed through Tall. friday going down there and reports say they were looking for Genl. Beauregard with reinforcements but I dont know that it is true. A squad of yankeys come out down here at one of the salt works and took all the men they could catch and broke up the kettles and went back. Well Sallie Cousin John wrote to me last week [and said] he would be here next wednesday if nothing happened. I am very glad to hear he is comeing. I will close for this time.

Give my love to all. I remain your affectionate brother James

1   The Battle of Olustee, also called the Battle of Ocean Pond, was the only major engagement of the war fought in Florida. The battle took place February 20, 1864, near Ocean Pond, a natural lake about 2 miles east of Olustee between Lake City and Jacksonville. The nine southern regiments and seven northern regiments were evenly matched with between 5,000 and 6,000 men on each side. However, the rebels took an early advantage by selecting the site of the battle when the 64th Georgia initiated the fray by engaging the 8th U.S. Colored Troops and the 7th New Hampshire Volunteer Infantry.

2   Official records number the losses at 946 Confederates and 1,861 Federals.

3   The chapter on the Gilmer Blues in *This They Remembered* names the killed as Berrien M. Matthews and the wounded as Captain Sampson Watkins Harris, "Corporal Smith" (probably William P. Smith), Private Jonathan Farmer, and Private Jethro Gibson Hansford.

4   Colonel John W. Evans, commander of the 64th Georgia, was wounded early in the fight and 22-year-old Lieutenant Colonel James Barrow assumed command. Barrow was felled with a bullet through the heart while leading a charge. He is buried in the family plot in Oconee Hill Cemetery in Athens, Georgia.

5   Of the 565 soldiers comprising the 8th U. S. Colored Troops, 343 were killed, wounded, or missing in the battle.

CAMP LEON
MARCH 24TH [1864]

Dear Sallie

I received your letter written the 16th yesterday and was glad to hear from you all. I thought you had received more than one letter from me, if they had not missed the rout some way, since you had written. I looked for a letter when Cousin John came, but he told me he had not seen any of you in several days.

He left home tuesday morning and got here saturday evening with all things safe. I did not look for him in two or three weeks, so I was disappointed twice. I looked for him when he wrote he was comeing, and when I heard he was going to marry I just [assumed]

then it would be a long time before he would come. he brought me the [supplies] you all sent. Shoes, vest, a bottle of brandy, & candle. The shoes are most too short for me, but I recon I can wear them. I was sorry he came back and did not see Eliza, as she was so anxious to see him before he left.

Well Sallie, I have no news of any importance to write. every thing is quiet down this way. We had quite cool weather for two days and nights. I [think] it was about as cold night before last as it has been since christmas and it is not warm today, but not as cold as it was yesterday.

Jack Edwards started home yesterday morning on a sixty days furlough. he went up to town and was examined by the board and they gave him a furlough. He has worked very hard for it, I think. he has not done any duty since last summer and I dont think he ever intended to do any thing more until he went home from the way he acted. he did not try to brake the chill on him from what I could find out. any one having chill can, by imprudence, keep them on him for a long time when they might other wise get shet of[1] them. it is true some will have them in spite of all they can do.

I believe I wrote to you Jim Hurt was sick. he got well of his first disease, but has been complaining of one of his feet [hurting with] something like the rheumatism. he has gone up to town to day to try to get a furlough. I will let you know if he gets one before I close this letter. I will send it by him if he goes.

Well Sallie, I had to stop writing to drill and will now try to finish this by fire light and my candle, but it gives rather dim light to write by with as pale lines as these. Cousin John received a letter from Sallie yesterday and I had a good laugh at him about reading it so often. I think he will read that one two or three times a day untill he get another one. he is getting along very well. I think [he] has written a letter every day since he has been here. I recon he will recollect how he used to talk to me about writing so much. Lieut Jarrells section is still down in Taylor County [Florida] and thirty of the boys are in town guarding the prisoners. They were relieved up there for about a week by Maj Capers Bat., but they have gone to Taylor after the deserters. Jim Hurt did not get back this evening. the Board gave him a furlough, but it was not approve by the commander of the Post the last I heard from him.

I will close for this time. I dont know when I [will] get home if they begin to let the sick go and stay there all the time like they did last year.

Cousin John joins me in love to you all.

Your affectionate brother   James

1   Misspelling of the colloquial term "shed of," meaning to get rid of.

CAMP LEON
MARCH 31TH 1864

Dear Sallie,

I received yours and Mary's letter day before yesterday and was very glad to hear from you all. I also received one from Eliza the same day. I expect from my feelings to write you a short letter. I have a boil on the back of my neck and it is by no means a pleasant feeling. It made it appearance about four days ago [as] a small bump not larger than a small pea and it still going on. I have to hold my head like old Mr Coil, but I hope it will get well in a few days. I am a well as I could wish otherwise. Cousin John is getting along very well. I think he has had a tuch of the blues for a day or two.

Well Sallie, I have no news at all to write, but I thought if I did not write you would all be uneasy about me. You know I wrote to you about transfering some of the company, but it has not been done yet. There is thirty of the men doing guard duty in town and Lieut Jarrel and his section is Still down in Taylor County and the rest of us here in camps. We have had some very windy weather for two or three day. it has not been very cold. I forgot to tell you I received the thread in your letter and you said you would send me some in the last one, but I recon you forgot it by the time Mary got through writing. Well, I will not write any more this morning, I will finish this evening. Your brother James.

Well Sallie, I thought I would write a few lines to Mary, but I will have to put it off this time. you can tell her this will have to suffise as an answer for both. It has been quite a windy day to day and a little cloudy. I am very sorry to hear that the fruit is all killed. You said I must make well of my dried fruit. I have not seen any thing of it yet. I started me a hat with the thread you sent me, but I did not have quite enough to make the crown. Tell Pa I have been chewing the tobacco he sent me, it is better than any I can get for less than three dollars a plug.

Well My neck dont get any better yet [and] as it is rather unpleasant writing, I will close for this time.

Give my love to all. I remain your affectionate brother James

CAMP LEON
APRIL 17TH 1864

Dear Mary [1]

I seat my self this morning to try to write you a few lines in answer to yours of the 7th, which came to hand friday evening. I intended to write yesterday evening, but about the time I thought I would commence, I heard my named called and thinks, what does that mean, but I very soon found out it was to cut up beef. So I and one of the other boys had two beeves to cut and weigh out, which was by no means a pleasant task for me, as I never was fond of that sort of work, even at home. I [only] think I have seen poor beef untill [now]. I am tired of it, but it is better to have a little of that to take occasionally than just to have the dry bread just so.

Well Mary, I recon you have heard [even] if I did not write to you, that our company was to be reduced to 125 privates, which left between twenty five and thirty to be transfered by the first of this month. but [it] was not done, from some cause I cannot tell. The Capt told us there would be a Genl inspection the next day, which was last thursday a week ago, and the inspector would let us know who would have to leave, so We looked for him every day for a week. The report now is he will be here next week and will reduce the company to one hundred and four rank and file, taking out sixty eight men. If that number is taken from the last of the company, or the last that joined, it will take me along. I have had my doubts whether there will be any transfered or not. I think from the start that has been made, the company will be scattered about all the year like it was last year we have not all been to gether since the first of february. there is about 60 in town now on guard & likely to stay there some time.

I recon you will hear before [you] receive this of Jim Hurt going home. he left here last thursday morning with forty days furlough. He said nine days of the time had gone when he got [it], which left him thirty one. Well Mary, I was thinking I would stand a pretty good chance of going home before long, but it will be some time yet agreeable to the orders issued by Maj Genl Anderson (the commander of the forces of this state).[2] It is this, All commanders of Companies, battallions, or Reg. making applications for furloughs must certify that the applicant has not had a furlough in two years and then he will only be allowed ten day at home. also any one furnishing a recruit not lyable to conscription will be entitled to twenty days furlough. No company will be allowed more than one on furlough for every twenty [on duty]. You all need not look for me before the latter part of August or first of Sept.

One of the company, J.W. Goolsby, received a furlough of sixty days from the Aj Genl Cooper. His mother[3] came down here some time ago and tried to get him a furlough. she called to see Genl Beauregard at Savanah as she came on and then went to Genl Gardner, but did not succed. I tell you the old lady worked very faithful, but did not dispair. she went back home and, having a sick family at the time, she waited until they got better and then put out to Richmond and saw the Secretary of War in person where she got the furlough. Who would have thought of an old lady sixty years old doing so much as that. She is the one, if you recollect about my telling you, put her age down at forty.

Well Mary, I have writen all I recon that would interest you at this time. We have very prety weather now, but it is quite cool for the climate. vegetation is making very little show as yet. I have not received that letter [of] Jimies,[4] I will try and plasure him a little some time when I have the chance to do so. I have not seen Cousin John since last sunday, but I hear from him nearly every day. he is at town on guard and is getting along very well. I will close. Give my love to all.

I remain your most affectionate uncle James

---

1   Jewel's niece, Mary Crowley.

2   James Patton Anderson entered the Confederate Army in April 1861 as Colonel of the 1st Florida Regiment of Infantry. Early in 1862 he was promoted to Brigadier General. On February 17, 1864, he attained the rank of Major General and was placed in command of the District of East Florida and the District of Middle Florida which were merged into a single unit, the District of Florida.

3   Jefferson W. Goolsby is listed in the 1860 Georgia census as a 30-year-old resident in the home of his mother Nancy N. Goolsby, a farmer in the Goose Pond District of Oglethorpe County. The name was spelled Goosby by the census taker. Nancy Goolsby's age was given as 55, and it was recorded that she was born in South Carolina. In the 1850 census, her age was listed as 42. J.W. Goolsby enlisted in the Echols Artillery March 1, 1862, as a Private and served until the end of the war.

4   Jimmie was Jewel's nephew and Mary Crowley's brother, James T. Crowley. On June 1, 1864, when Crowley was barely 16 years old, he enlisted in the Confederate Army and joined Co. D, Cook's Battalion, commanded by Major Ferdinand W.C. Cook and manned mostly with employees of the Cook and Brother Armory in Athens.

CAMP LEON
APRIL 18TH 1864
[6 MILES BELOW TALLAHASSEE]

Dear Sallie

I seat myself this evening to write you a few lines to let you know that I received your kind letter of the 10th yesterday evening. The eastern train ran off the track, or I would have received it saturday.

and they broke down friday and were about five hours behind time. The St Marks train is two hours behind this evening. I recon the other train was behind again.

I have but little news of importance to write this evening. I recon you have heard that Jim Hurt was at home before you got this letter. You know I wrote to you sometime [ago] about his going before the board and got a furlough. it was sent up to be approved and they neglected to send it to him untill it was nearly half out. it was for forty days. he left here last thursday morning on a crutch complaining of his foot. it is the opinion of a good many here that he had no more use for a crutch than I have. he told some of the boys the morning he started at the depot if that blamed old crutch bothered him he would throw it away. I think he will hold to it untill his furlough is out so he can get it extended again. if he dont think of that, I have no idea he will carry it home with him. I recon I had [best] not say much more in that respect, for fear you might think he is playing off.

Well Sallie, I have been thinking there would be a chance for me to get home before long, but I fear I have been mistaken. Capt Tiller had some orders read here friday evening from Genl Anderson. He says there will not be any furloughs approved unless the Capt, Maj, or Colonel of the regiment will certify the one that has applied for a furlough has been from home two years, and only allowed ten days at home at that. and any one that furnishes a recruit not subject to conscription shall be entitled to twenty days furlough. According to that order, I will not stand a chance until about the last of august. also no Reg or company will be allowed more than one at home for every twenty [on duty]. I believe from the way they are going on now it will sorter like it was last year, so many of them will get home on sick furloughs and stay there, that some of us will not have any showing   Wilie Young and H H Colquet[1] went before the board today and got furloughs and sent them up to have them approved. I dont know what will be [the] consequence. Wilie has been in bad health ever since last summer. he looks very thin and bad, but Colquet, I think, might do if he would. I know there is plenty [of] men here that is in as bad health as he is. Cousin John sent Antwine[2] down here yesterday, he is well as far as I know. They have called on us for twelve more men for guard in town.

Well Sallie, I received the thread you sent me, but I cannot get any palmetto to make anymore hats. the Capt will not let any of the boys go to get any. I will close as [I have] nothing more of any importance to write. You must write often. Give my love to all. I remain as ever your affectionate brother James

1   Hopson Hope Hull Colquitt joined the Echols Artillery as a Private on March 1, 1862, and served until the end of the war. He is listed in the 1860 Georgia census as the 23-year-old son of William H. and Elizabeth Colquitt, farmers in the Grove Creek District of Oglethorpe County.

2   Antwine's identity is uncertain. He may have been someone John Jewel was attempting to hire as a substitute or he may have been Jewel's slave.

CAMP LEON FLA
APRIL 24TH 1864

Dear Sallie

I seat myself this evening to write you a few lines in answer to yours of the 20th, which I received yesterday. I also received one from Mary C written the same day. I was very glad to hear from you all. Those two letters came sooner than any I have got in sometime. I very seldom ever get one in less than a week after it is written. I have no news of any importance to write. I am in very good health at this time.

I am in hopes they are done with me for a season. You recollect I wrote to you we were looking for a Genl inspection for some time, as the Capt had told us we would all know then who would be transfered. we were anxious for the time to come on and sure enough it came of last friday morning. not a word was said about transfering any one. I was out looking for my horses and was not here. I left thursday evening and traveled till neerly midnight and thought I was about to catch up with them for some time. Evans[1] was with me. we got supper at a soldiers house who had just come home a few days before on a furlough, and about nine Oclock we came to a house and inquired for the horses. they told us that two passed there after night, which I thought must be mine from the description. we were then fourteen miles from Camps. We went on three miles further and lost the track of them and concluded to stop till morning. we called at a house and got some fire and went out built up a fire and stayed till daylight [the] next morning. I thought from what I heard there [that] we would soon find the horses. but we lost track of them after going on a while, so we thought we would get breakfast at a house. but they told us we would have to wait till nine oclock.   we fed our horses and waited a while, but I thought it would not do for us to wait so long so I left them and turned home ward. [I was] then not less than twenty miles from here. We did not get any thing to eat untill we got to town where the boys were on guard, about one o clock. dont you recon I was sorter hungry. I would have thought I never could have [endured] such a trip as that before I came to the war. I suppose we were tracking some body else horses as we found mine about a mile this side of town in an old field.

There is an officer here in town recruiting for the navy at Charleston. nine or ten of the boys have joined and will leave us if they can be transfered by Genl Beauregard. I think it is quite a take in with some of them. I think they will find it is not the thing it [is] represented to be to them. I think they will not be as well satisfied as they have been with the life insurance company as it is called by some. Our officers are trying to get the company moved out of this state, but I dont know whether they will succeed or not. Well Sallie, I saw some large plantations the other day in my travels, the most of the people plowing and hoeing corn. Some places the oak and hickory leaves are grown.

The orange trees were kill last winter. they are just putting out now. there will not be any oranges here this year I recon. Well Sallie, I recon I will have to close for this time. It looked very much like rain this morning, but is clear and warm this evening. You must write often. let me know how Jim H is getting along. Give My love to all. I remain your affectionate brother James

P.S.
I heard to day Jim [Hurt] got home saturday and went to Adkissons to see Babe, his sweet heart as some calls her, be sure and let me know if he went on his crutch.

1   This was probably N.H. Evans (already cited).

CAMP LEON
MAY 3RD 1864

Dear Sallie

I have taken Seat this evening to write you a few lines in answer to yours I received today, which you sent with Cousin John. I was in town yesterday, but I left before the mail came in. I have news to write to you of interest, More than I am well and fattening on cornbread. The boys talked about my fattin so much it excited my curosity to know how much I weighed. I weigh 160 pounds. as much as I ever weigh before with my overcoat on. I think my health is as good now as it was last spring at this time.

I recon you have heard that Wilie Young went home. he left here friday and got to Antioch sunday, if he made the connections on the roads. Cousin John is well and getting along very well, I think. He told me to write to you to tell Pa he wanted some of his tobacco if he had any to spare, or for me to write to him to send some so he could get it from me. I have not used all that Pa sent me yet quite   I think it is very good. Tell him I will be very glad to get some more of it if he has a plenty of it, but dont disfurnish himself at all.

Billie Davis has quit the salt works and joined a Calvary company in Colonel Hoods Reg.[1]   he and two more passed here sunday evening with four men they had taken up down towards the coast for some of their meanness. One of them was a deserter, I believe. It has been very warm for several days. it seemed hot enough for summer, but last night it turned cool and has been so all day.

Well Sallie it has [come] to be very fashionable here now a day to wear silver rings. every one that can get a five or ten cents piece is having rings made. they sell them up in town from 10 to 15 dollars a piece. If you can get any, send them down. If you can find any old pieces of gutapercha combs like those long crooked combs you used to wear I will make you all some rings. rings like those I sent you last year are worth from $3 to $5. I saw some today made of an old silver spoon that looked very nice.

Well Sallie, [I] have been about out of money ever since christmas, but have borrowed and wored [worried] along some how. I recon we will draw some before many days, as they are making out the payroll. The government is due me twelve months wages up to last saturday and about 75 dollars for clothing, but I think it doubtful whether we [will] ever get all of it or not. I think they ought to pay us for our clothes, as some of them drew them last fall and the rest of us did not get any.   I think they ought to make us even some way. I have not done much at hat making yet, it dont seem to be very profitable this spring. the boys are not willing to pay as much in proportion to other thing as they were last spring. They are not as eager to get them, no ways..

Well Sallie, I have just received a letter from Sister Jane and Lemmie.[2] They are all well. Well Sallie, I am out of stamps and there is none to be bought here now, so I will have to send my letters without paying the postage on them, I recon.[3] I dont know what to do. you can get them that way. if not, you will have to deposit a fund in the office. I will have to close.

Write often. Give my love to all. Also to uncle Sill.

Your affectionate brother James

1 Lieutenant Colonel Arthur Hood served in the 29th Battalion, Georgia Cavalry, and the 2nd Georgia Cavalry.

2   Jewel's sister Jane Edwards and her oldest child Lemuel, listed in the 1860 Georgia census as 11 years old. In 1864, at age 15, Lemuel J. Edwards joined Co. D Cook's Battalion along with his 16-year-old cousin James T. Crowley (previously cited).

3   The Confederate Government permitted soldiers to send mail without postage, which had to be paid by the recipient. Usually, patrons were required to keep funds on deposit at local post offices to pay for such mail as it came in.

CAMP LEON FLA
MAY 12TH 1864

Dear Sallie

I have again seated myself to write you a few lines in answer to yours written the 5th, which was gladly received.

I dont think I can hardly write enough to be worthy of calling a letter, as the old saying used to be, for the want of soap. I am glad to tell you that I am still enjoying good health, as good as I ever did in my life. Our company is in very good health now. I dont think there is more than five but what is [not] able for duty.

We hear some little war news occasionally from the North and west, but it is not worth while for me to try to inform you any thing about it as it is all old with you by this time. I have not heard from Cousin John in several days. he was here last week one night. I am not doing much in the way of hatmaking, there is but little demand for them yet. Money is getting scarce with the most of us, and what little there is in circulation wont buy any thing hardly. I thought we would draw our money the first of this month but it very uncertain when we will get any.

The wether was very warm last week and the first of this week, but it is very cool now. I think it was very near cold enough for frost this morning. the wind blows cold now in the shade. It is nearly twelve Oclock and I feel cold in the house with out fire. Eliza said there was frost enough to bite the potatoe tops the morning of the 4th. I [think] the weather certainly has been colder this spring than was most ever known. I dont think there will [be] any oranges in this country this year. the trees were all killed, or at least all the small twigs. I recollect passing by a house last year coming down to Tall. about the middle of february and I thought the yard was as green as I ever saw one in the middle of summer with orange and Oleander bushes and flowers. I saw the same place this year in april and [it] looked like it had been burnt almost.

Well Sallie, three of our company were transfered to the navy at Charleston last week. I suppose they were building a new gunboat there and wanted two hundred to man it. There is several more that joined, but the officer could not receive more than three from one company without a hearing from Genl Beauregard. I think we are doomed to stay here this summer, or some where in the neighborhood. Our horses are still going down every day. We have not got enough to drill, so we have to turn them out to graze two hours in the morning and two in the evening and guard them to keep them from going off. The drivers have to spend two hours feeding and currying every day and every third day [they have to spend] four hours to watch them. it will sorter break into my hatmaking business.

I believe I wrote to you to send me all the Gutapercha you could get that would make finger rings. I have got two silver rings I swoped for, but I dont know who of you to send them to. I want to get two or three more so I can send one for all of you. Send me all the ten and five cent pieces you can get. they sell at from five to ten dollars here. I saw a nice silver spoon that some of the boys got some where to make rings, they cost about forty dollars a set in good times. I guess some negroe stold it and sold it.

Well Sallie, I will close, for I think I have been long enough writing without it was worth something.

Give my love to all. Your affectionate brother James

*[This letter is in the collection of the
Robert W. Woodruff Library at Emory University]*

CAMP LEON FLA
MAY 15TH 1864

Dear Sallie

I again seat myself this pleasant morning to write you a few lines in answer to your welcome letter I received friday evening in which I found the dime and postage stamps you sent me, for which I am very much obliged to Pa for sending, me as there is no chance to get any here now. I was a little supprised at getting two letters from you two evenings in succession. The last one came through very quick it was mailed wednesday the 11th and I got it friday evening. I received one from Eliza yesterday which come in the same length of time. She said she exspected to go up and stay with you all next week or this week as it is now. I hope she will have the chance to go. she said she had been waiting for me to come home so we could go together but you may tell her not to wait for me for she can go when I come any how, and maybe go again a time or two more, yet. I dont make any calculations about when I will come as I have been disappointed so often. I recon Jim Hurt must have got his furlough extended as he has not come. I did not look for him much. The surgeon of the hospital that gave him the furlough sent a notice here that his furlough was for sixty days and it was put down that way on the muster roll and payroll. if he had known it, it would not [have] made any difference about trying to get it extended, but I have no idea he has heard any thing about it. I dont understand such doings myself. some of us have not forgot the time he went from Atlanta on a three days furlough and stayed six weeks. I recon I will have to take the rheumatism or something so I can get a furlough.

Well Sallie the war news is very favorable on our side it seens we meet with great success at every point. Old Pappa Price as he used to be called has captured Steel and his army[1] and Genl Beauregard gained the victory at Petersburg.[2] also Genl Morgan has gave them a thrashing. We ought to be very thankful for such success.

Well Sallie I had you a ring made. I thought for fear I might spoil it, I would get [some] one to make it that was used to making them it is rather difficult to make them the right size every time. he made it a little larger than I told him. I will send two the largest one is the one I had made for you but you can take [your] choice and let Eliza have the other one. I have got two gutapercha rings but one of them is too small and the [other] too large for any of you. I [will] write a little for Eliza and send in this letter. I will send it by Whit Johnson[3] if he will take it and you will get it sooner.

Give my love to all.

Write often I remain your affectonate brother James

1   Old Pappa Price was Confederate Major General Sterling Price, former Governor of Missouri. Steel was Union Major General Frederick Steele, a West Point graduate and professional soldier. Price and Steele commanded part of the forces that clashed during the Red River Expedition waged in Louisiana. Contrary to the rumors, Price did not capture Steele and his army during the campaign.

2   Against almost overwhelming odds, Confederate General P.G.T. Beauregard did successfully defend Petersburg during the spring of 1864. The city did not fall to Union invasion until almost a year later in early April 1865.

3   Whit Johnson probably was Mid Johnson's older brother, Whitson G. Johnson. Whitson Johnson had served in Co. B, 1st Regiment, Georgia Volunteer Infantry; Co. A, 12th Battalion, Georgia Light Artillery; and Co. A, 63rd Regiment, Georgia Volunteer Infantry. He had resigned April 3, 1863, with a disability due to acute rheumatism and may have been visiting his brother in camp.

CAMP LEON
MAY 22ND 1864

Dear Sister Sallie

I have taken my this evening to write you a few lines in answer to your kind letter which I received yesterday with Eliza's written, the 18th. It seems that the letters You all write come in a short time now to what they did some time. I am well with the exception of a slight cold and a little sore throat which I took last night. it was quite warm in the forepart of the night and [I] lay down with out any cover and went to sleep and got cool. I expect to write you a short letter this time as I feel a little drowsy. I have taken a nap of sleep since dinner which I very seldom do from the simple reason it is most sure to make me feel bad all the evening.

Well Sallie, I wrote to you all a good deal about our company being reduced, but that has all died out. Those three that went to the Navy at Charleston stoped all transfers. There has been two or three letters received from them since they went there. instead of getting such great rations they only get one sea cracker, as they call them, a day, and a little beef. one of them said he would give every thing he had just to get back to Fla again. Instead of that, now the talk is about going to Andersonville Georgia to guard the prisoners.[1] You may know where it is, but I did not know there was such a place till they commenced sending prisoners from here up there. it is a small town above Albany where we have some 18 or 20 thousand prisoners. It is the opinion of a good many that we will go there. I think it is very uncertain. I have no doubt but our duty would be heavy there but then we would get back to our old native state again and be so much nearer home, and a railroad all the way.

Now I will tell the chance for it. Capt Gambles company was sent from here up there and they are trying to make the swope with us. They have a good set of horses and they are not needed there and we have but few horses and more men.

Mat Briscoe[2] is there and he wrote to John Kinnebrew they were trying to make the swap. The Commander of that post is willing to it.

Well Sallie, I recon you got the letter I sent by Whit Johnson with those rings in it the day you wrote to me. I expect to send this one by Lieut Glenn as he exspects to start home to morrow. I dont know how long his furlough is, but I expect he will stay a good while. he has been home this year and stayed two months and has not done any thing since he came back. Cousin John is getting along very well. I dont think it is worth while for any one to go from here home to get over the chills   they all seem to have them as long as they stay there and come back and get well of them at last. It is very warm to day. I think it will do for a summerday. I will close.

Give my love to all.

Your affectionate brother James

1   Andersonville was the infamous Confederate prison in Sumter County, Georgia. A stockade enclosing 26½ acres was hastily constructed early in 1864 to hold up to 6,000 prisoners, but as many as 33,000 were confined there at one time after Grant and Lincoln ceased prisoner exchanges. Of a total of 45,613 Union soldiers incarcerated there in just over a year, about 13,000 died, mostly from disease and malnutrition. Captain Henry W. Wirz, prison commandant, was the only southerner executed as a war criminal after the war.

2   This probably was Madison P. Briscoe, a Private in the Stocks Volunteers from Greene County, the same company in which Jewel's brothers-in-law Thomas F. Colclough and Franklin W. Colclough were serving. Briscoe was listed in the 1860 Georgia census as the 17-year-old son of John and Elizabeth Briscoe (already cited).

CAMP LEON
MAY 29TH 1864

Dear Sallie

I thought I would write you a short letter this morning to let you know that I am still well, though I am troubled some with cold. I feel so dull and stupid, I think I will not write much. When I tell you our condition, I think you will excuse me. I feel as if we were just about to start to the war.

We carried our horses up to town tuesday and turned them over to the government and Yesterday our guns, amunition, and harness were sent of and we are to be armed with musket in a few days. The order was that we would be changed [to infantry] for a while, as horses were hard to get. We are exspecting orders every day to go up to town where the other boys are, and then all be put out doors without any shelter at all. There is twenty of the last recruits that come to this company to leave in the morning for the conscript camp at Madison in this state and they will be sent to some Ga Compy or the conscript camp in Georgia. I think the most of them hate to leave about as bad as they did to leave home. There is a talk of Hoods cavelry being dismounted and we will be put in that regiment, as they lack one or two companies of being full. It is the opinion of a goodmany of us that our officers are looking up for promotion. Hood is only lieut Col and if he get a full reg he will be Col and the Major will take his office and of cours as Tiller will be seignior Capt, he will be the Major.

You recollect this is just supposition with us. We may go to town and stay there this summer to guard those prisoners, or we may go to Atlanta. there is no telling. all the infantry has been sent from this state to Johnsons army some time ago. The state troop have been sent from Atlanta to Andersonville to guard the prisoners and those that were there sent to Atlanta. I heard a day or two ago that Gambles Artillery had been dis mounted and ordered to Atlanta. I dont know [if] that is true. Now you see how we come out with the swop at Andersonville I wrote to you about. I didnt think it would be made, but it has turned out a little different from my exspectations, or rather a little sooner than I exspected. I have been thinking for sometime that we would have to shoulder musket. I do hope we will not have much marching to do in this sandy country. We have not heard any thing from either of the armies in several days. I would like very much to hear how they are getting along.

Well Sallie, I was in hopes I would hear from you all yesterday. I have not heard from the letter I sent by Whit Johnson two weeks ago tomorrow with two silver rings in it. I sent two little fans by Lieut Glenn last monday, one for you and the other for Eliza. I did not think I would send them when I was at work at them, I merely thought I would try [to see] if I could make one. I thought I would make some more and send, but I will not have the chance to do it now I am afraid. I have nothing more of any importance to write so I will close, hoping to hear from you all in a few days. Give my love to all.

I remain your affectionate brother James

Cousin John was well a day or two ago.

CHAPTER VIII

On the Move

*"I think of all the country in the Confedracy,
this down this way is as sorry as can be found"*

Dear Sallie

I thought I would write you a few lines this evening to let you know I received your letter monday written the 25th, also one from Mary C., and I thought I would write to send it by R.L Hargroves,[1] as he is going to start home to morrow.

Well Sallie, we left Camp Leon this morning and marched up to town with our knap sacks on our backs. I tell you it was very warm walking. I thought then if I had to start on another march and have to take a gun and cartridge box I will not have quite so many clothes. I have seen enough of infantry to know I will not like it. we have not got our guns [muskets] yet. I recon we will get them in a few days. It has been thundering about all the evening and I thought we would have a hard rain on us in the wood. We have just commenced the soldiers life, I think. I hope this war will not last long if I have to carry a musket. I heard that the news was very favorable for us yesterday. I have not heard any to day. All the gards are ordered from here but our company. There is no telling how long we will stay here. I will have to close for this time. You must excuse this short letter. Give [my love] to all.

I remain your affectionate brother James

1   Richard L. Hargroves enlisted in the Echols Artillery as a Private in March 1862 but eventually became 2nd Sergeant and served until the end of the war. In the 1860 Georgia census he was listed as the 29-year-old overseer on the farm of Charles J. and Martha Hargroves in the Grove Creek District of Oglethorpe County.

TALLAHASSA FLA,
JUNE 12TH 64

Dear Sallie

I have taken my seat this morning to write you a few lines so that you all may know where we are. I am still enjoying very good health. I thought I would have received a letter from you before this time. I have not received one from you since I left Camp Leon. I received a letter from Eliza friday stating that Mattie was very sick and she did not think she would live if she did not get better soon. I hope she has got well by this time.

Well Sallie, I wrote you a short letter last week and sent [it] by R.L Hargroves, which I recon you have received. I told you where we was which was about all, as I had but a few moments to write. I dont like this camp at all, it is too much like a swamp. the growth is Magnolia, sweet gum, and beech. The woods is so thick there is but little air stirring at any time and the ground dont get dry from one rain to another. We are on guard every other day and night, so you see we dont have much time to spare. Cousin John was complaining yesterday morning with cold and did not go on duty, but I have come to camps this morning and have not seen him. he has gone to town to see Jos Armstrong. he is at the hospital sick and [has] been there two weeks to day. I dont think he is as well as he was when he went there. There is at least a half a doz of the boys taken sick since we come here.

Well Sallie, I saw John Colclough friday. he is express agent on this railroad from Madison to Quincy. Our camps are on the road about a mile from the depot and as he passed by friday going up to Quincy he droped me a note. So I went up to the depot to see him. he has grown a gooddeal since I saw him. He says he did not like to come down to Fla., but as it was a new line established he was detailed to take it. he will pass here every day I recon, as the trains go up one day and down the next. There is a dispute in Oglethorpe about there being an express line here. Cousin John wrote to his

Pa to send him some things by express and he wrote back to him that he could not get them to take them and told him there was no express in Fla. It is true it has been established but two weeks, but I thought they would have known it. It will cost 20 dollars on the hundred from Athens Ga to this place. I want some flour if there is any chance to get it, as I am getting real biscuit hungry. We have not drawn any flour in a long time. It only cost $1.50 to $2.00 now. it has been as high as three, but you know it will not do for a soldier at that price, that never draws any wages. I dont believe they intend to pay the soldiers any more money in this country from the way they act.

The people there in town are as kind toward our company as could be exspected. Some of them have been up here two or three months. They let us have milk and all the vegetables they have to spare and will swop us bacon for our beef. some of them will [swap] pound for pound and others one for two. I think the most of them do it for an accomodation. I had rather have one pound of bacon than three of the beef we get. I wrote to you some time ago to know if John Kinnebrew could get five lbs of wool to make him a suit and what price. he has asked me to write again as he is anxious to know. I expect to send this letter by Lieut Jarrell tomorrow as he is going home on a furlough. I will close for this time hoping to hear from you soon. I recon Jim Hurt will come back next week.

Give My love to all. Your affectionate brother James

TALLAHASSA FLA
JUNE 20 [1864]

Dear Sallie

I seat my self this morning to write you a few lines. I received a letter from you a day or two ago written the 5 of this month. that is the only one that I have received from you since the 25th of May. so you see, if I dont get another one in a few days it will only be one this month. I am very anxious to hear from Eliza as Mattie was very sick when I heard from her, which was the 7th.

Well Sallie, I am happy to tell you that I still enjoy very good health. There is seven or eight of the boys at the hospital, but none of them very dangerous. Jos Armstrong is mending some I think. Mat Norton has been there about a week. I would not be surprised if he has a bad spell before he gets well. We moved from the Magnolia grove last week. It was in between two swamps and the grove was so thick the ground and leaves would not get dry from one rain to another. The Musketoes looked like they would use us up of a night. We are camped about a mile and a half from town in an old field with a very pretty grove of liveoak. we have tolerable good spring water for this country, but it would not be good up there.

Well Sallie, The weather has been very wet for some time. it rains every day more or less. the railroad from here down east has washed away in several places and in some of the swamps, has given way. so there is no passing, and not likely to be in some time. I think it doubtful about our getting any mail by that rout. nearly all of our mail comes that way.

I have got a good joke on cousin John. he wrote to you on the 21st of May, and was looking for an answer for several days. The post Master Told him there was a letter at the office for him, so he went to get it and found it was backed to you, and had not been sent off. he did not have any postage stamps and he, instead of signing his name at [the] top of it, put J. Jone's Echols Artillery. I think that a wide mistake. the postmaster said he did not notice the name on it. We have been looking for Jim Hurt several days, but have not heard any thing about him. he got his furlough extended thirty days from the 14th of May, I understood, and surely he has not got another extension.

I do wish I could come home, but it looks like the chance is bad. I cant tell you any thing about when I will get there. Tiller will not give any furloughs at all. All those that have gone home were furloughed from the hospital. The new issue have gone into camps here in town. they are quite a poor looking chance for soldiers. I think they will take our place here on guard. I do hope if we have to leave here we will go up in Georgia. I dont want to have to go down south again. We may stay here this summer for any thing I know. I will close for this time hoping to hear from you again soon. Give My love to all. Your brother James

TALLAHASSA
JUNE 26TH 1864

Dear Sallie

I have taken my seat this morning to write to you a few lines to let you know that I received your kind letter written the 17th. I was very glad to hear from you all. I thought you had quit writing to me or something was the matter, as that was [only] the second letter that I have received from you in a month, from the 25th of may to yesterday. I also received a letter from Eliza yester, they were all well. Well Sallie, I have no news to write at all. I am still enjoying very good health Cousin John is well.

There is a good many of the boys in camps complaining some. Jos Armstrong is mending some. he is able to walk out in town occasionally. The guard duty is not so heavy on us now as it has been. The new issue have gone into camps here in town and they are now on duty. I think the name suits some of them very well. One of the Lieut was officer of the guard the other day when I was on. You can just think what sort of an officer Jimmie Crowley would make in a company of fifty men and boys and you will have a very good idea of their first and second Lieut. their Capt is an old man. I could tell you more about them if I could see you. The weather is very hot now, it has stoped raining again. it rained every day for about three weeks. it has not rained any in three or four days. I am afraid there is so much rain the wheat crops will be injured. We bought some flour yesterday and had buiscuit for supper and breakfast for the first I have eat in a long time.

I commenced writing this morning but I felt too stupid to write as I had just got up from taking a nap. it [is] very hot this evening.

The corn crops are looking tolerable well, but in some places it has been most too wet for it. I cant think of any thing to write as there is no news down this way at all. We were looking for Jim Hurt back last week, but I suppose he has got another extension. One of the Company, Charlie Broach got back here yesterday. he has been home on a sixty days furlough. he saw Jim and Jack Edwards. Jack was going to the hospital at Greensboro. I suppose Jim and Babe are to be married next thursday night. I heard it from one of the Johnsons and I guess it come from his sister. Mid Johnson had to leave here to go to the conscript camp and got a furlough to go home and has got married and got out of the war by getting the appointment of balif in Lexington.[1] I wonder if it would not be as fair for me to go home and claim my commission as a justice of the piece. Well Sallie, I bought me a pencil yester day and payed a $1.50 for it. My ink is so pale and so much trouble I thought I would try a pencil. I do wish I could get a furlough, but it looks like there is no chance. I will close for this time.

Cousin John Joins me in love to you all.

Your affectionate brother James

1 Middleton W. Johnson married Hophie N. Lumpkin in Oglethorpe County on June 9, 1864.

CAMP LIMPKINS
FLORIDA
JULY 17TH 1864

Dear Sallie

I have taken my seat this beautiful sabbath morning to write you a few line to let you know where we are. The last time I wrote to you we was on our rout to the obstructions on the Appalachicola river. I wrote and mailed my letter at Chattahoochee. I recon you will be a little surprised when I tell you where we are now. We went down to the Narrows and brought up five siege pieces and dropped them

at Chattahoochee and got back to Tallahassee friday Morning. I
stood the [trip] very well untill my left foot commenced hurting me
in the joint below my ankle, which I think was caused from walking
so much. I have been limping ever since, but it is nearly well now.
it does not hurt me any, only when I walk, and I have made it
convenient to ride in the place of Marching. Other wise I am as
well as ever. We have had two or three meals of our flour and meat
from home. I was so glad to get some biscuit, but as it happened,
we have drawed a little flour for the first time in about six months.

Well, I will now tell you about our trip to this place. We got
orders soon after we got back to Tallahas. to move again, so we
came back to the depot, took the train at two oclock and came to
St Marks were we put our baggage on a flat and carried it about
three miles up the St Marks river. I got on a small boat with six
others and went up. The company marched here by land. We are
in very good cabins near the river, where I think we will very apt
to spend the summer, though I dont [know]. If you recollect the
place called Camp Brokaw where we were camped last spring was
a year ago, about a mile from Newport. we are now about a mile
below Newport on the St Marks river.

We will have to get our mail from Newport. I hate to be down in
this country on account of it being so much trouble about getting
our letters although they get a daily mail at St Marks.

Well Sallie, I have not been around to see anything about here
so I cannot tell you much about the place. I know one thing, there
is a plenty fleas and musketoes here if nothing else. It is said that
we have come down here to do picket duty on the coast, but I can't
tell any thing about that yet. all the Calvery that was down here
picketing have been sent off.

Well Sallie, I got acquainted with Cousin John Bell (Uncle Sills
son) of Coweater [Coweta County, Georgia] while I was down on
the river. he belongs to a calvery company there. he has been living
here in this state three years.

Well Sallie I heard the other day that Jim hurt had got a detail
in Madison. Sallie wrote to Cousin John about it. Lieut Wade and
one of the Tillers is going to start home on furlough this evening. I
do wish I could get a furlough and come home to see you all. I had

rather went to Atlanter in Johnsons army than to come any further down in this state. I will close for this time. The last letter I received from you was written the 25th. write often.

Give My love to all. Your affectionate brother James

P.S. I forgot to tell you Wilie Young has come back, also Dick Hargroves and Lieut Glenn.

[This letter is in the collection of the
Robert W. Woodruff Library at Emory University]

Darby Station[1]
AUG 25TH 1864

Dear Sallie

I have taken my seat this evening to write you a few lines to let you hear from me as it has been some time since I have written. I have been anxiously expecting a letter from you but have not received one since the 25th of July. I have no doubt but you have written since that time if you have they have not come to hand. I have received them tolerable regular from Eliza though the most of them are a good while on the road. I am at this time enjoying very good health. I had a little sick spell for a few days since I come down east.

We left Camp Jackson yesterday and come to this place about six miles where there was a large turpentine distillery but the yankeys have destroyed it entirely and we are five or six miles above Baldwin. It is thought that the yankeys have all gone back to Jacksonville. They left Baldwin and attempted to make a rade round south of us by Stark and Gainsville on the Fernandena & Cedarkeys railroad and then to Lake City. but they met with about eight hundred of our troops comd by Capt Dickerson at Gainesville. he routted them completely taking 200 prisoners. I never learned the number killed and wounded. no losses on our side that I learned.

Well now I will tell you something about our trip to that battle but it came off the morning we started. Nearly all that was here went (it was last wednesday morning). We marched hard all day and the next morning rose at 2 Oclock in the morning and put out again. about ten oclock we met a curier that told us of the fight and we change our course to meet them but soon found it was no use and change our course *again* and marched till nine oclock that night resting about two hours at twelve and a few minutes occasionally.

We lay over at a place called Waldo friday and saturday till two oclock after marching about 50 miles in two days. I got along very well but raised a bad blister on the bottom of one of my feet. We took the train saturday evening and rode about twelve miles to Starks where we got off and took it a foot in as hard a rain as commonly falls, for about two hours. The roads was very wet and we had several creeks to wade. We have been in service over two years but we have not been soldiering very long. I was in hopes when the yankeys left here we would go back to middle Fla. but they have gone to repairing the railroad and we have move below them for protection, so I recon we will stay down here untill there is some demonstraton made some where else.

The infantry is made up of dismounted cavelry, artillery, and the new issue about one common regiment under command of Lieut Col McCommac. We have a small force of cavelry and one battery of artillery. The most of the cavelry and artillery that have been dismounted on this occassion think they will take their horses again before long but I would not be surprised if some of them are like we are, dismounted for good.

I have not seen Cousin John in some time. he went to the hospital at Lake City. I got a letter from him last week. he was getting along very well and thought he would come back to the company in a day or two but the Dr sayed he had to go to Tall. the next day. They have sent all of our sick from there to Tall, and as soon as they get able for duty they put them on there and have not sent one of them from there to the company since we come down here. there is nearly half of the company up there now and they keep sending them up to the hospital. I recon that will be the way the most of the crowd will get back and then maybe they will order the others up there. I would not mind staying here so bad if we could get our letters in time.

Well Sallie I must close for this time. I dont know when I will get this off. there is no post office this side of Lake City. they bring the mail down by hand on the train every day to camp Jackson. I dont know how we will get it from there [except] by the wagon train that bring our rations. I am out of stamps again and no chance to get any this side of Tall. I must close.

Give my love to al. I remain your affectionate brother James

Dear Sallie

I have just received your letter written the 8th but it is near night and I have not had time to read it all also two from Eliza I am so glad to hear that you are well. Yours truly James

1   Darby Station was the old name for the present town of Macclenny, Florida, on the railroad about 28 miles west of Jacksonville and is the county seat of Baker County. The community also was known as Darby Ville or Darbyville.

DARBY STATION
SEPT 20TH [1864]

Dear Sallie

I Seat my self to night to write you a few lines as I have a chance to send it by hand. James T Johnson is going to start home in the morning on a (15) fifteen days furlough to get Married.[1] he will have a very short time to stay, it will take him four days to go and four to come back. his time will be out the 6th of Oct. I exspect he will be very apt to come in a day or two of the time, I recon.

I have no news to write at this time, as I wrote to you last Thursday or friday yoar last that I have received was written the 2nd. I thought I would have got a letter from you before this time. I want two pair of yarn socks and some cake soap an would like to have a Shirt and pair of drawers, but I recon from what he says he cannot bring more than the socks and a small cake of soap. I am not needing the other things now and if we draw as we exspect, I can make out without them. I would write to Eliza for the things, but I thought she would not get the letter in time. I will send fifty dollars in this letter for her, as I have more than I need here.

I received a little note from Cousin John this evening. he did not say any thing about his health. I would have written this evening but I was out on detail and did not get back till night, therefore you will have to excuse me this time. James Johnson says he will leave home the third of Oct., or at least that is the time that he exspects to start back. So any of you can meet him there that day. I dont know any thing about when I will get there. Tell Ma I thought I would get to come to see you all when the two years rolled round, but the time has past and I see no more chance now than was before.

I will close for this time.

Give my love to all. I remain your affectionate brother James

1   James T. Johnson married Harriett Elizabeth Carithers in Oglethorpe County, Georgia, September 28, 1864.

BALDWIN EAST FLA[1]
OCT 2ND 1864

Dear Sallie

I seat myself this morning to write you a few lines to let you know that I received your most welcome letter last thursday, written the 23rd. I was very glad to hear from you all. I am sorry to hear of so much sickness and so many death in that neighbor hood. it seems like there has been a great deal more sickness in that country than there used to be before the war. I am glad to inform you that I am still in good health. I am fearful that our health will not be as good, even as it has been.

I have been hearing talk of Baldwin for sometime and now I have seen the place at last. There is one old brick chimney on the place. I suppose from the sine [sign] there has been some few old houses there. The railroads cross here. I think of all the country in the Confederacy, this down this way is as sorry as can be found. it looks like it might nearly all be covered in water in wet weather. it has been dry for sometime and nearly all the ponds have dried up. It is but very little trouble to dig wells, but then the water is not good when we get it. We had spring water at the other camp we come from. We left there thursday morning and came to this place and have been busy fixing up our shelters since that time.

Well Sallie, I have no news worth writing this morning. We keep moving a little nearer the Yankeys. I recon we will get near enough to see some of them before a great while. I think when the railroad is completed down here and they get to work taking up the Fernandena railroad again, the Yankeys will be very apt to run us I think, though we can not tell. they may rout us before that time. We have not got force sufficient to contend with many of them. We only have about 250 infantry, 100 calvery, and one company of Artillery. the others have gone back to Middle or west Fla. Our company is now left with the new issue battallion. I do think it a perfect disgrace for a company that has been out nearly three years to be attached to a Fla new issue Battalion. I think if our officers would try they could do better, but all they care for is to go home. Capt Tiller has gone home again, the plea was that his wife was very sick. I would like to know what more his wife is than mine or any other soldiers. just because he is an officier he can go when he wants to go. Lieut Wade is the only officer that we have that will stay with us.

Well Sallie, we have just been out on inspection with a new issue Capt in Commd of the Bat. he did not know how to give the first command right. he can say uses and youones,[2] that is the way the most of them talk. I believe there is about half of the officer that might drill till they get to be a hundred years old and would not learn to drill correctly. I hope something will happen so that we will not stay here with them long. I and George Martin have applied for a detail on the railroad to Oversee some hands getting crossties. They were needing two men and one of our company was at work at the bridge with the Superintendent and he says they would take us and let us know in a few days. I thought we would have been detailed before this time from what he said. I will have to close for this time hoping to from you again soon give my love to all.

Your affectionate brother brother James

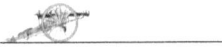

1   Baldwin is a small town in Duval County on the railroad about 20 miles west of Jacksonville.

2   The plural of us and you.

BALDWIN EAST FLA
OCT 16TH 1864

Dear Sallie

I will write you a few lines to let you know that I received your most welcome letter friday evening dated the 14th. I recon as I received it the fourteenth, you must have written it the 4th. I have no news of any importance to write. I feel like it will be a task for me to undertake to write a letter that is worth anyone reading, as there is nothing new transpired since we have been here. I am enjoying tolerable good health, though I dont feel altogether as stout as I have done some time ago. I received a letter from Eliza a few days ago. She was complaining of the rheumatism. I am fearful she will have a bad time of it this winter. I am sorry to hear of so much sickness in that country.

Well Sallie, we had preaching here last night. it was [a] much better sermon than I exspected to hear from the appearance of the man. He reminded me of Old Willis Eidson[1] very much. he claims to be sent out by the Methodist conference to preach and goes with his bugel on his back and stick in his hand. he is the shabbyest looking chance that I ever saw to be going about to preach, without any exception, though I dont pretend to say that he is not a good man. he said he would preach again to day for us. We received orders the other evening to pack up and be ready to move in a minute. we thought the Yankeys were coming and we would have to run. The calvery went out to see what was the matter but found nothing. There was some of them seen by our pickets scouting about to see what they could find.

Well Sallie I dont hardly [know] what to write to you. I sometimes write something about coming home, but not often, for the simple reason I cant tell any thing about when I will be permitted to enjoy that privelege. If I was to do as some of them have done here, I might get there. I copied two furloughs for Lieut Jarrell a day or two ago for two of the company here, and one of them gave as his reason for wanting to go home was that he had not been at home in twenty nine months. also his family had no body to provide for them and he wanted to get provisions for them the year. I dont think that I have been from home that long[2] and he came from there sometime after I did. and besides he has his wifes farther there to help her. I dont feel disposed to tell such tales if I can help it. So you see, that is the way some men get along. I expect I will find a many one here that will say they have been from home longer than I have to let them tell the story.

I have not heard from Cousin John since I wrote to you last. I heard those boys were all ordered to return to the company and have heard since that they were all sick. The Dr has sent about a doz. of our com. to the hospital this last week. he did not have anything to give them here.

It is reported here that the Yanks have burnt Atlanta and Forest captured Sherman but it is not reliable. I am sorry to say it but [I am] getting very much out of heart some way. I have no doubt but we would all cheer up if we could leave this country. I will close for this time, hoping to see you all before a great while. I am going to try some way. Give my love to all.

Your affectionate brother James

P.S.
Direct your letters to Lake City or Baldwin East Fla; either will do, I dont know that there will be much difference.

1   Willis Eidson is listed in the 1860 Georgia census as a 62-year-old resident of the Falling Creek District of Oglethorpe County. Oglethorpe County records show that Eidson married Mary Richardson August 30, 1840.

2   Jewel's last furlough had been slightly more than 2 years previously during late August and early September of 1862 to be with Eliza when Mattie was born August 31, 1862.

[This letter is in the collection of the
Robert W. Woodruff Library at Emory University]

BALDWIN EAST FLA
NOV 20TH 64

Dear Sallie

I seat myself this morning to write you a few lines to let you know that I received your kind letter of the 11th written up at Sister Janes. I was glad to hear from you all and hope all may be well by this time. I am sorry to hear that the fever is got in the family. I am afraid you all may have a hard time if it is like some of the families.

Well Sallie I have just as good health as I could wish for. I have no news of any importance to write so I dont think [I] can hardly write a letter worth reading. but I know if you all are like I am you want to hear if it is nothing more than to say that you are well or how you are getting along. I heard a few days ago that the yankey had burnt Atlanta and left it or about to leave and our Malitia were ordered there. We never know how to take such reports and the next day we heard the yanks had taken Griffin.[1]

You say you heard there was some prospect of my coming home before long I think there is some. I am in hopes of getting there between now and christmas if every thing goes on peaceably as it has done for some time but then we never know what may happen or when we may have to move. Lieut Jarrell has promised to let me [come home] before long. three of the boys started home last friday. They were wagon drivers and got their furloughs from the Quarter Master. There is none on furlough from the company now. If I can I want to get there to spend the christmas with you all. I received a letter from Cousin John the first of the week. he was sick and sent for a discriptive list to go in the hospital. he had been sick about a week. Our company is in very good health at this time or those that is here. There is a good many at the hospitals and off on details. Our boys are all anxious to leave this place and most every day there is some talk of our going back to Middle Fla or Ga. The officers here say that we will go to Tall. or Mariana in West Fla. Col Turney told Capt Tiller yesterday we would go back there but I dont put much confidence in it.

Well Sallie I will close for this time as I have nothing of importance to write and my paper is getting scarce. I hope to see you soon. Give my love to all. I remain your affectionate brother James

1   The stories were true. Union Major General William Tecumseh Sherman captured Atlanta in September 1864. After pillaging and burning the town, Sherman's 60,000-man army started to Savannah, 250 miles away. They cut a swath of destruction 30 to 60 miles wide diagonally across the state, living off the land and destroying provisions they did not need. Available Confederate forces, including the Echols Artillery, were assembled to defend Savannah but were easily defeated and driven across the Savannah River into South Carolina and beyond.

SAVANNAH GA
DEC 4TH 1864

Dear Sallie

I seat my self this morning to write you a few lines to let you hear from me. I have no news of any importance to write. I am still enjoying the best of health. We have once more got in our native state. I have rather neglected writing to you, but it has been reported here the rail roads was cut and no chance to get a letter through.

Well, we left Baldwin a week ago, day before yesterday and came to Madison [Florida] that day. saturday we Marched to Quitman [Georgia] on the Gulf road [and] sunday we came through to Savannah. The company is divided and [is] about three miles from town on the Central rail road and the Augusta road. We have charge of two siege batteries of three guns each, and our small arms also. Cousin John is here. he has had three chills since he left Tall. Fla. There is a little fight near Pocataligo [South Carolina] about twenty miles from here on the Charleston road. The first Brig: of Ga. Militia volunteered and went in the fight. They came back night before last, and went up the road toward Augusta. Some of our boys went over to town to see them. Brother was along, I was very sorry I did not go there so I could have seen him. he told the boys to tell me he was well. The company that Jimmie [Crowley] was in was left over in South Carolina. I will have to close for this time as the mail boy is now going to start to town and will not wait for me.

I thought I would have longer to write when I commenced. Give my love to all

Your affectionate brother James

JAMES ISLAND[1]
JANUARY 1ST/65

Dear Sallie

I recon you will be glad to hear from me at this time. I know I would be glad to hear from you all. I have not received any letter from you since the tenth of Dec. I am still enjoying good health. The weather is very cold today. Yesterday it rained a little and blew off very cold with the wind from the north and [I] tell you it was cold this morning. Cousin John had a chill to day. we had to go out to the breast works and stay there without fire and got so cold, I recon was the cause of his having a chill. I think of all the places we have ever been this is the worst. We cant get but little wood to burn and [have to live] out doors. there is some few pine trees here but we are not allowed to cut them, so we will have to haul [firewood] about a mile when we can get a wagon.

Our rations are very short. we dont get any meat. we have been on the Island a week and have only got one pound of beef. we get some flour, meal, and rice, but not enough to hold out. we ought to have drawn rations yesterday evenin and it will soon be night and we have not drawn. We eat [our] last rice and bread we had about this time yesterday. I bought thre dollars worth of potatoes just now and eat them. They sell four & five about the size of my finger for a dollar. Cousin John wrote home for a box of provisions to be sent by Lieut gibson. When he comes he said he would pass Antioch the 4th or 5th of this month. I wrote to Eliza to send me some thing to eat by Gibson. he told me he would bring any thing for me. I do hope the time will soon come when I can meet you all at home, there to stay, but we can not tell how long [that may be]. I will close for this time, hoping to hear from you all soon. Give my love to all.

Your affectionate brother James

Direct your letters [to] Fort Johnson, James Island, Charleston S C.

1   James Island is on the South Carolina coast near Charleston. Fort Johnson was located there.

JAMES ISLAND
JAN 27TH 1865

Dear Sallie

As I have an opportunity, I will write you a few lines to let you know that I have received yours of the 18th a few days ago. I would have answered it before, but the next day after I received it I had to go out to work, and yesterday it was so cold all day I could not undertake to write. The wind feels just like it come from a snow bank, it is so cold. I am getting along tolerable well now as to health. Cousin John had a chill day before yesterday. Well Sallie, we have not heard a word from our boxes yet, since Gibson left them. We telegraphed for them last saturday and thought they would send them in a day or two.

Cousin John, George Martin, Evans, and I all mess together, and three of us have boxes on the way. we would have a plenty for a little while if we could get them. There has been several of the boys come from home since Gibson and brought a lot of boxes for the boys. I wish Gibson had brought ours with him, but they told him they thought it would be a week before the railroad would be repaired. We dont draw rations enough to make out on and of course have to buy [food] when we find any thing to buy. we dont get enough for more than four days out of five. it is a general complaint all over the island. I hope we will not have to stay here long, everything is too scarce. it is a hard matter to get wood to make fires and that we get is green pine and sweet gum, and you know that is a bad chance for fire. There has been a talk of our drawing money for some time, but we have not got it. We drew clothes for part of the camp, but there was not enough on hand for all and I dont know when we will get them.

I wrote to you of hearing of Brother's[1] death. I was very sorry to hear of it. I did not think he could stand the service. They are all left in a bad fix. I will close for this time, hoping to hear from you often. My love to all. Your affectionate brother James

Well Sallie, I have just heard that our boxes have come to town this evening. we will get them tomorrow I recon.

1   Jewel's brother-in-law Benajah Crowley was exempted from service for most of the war because of his age. The Conscription Act of February 17, 1864, lowered the minimum age from 18 to 17 and raised the maximum age from 45 to 50. Various sources disagree on Crowley's age, but he probably was more than 50 years old when he joined Co. K, 3rd Georgia Militia, late in 1864. He died from pneumonia in Augusta, Georgia, on January 12, 1865, and was buried there. His wife Elizabeth was left with 11 children at home.

JAMES ISLAND
FEB 13TH 1865

Dear Sallie

I have taken my seat to write you a few lines to let you hear from me, if there is any chance for the mail to get to you. I dont think it is worth while for me to write, but it may find a way out some how. The Yankey have got the railroad so our communication is cut off. We are still on James Island yet, but I can not tell how long we will stay here. there has been a good many troops sent from the island and [it] has been reported we would leave it, but not yet. I have been uneasy for fear we would have to leave some of our meat that we got from home, but I think we could come very near carrying all of it with us now. The Yanks landed troop down on our right last thursday night or friday morning and drove in our pickets. [They] took possession of our lines, but fell back that night to their gunboat. They came out [on] about forty barges to Fort Johnson with about seven hundred men. Our batteries fired a few shots at them and they soon went back. I will close for this time. This leaves Cousin J and I well. I would write more if I thought you would get it.

Your affectionate brother James

James Jewell's letters ended here,
but his story was not finished.

James Jewel's fate and that of the Echols Artillery is chronicled in a book published in 1965 by the Oglethorpe County, Georgia, Chapter of the United Daughters of the Confederacy. *This They Remembered* was published as part of the commemoration of the centennial of the War Between the States. It was compiled by Miss Gussie Reese from articles printed in early editions of the *Oglethorpe Echo,* published weekly in Lexington. From the 1870s through the early 1900s, local Confederate veterans supplied articles to the paper recounting their experiences during the war and giving accounts of later reunions. C.M. Witcher and M.B. Amason provided a short history of the Echols Artillery in the August 7, 1885, issue.

According to Witcher and Amason, on the night of February 17, 1865, all the Confederate forces around Charleston were evacuated. The Echols Artillery and other units under the command of General William J. Hardee marched northward all night and camped at Monck's Corner, South Carolina, the next evening. From there they followed the track of the Northeastern railroad through Kingstree to Cheraw, where they rested for 3 or 4 days. They were joined by other detachments and attempted to make a stand against Sherman's army but were forced to retreat across the Pee Dee River. After a short battle, the Confederates burned the bridge and retreated across the border into North Carolina. Their march took them through Rockingham to Fayetteville. There the weary Southerners met the enemy again as they crossed the Cape Fear River. Hardee's men exercised their acquired expertise in bridge burning and retreated toward Raleigh. General Hardee made a stand on March 16, 1865, near the little village of Averasboro. There, just 25 days before Lee's surrender at Appomattox, James Jewel disappeared.

How he met his end is unknown. Witcher and Amason reported that in the battle at Averasboro "Nathan M. Eberhart was killed and I.H. Webb and J.H. Tiller, Jr. wounded, and James Jewel missing and never afterwards heard from." Witcher and Amason further reported that about this same time that "a very fatal disease something like brain fever" broke out among the troops. Jewel's longtime friend G.W. Martin died of this malady.

When pensions became available for widows of Confederate soldiers, the affidavit that Eliza filed with her application in 1891 stated that James "was sent from near Smithfield North Carolina to the hospital at Smithfield N.C. and that he has never been seen or heard from since that time." Did he have a relapse of malaria, brought on by exhaustion and malnutrition? Did he contract the "brain fever" or some other disease? It seems certain that the answer will never be known.

CHAPTER IX

Letters from Home

"I hope these lines may find you well. Good bye my dear brother"

My Dear Brother

I received your dear letter this evening and was so glad to hear from you. You spoke of having snow. We have had real white, hard snow. I will commence at last Sunday and give you a short sketch of the events of this week.

Eliza and Sue[1] came to Antioch Saturday and then here. John Christopher and Cousin Becky[2] and Bud[3] came also. Sunday it rained in the morning but stopped [in] time enough for us to go to Antioch. the sun shown out and we thought we would have a good day, so off we went to church and found quite a large congregation, and in a few moments it was raining hard. Brother Marshall, Sis Jane and the children, Mrs Pass and Lou[4] came down on the [railroad] cars. I was sorry it was such a disagreeable day. Williams funeral[5] was preached. Mr. Mell[6] preached more of a funeral sermon than he generally does. his text was the 28th verse, 14th Chap. of Johns gospel.

Monday was a clear, beautiful day, first rate weather for work. I wove as fast as I could all day and was out getting supper when Aunt Sallie, Cousin Lizzie, and Babe[7] came. Tuesday it blew up cold weather. Aunt Sallie and Babe went home, and Cousin Lizzie staid with us. Wednesday we went over to Brothers, it was cloudy and cold. that night it commenced sleeting and by morning the ground was covered with white, round snow. Thursday we had to stay in the house, it was so slick we could not walk well. and you can just imagine how we spent our time sitting around the fire pitying the poor soldiers, slipping out once and awhile to get some ice to eat. The children had quite a jubilee over the snow.

Mary[8] has been quite sick since christmas, that abscess has stopped running and her body has broken out in red rough spots. what it is, time alone can prove. It has been reported all over the county that she had the consumption and was not expected to live. but she is not that bad off yet. She looks better now and does not cough. We were all uneasy about her because she had such a cough and that rising is thought to have come from her lungs. She has been very low spirited. I think if she will only take care of herself during the cold weather she will get over it, at least I am in hopes so. I have heard of 4 or 5 deaths this week and the last week, old Mrs Martin,[9] Mrs. Marable,[10] Mrs. Gibson,[11] and Alvin Robinson. Malcolm Landrum[12] lost a valuable negro woman last night with the Pneumonia. old Mr Christopher[13] is very sick. he had a breaking out on one of his legs and it has inflamed and spread. the Doctor says mortification has taken place. He was almost speechless the last account I had from him.

Bud Jimmie, I had the real genuine mumps. I tell [you] it made me sick. I was confined to the house longer than I have been for a long time, that was a week. I had no idea how bad the mumps was. I am afraid the smallpox will be scattered [around here]. that is one disease I hope will pass by. Jim Drakes[14] family has it and he was in Lexington last week. the men there asked him to go back home and he went back. I don't think he has any business travelling about. The people are being vaccinated all around. I think it must be the real vaccine matter, for I have heard of none that tried it but what it has made them sick.

I almost forgot to tell you Uncle Sill[15] came up last Friday week and took his old hack away. he bought a horse from Jim Drake and give the enormous price of $60 for him. he is a poor looking chance. Uncle John[16] paid part of the money for him and I reckon he sold his overcoat for I do not know what he has done with it. he will not tell when we ask him where it is. He was off bright and early Saturday morning for Mr. Sanders.[17] after bidding us farewell and presenting May with his Bible he jumped in his carriage and was off. In a few moments he came back to get some one to help him along.

his wheels had locked and he could not get them to run. Sam[18] got them loose for him and the last I heard he was going on. Liza[19] met him as she was coming to Antioch. She took a hearty laugh. she says she never expected to see him ride in it again. He talked of going to Monroe [Georgia] to teach school but I expect he will be back before long.

I have not seen or heard from Cousin John this week. I do not know when he expects to start. Liza brought some shirts and drawers and we will send them by him when he goes. I had not heard anything about Mrs. Camps marrying before. I hardly ever see or hear from any of them nowadays. The weather is moderating a little, [but] the snow has not melted any hardly, it will take a day or two of warm weather to melt it off. Pa's hogs are dying but they do not die as fast as they did when they were sick before. he has not lost any big hogs yet, it is the pigs. some of his large ones are sick, I hope it is not the cholera. nobody has taken the mumps from one yet.

Sunday. The snow is still on the ground. Bud Jimmie, it had been such a long lonesome day. Cousin Lizzie is with us yet. Brother came over to see us this morning. him and pa went up to Mr. Martins this evening. Franks remains were brought home and they were going to bury him.[20] there was so much ice and water on the ground we were afraid to go. Ed came by this morning and told us.

Bud & Mat[21] have both had the mumps. Mat was right sick. Jerry[22] came up this week to get a plow horse. they were all well down there. I hope Liza will get through with her work and come and stay with us some. it seems like she has almost got to be a stranger. Mattie is lively as a cricket and always ready to laugh. she got so many kisses Saturday at Antioch her face was chapped all round. she is quite a noisy little lady, she got up almost as high as Mr. Mell singing and playing Sunday. I am in hopes the snow will soon melt off so I can get out and see what is going on. I have been looking for Cousin John all day but he has not come yet. he promised to let us know when he was going away and he expected to go tomorrow. I reckon he certainly has given out the idea of going then. I have not received a letter from Mark[23] since christmas. Lizzie[24] heard from Berry a few days ago, he is well. they were camped in a good place. Berry sent Alf Brooks,[25] Mid Davis'[26] substitute, back. he says he has no use for him. Mid had been trying some other way to get out. he is justice of the peace now.

Aunt Lucy Lumpkin[27] had a letter from Mrs Varner. Matt Varner is dead.[28] I did not learn when he died, but it was some time very lately. four of that family have died since they left here. Well bud Jimmie I have written enough without it was something more interesting to you. it is getting late. Ma, May, and Mary are asleep. Cousin Lizzie is near about it.

I hope you will have the chance to come and see us before long. I am glad to hear that you fare so well. I wish I could get some of that good syrup that you have down the country. I forgot to tell you I had a potatoe pudding for dinner sweetend with home made syrup. it was good. I liked to have eat too much. I will try and send this by tomorrow mail if I can. I dont expect you can read this for I have written it in a hurry and my pens are all bad. do you have any good ones down about Quincy? If you have I wish you would send some up this way. I must stop writing now. Goodby, all send their love.

I remain Your Affectionate Sister Sallie.

1   Sue was James Jewel's sister-in-law Susan E. Colclough, Eliza's younger sister.

2   Cousin Becky may have been Mary R. Campbell, John A. Christopher's wife, whom he married September 9, 1856.

3   Sallie was referring to her brother William. She also sometimes used the nickname Bud for her brother-in-law Marshall Edwards and possibly her brother-in-law Benajah Crowley.

4   Mrs. Pass may have been Nancy Pass, listed in the 1860 Georgia census as the 51-year-old wife of M.J. Pass, a 66-year-old farmer in the Buck Branch District of Clarke County, and neighbor of Marshall and Jane Edwards. M.J. and Nancy were the parents of Matthew J.H. Pass (cited elsewhere). Lou was her daughter Ludie Pass.

5   William is unidentified.

6   Mr. Mell was Reverend Patrick Hues Mell (already cited).

7   Aunt Sallie was Sarah Jewel Parris, sister to James Jewel, Sr. Cousin Lizzie was her daughter Elizabeth. Babe is unidentified but may have been Sarah's daughter Adeline. Sarah Jewel married Nathan H. Parris on December 11, 1819. In the 1860 Georgia census,

the family name was spelled Parrish, and Sarah was living with her son Henry C. Parrish, a 34-year-old farmer in the Falling Creek District of Oglethorpe County. Also in the household were Henry's wife Mary, their two children, and Sarah's daughters, Elizabeth, age 29, and Adeline, age 21.

8   Mary was Sallie's older sister, Mary Jewel.

9   This was Sarah Martin, listed in the 1860 Georgia census as 87 years old and in the household of John and Nancy L. Martin in the Wolfskin District of Oglethorpe County. Her tombstone in the Martin family cemetery gives her birth date as August 21, 1770, and her death as February 1, 1863. The inscription further states that she was the wife of Gibson Martin, born September 21, 1770, and died May 2, 1809.

10   This probably was Frances Marable, listed in the 1860 Georgia census as a 76-year-old farmer in the Wolfskin District of Oglethorpe County. She was the only resident in the household and was further identified as having been born in Virginia.

11   Mrs. Gibson is unidentified.

12   Malcom M. Landrum was listed in the 1860 Georgia census as a 26-year-old farmer in the Wolfskin District of Oglethorpe County.

13   This probably was Richard Christopher, listed in the 1860 Georgia census as a 67-year-old farmer in the Wolfskin District of Oglethorpe County. He was the father of David and John A. Christopher (cited elsewhere).

14   This probably was James V. Drake, listed in the 1860 Georgia census as a 49-year-old farmer in the Woodstock District of Oglethorpe County.

15   Uncle Sill was Sylvanus Bell, brother of Rebecca Bell Jewel, Sallie's mother.

16   Uncle John was John A. Bell, another brother of Sallie's mother. He is listed in the 1860 Georgia census as a 40-year-old farmer in the Falling Creek District of Oglethorpe County. Others in the household were Mary, 38, three daughters, ages 5, 7, and 12, and Sarah Humphries, 78.

17   This probably was Jonathan Sanders, listed in the 1860 Georgia census as a 65-year-old clerk in Lexington, Georgia.

18   Sam probably was a Jewel slave.

19   Sallie sometimes referred to James' wife Eliza as Liza.

20   John Franklin Martin died August 22, 1862 (already cited). Apparently his family removed his body from the Atlanta area and had him re-interred in the family cemetery in Oglethorpe County.

21   Bud and Mat probably were Sallie's brother William and his wife Martha.

22   Jerry probably was a slave of William Jewel.

23   Mark was Sallie's cousin, Marcus de Lafayette Jewel, brother to Cousin John (already cited).

24   Lizzie was Berry Bowling's wife Elizabeth (already cited).

25 Alfred Brooks was listed in the 1860 Georgia census as a 30-year-old resident in the household of the William H. Puryear family, farmers in the Georgia Factory District of Clarke County, Georgia.

26 Middleton Pope Davis enlisted in the Oglethorpe Rifles as a 1st Sergeant May 15, 1861, but was recorded as later discharged by furnishing a substitute. Davis is listed in the 1860 Georgia census as a 28-year-old farmer in the Bowling Green District of Oglethorpe County. Davis served as sheriff of Clarke County during the 1870s.

27 Lucy Lumpkin has already been cited. Sallie's reference to her as "Aunt" may have been a pet name.

28 Mrs. Varner and Matt Varner are unidentified.

FEB. 24TH, 1863

My Dear Brother,

I received your letter Saturday evening dated the 17th, and I thought I would write to you but I have nothing of interest to communicate. We are all well except the mumps. Sis May took [the mumps] Friday [a] week ago and she has not been able to be up any at all hardly. she has eat more today and sit up longer than she has for a week. I think she will be well before long. Mat Crowley and John[1] have had them and are getting well. Marys health is better than it was some weeks ago, but that breaking out is still on her body. I have not heard from Bro. Marshall since they were at Antioch.

The weather had been bad all the week, it rained nearly every day. Saturday it was stormy, the wind blew very hard and it thundered heavy. It was cloudy all day yesterday, it blew up cold last night and today it is cloudy again and the wind from the east. I would not be surprised if it snows again.

I do not blame you for being sorry to leave there. I expect Cousin John will be sorry he missed the party though he was doing so well at home and that is dearer than all other places. I have not heard from Eliza since the 3rd Sunday. they were well down there and had not taken the smallpox, but I do not know how they are now. We have heard from that neighborhood several times and have heard that Bryants children[2] were both dead, but the last reliable account I had, they were getting well. Miss Camp was not married when it was reported. it was the talk over the whole neighborhood. I have not heard from her since the 3rd Sunday.

"Well" Bud Jimmie, the conscripts were ordered to cook 3 day rations and be in Lexington 3 days, but I do not know what they are going to do - the halt and blind, all classes. I reckon there will be many a one that is diseased.

John Powers[3] came in here about a month ago and he was in Athens last week and Mid Davis said something to him about being a deserter when he plunged a knife in him, but I do not know how badly he was hurt and they have "posted him off to the wars." He was riding a fine horse and pretended he belonged to a cavelry company but it was proved that he belonged to an Infantry. It is believed that the horse was stolen.

I commenced writing this last night and I could not see the lines as you might suppose from the looks of it. It is cloudy again this morning. it has not snowed any yet, but it is cold enough. Ben Gilham is at home trying to get up recruits but I dont think he will get many, but there is some around us here that I think had just as well go as not. some that are entirely out of business and have nothing to do but to make money off of poor old men that are at home minding to their own business and harming no one. Ben says his company is enjoying better health than they have been before. I received a letter from Cousin Mattie[4] the other day. the boys are well and in fine spirits. I suppose they are daily expecting an attack on Charleston and Savannah both. I hope the war will end before long. I hope the prospect will still grow brighter. do you reckon there will be any chance to get furloughs any more? I was dreaming the other night that you came home and was fixing to have a long chat when I found it was only a dream. do you ever see the Yankees or hear of them about where you are? If you can send any little curiosities in a letter you must do so. I know you will think I might have written more but I have no news. You must write a long letter. You see so many new things to write about, and I hope I shall have more to write next time. We have been looking for Liza to come up. she promised to come and stay a week. all send their love to you. all of our friends are well as far as I know.

Brother will be here directly to shoot a beef for Pa, and I must have my letter ready to send to the office. I remain Your Affectionate Sister Sallie

excuse the scribble

1   Mat and John were Martha and John Crowley, children of Sallie's sister Elizabeth.

2   The Bryant children are unidentified.

3   John Powers is unidentified.

4   Cousin Mattie is unidentified.

MARCH 2ND 1863

Dear Brother Jimmie –

I received your letter yesterday at Antioch and was very glad to hear from you. You said you had received only two letters. I have written several to you since you left Atlanta. I cannot tell why they never reached you. Liza too has written several. We have had rainy weather for several days almost every day for two weeks it had been raining. the roads are so muddy that it is difficult to travel. We went to church yesterday. there was only a few people out. Mr Mell gave us another bate of hard corn but not quite so hard as the last. I think his sermon suited the times very well, although it did not suit everybodys taste. His text was the 8th chapter, 36 verse of John. If the son makes you free you shall be free indeed. it was the same text that Brother White[1] hammered at so long when he preached. He spoke of natural freedom, spritual, and religeous freedom. it was partly a war sermon. Mr Threldkeld[2] lead in prayer. I think he is the strickest old gentleman I ever saw.

well Bud Jimmie, the conscripts met in Lexington last week but I do not know what they done. I have not heard who they are going to send off. the militia officers were all ordered to go to Savannah. Bud came up and staid with us Friday night and expected to leave tomorrow morning but the order was countermanded and we do not know when he will start. Maggie and Jimmie[3] went down there yesterday evening. May went to stay with Mat. Mr Colcloughs family are well. I hope the weather will be good so Liza can come to see us. if she docs not come I am going to start down that way if I can get off Saturday. Mary and I made arrangements to go there the 4th Sunday but it rained and we were disappointed.

I have not heard from Brother Marshall since I wrote to you. Brothers family are not well. Mary, Maggie, and Will[4] have the mumps. Sis Mary has just got able to go to work. She was very sick and Mat was sick with them nearly two weeks. I think it will go through before it is done with. it is all over the county. I thought nearly all of this neighborhood was through with it, but it is in Columbus Landrums[5] school at the Shanty and Cousin Henry Paris [Parris] and Mr. Gilhams.[6] Ben [Gilham] was at church. I do not know how many recruits he had made up. I dont think he could get many.

Davy Patrick[7] is at Mrs Chappels[8] so I heard, but I have not seen them. he was at Uncle Billies last week. I reckon he dont know we are his kinfolks. he is always so shy. Jimmie Crowley started to school at Mordecai Edward's to Mr Sly.[9] how do you come on sewing? I understood Cousin John received a nice needle case. did you get any needles? I want you to write what Cousin John got in his box at Griffin. I understood he had nearly all of Griffin out to welcome him.

Malcom Landrum is very sick. he was taken last Friday. they found him lying on the floor insensible of anything and [he] has not known anything hardly since. Brother says he was taken different from what he ever was before.

I was surprised to hear that Jim Barrow had not spoken to you. I always thought he was friendly and was so much like his grandpa he wouldn't think about being so much above speaking to his old acquaintances. We have not heard anything new from Savannah and Charleston. there was a great deal of fuss about men being ordered there last week and some people were prophesying for your company to be sent there and almost had you there anyhow but I did not think it was so. Pa has cut your shoestrings and I will put them in. I must conclude by saying we are all enjoying good health and hope these lines may find you enjoying the same blessing. All send their love to you. You must write as often as you can and I will do the same.

I remain Your Affectionate Sister

Sallie

1   Brother White is unidentified.

2   Mr. Threlkeld probably was Thomas Threlkeld, the Baptist preacher from Griffin mentioned in an earlier letter from James Jewel.

3   Maggie and Jimmie were Margaret and James Crowley, children of Benajah and Elizabeth.

4   Mary, Maggie, and Will were the children of Benajah and Elizabeth Crowley.

5   This was probably C.J. Landrum, listed in the 1860 Georgia census as a 33-year-old farmer in the Bowling Green District of Oglethorpe County. Others in the household were Elizabeth, 26, Parthenia, 9, and Leonidus, 7.

6   Mr. Gilham probably was William Gilham, the father of Benjamin F. and Thomas D. Gilham (cited elsewhere). William Gilham, 52, and Isabella Gilham, 55, were listed in the 1860 Georgia census as farmers in the Bowling Green District of Oglethorpe County. Also in the household at that time were Thomas Gilham, 28, and Mary Gilham, 20.

7   David A. Patrick is listed in the 1860 Alabama census as a 24-year-old living with the family of Reuben H. McCoy, ambrotypist [photographer], in the Ridge Grove District of Chambers County. David Patrick was the brother to Mandy Patrick and Mary Ann Patrick Seals (cited elsewhere).

8   This probably was Margaret Chappell, identified in the 1860 Georgia census as a 67-year-old resident of the Falling Creek District of Oglethorpe County. Others in her household included John M. Gilham, 29, and Matilda [Campbell] Gilham, 26.

9   Mordecai Edwards was identified in the 1860 Georgia census as a 51-year-old farmer of the Wolfskin District of Oglethorpe County. Others in the household were Martha J., 34, and 8 children from 3 months to 13 years old. Mr. Sly undoubtedly was a teacher at Rose Hill Academy, established by Mordecai Edwards to provide schooling for his children and others in the neighborhood.

MARCH 18TH 1863

My Dear Brother,

I received your letter of the 9th last Friday evening. We have beautiful weather for planting, clear and warm. Pa commenced planting corn yesterday. some in the neighborhood have nearly finished. there is such a cry raised for provisions I think the farmers ought to plant everything that will do to eat. The soldiers from every quarter are writing for the folks out here to keep their horses fat for they expect to have to eat them before a great while. It is really distressing to read the letters from the soldiers in Virginia and I suppose it is the same way in other places where there has been an army stationed.

Uncle Billie received a letter from Cousin Mark Saturday evening. no such letter has ever been written by him before. he says he was marched almost to death with nothing to eat but crackers and a poor supply of them. I heard somebody say that they thought a very poor cow in Jackson County was carried off to the army. there was a many one on the [railroad] cars last week and added to all this the extortioners [charge] such prices as is now put on everything. Irish potatoes is selling at $10 a bushel and every thing else in proportion. what is to become of the soldiers families that are left behind. it is indeed distressing times.

The militia officers have not been called out any more, but are expecting orders. Col Nichols went down and got the quarter masters place. he is at home now trying to buy provisions for the government. he is offering $18 a gallon for brandy. I do not know what had become of Nat Hunter[1] but he got some office I reckon.

Well Bud Jimmie, our gardens are looking very well and I am in hope we will have good seasons. Ma planted corn Friday in your garden and we have peas, onions, irish potatoes, all in there. we had some potatoes left and wanted to send them to Eliza if we had any chance. they did not have [any] and could not give the price of

$10 for them. I have not heard from there since she was up here.
I heard from Brother Marshals folks last week. they were not well.
Sis Jane and Brother was both sick. I have heard of several deaths
amongst the negroes lately of pneumonia and measles. Fielding
Dillard[2] lost two negroes friday. one of them, the likeliest he had,
with the measles. he was so hard headed they could not control
him and he exposed himself too much. I do not hear any thing of
smallpox now and I hope we will not hear anything more of it. I
have no news to write, only we have a great deal of work to do. Ma
is busy making soap, Sis May is weaving, and I have been spinning.
I have the old piano in splendid tune. factory thread is selling $4
1/2 a bunch, but you can never get any of it for when you go after
it they will not let you have it for anything but provisions. carry that
and they want money. Take cash and then they will say they cannot
let you have any for they have got to pay their debts. and so it is you
have to go back home and take to the cards and wheel. but what
is the worse of all, you have to give $10 for a [spinning] wheel and
$18 or $20 for a loom, and $18 for a pair of [cotton] cards without
any backs, and by that time you can spend a pocket full of money.

Brothers family is well. Sis Lizzie has got over the mumps.
Malcom Landrum is still sick. he has spasms every day almost. Dr
Tom Landrum is tending to him. I reckon he will [do] something,
he goes up there every day.

I was glad that you got your shoestrings. I was afraid some body
would open it before it got to you. I was in hopes you could remain
at Quincy and not have to go to Alum bluff. I know you all would
be much better satisfied there than in that "out of the way place."
If you can only have good health and get enough to eat, it will be
more than many a poor soldier has. Jabez Brittain was to start to
Virginia Monday but I have not heard whether he has gone or not.
I reckon it went hard with him to have to give up his office. I went
to Antioch Sunday. there was a good many people out. Uncle
Billie, Joe and John's famlies were well. Bud Jimmie, if I could see
you I could tell you a heap that I can't write. I am in hopes you will
get letters oftener than you did at first. I have written as often as I
could and will write as often as I can. I am nearly out of paper and
will have to get some as soon as I have the chance. it was $2 a quire
several weeks ago. I do not know what it is now.

All join me in love to you and Cousin John. Write soon.

I remain Your Affectionate Sister Sallie

1   Nat Hunter was Nathaniel Harrison Hunter, who joined the Oglethorpe Rifles as 2nd Lieutenant on May 15, 1861, and resigned in September of that year.

2   Fielding Dillard is listed in the 1860 Georgia census as a 44-year-old farmer in the Wolfskin District of Oglethorpe County. Others in the household were America, 35, and 10 children. At the time of the 1860 Georgia slave census, Dillard owned 33 slaves.

MARCH 29TH, 1863

My Dear Brother

I have just received your letter dated 22nd in answer to mine, though not to my last letter. I wrote one and sent [it] to Quincy a few days ago before you left there. Sis May and I went to Uncle Billies Saturday week ago and heard there [that] you had gone to Jacksonville, or at least had been ordered there, and that was all we heard until Mary received a letter which amused as well as interested us for some time. I think those men certainly are more industrious than a great many are to be so well fixed up. they beat all the soldiers I ever heard or read of.

Bud Jimmie, we have had rainy weather for a long time. yesterday it rained all day and nearly all night, and today it has been cloudy and it seems to me a long dreary day, but it was owing to my disappointment I reckon. Mary Crowley and I intended going to see Eliza and Bud, so we were out this time. we made arrangements to go on Saturday but it sleeted all the morning and was such bad weather we did not get off and it is put off until tomorrow morning and I think by that time it will rain, so it is very uncertain when we will go. but it will not be because I do not want to go. I am very anxious to see them all. we heard from Eliza at church Friday. Mary Gilham[1] saw her at the factory.[2] they were all well. sister Mat has been very sick all last week with the Pneumonia, I suppose. Last Friday was fast day, there was a meeting at Antioch. Sis Mary, Mat, and Brother went. there was no preaching, only a prayer meeting. there was quite a large congregation out.

I have not told you about our trip to Uncle Billies. it was so bad we could not go down in greene [County], so we concluded to take a trip there [to Uncle Billie's]. we found all well. they had just received letters from Cousin John, Mark, Edger, and Emily.³ I was very much interested for a while reading letters. Cousin Mark was doing well. Cousin Nannie⁴ left for Alabama Wednesday. Cousin George had fun teasing her about her staff, as Cousin John termed the old widowers. She has left Georgia with the expectation of returning next fall. Cousin Camiller's⁵ family was well. I do not know what she will do for company. Cousin Nannie was [a] great crony with her. Berry Bowling, Nat Brightwell, & Jut Norton⁶ came home Thursday. they are on furlough for 30 days. Berry had a chance to come and put out. Mark [Jewel] does not want to come without he could stay. Their company had hard times on their march to Richmond. they were marched down and [had] nothing but crackers to eat. Nat looks as well or better than he did before he left here. I would like to see him. I reckon he will have a great deal to tell. It has been 22 months since him and Jut left home.

Brother [Benajah Crowley] has been over here today. they are all well except Emma.⁷ she has the mumps again. she had them in one side. We have 3 or 4 cases of the mumps. Laura, Will, Ann, and Dollie.⁸ I was in hopes we would not have any more, but it will go through now. Pa commenced planting corn two weeks ago. he has [planted] most of the lowgrounds and the newgrounds. there has been so much rain and cool weather, vegetation is very backward. during the first two weeks of ploughing times it rained so much that we could not plough more than three or four days. he expected to get [it] all planted in this month, but cannot do it now. There is a great cry for provisions. I hope everybody will plant provisions of every kind. Wheat is selling at $13 a bushel, corn $3 1/2. I do not know what the poor people will to. salt had gone up $.50 per bushel. every thing is advancing. Ma sent butter to Augusta and got $1.20 for one can and $1.30 for the last. dried peaches $7 and $8 per bushel. The fruit is not killed, but according to the old rule there will be four frosts in May and it is not out of danger yet. Wheat looks very well for this season. The winter oats are partially killed but most of the places [have] a stand. Mr Youngs[9] property was sold at high price, a large wash pot went for $30. Beegums $8, and other things in proportion. Mr. Colclough came up there to buy a horse, but they were too high for him. I believe he came to the conclusion he had better go home and turn out a part of his crop.

I staid all night at Mrs Lumpkins[10] with Lucy Moore Thursday night and by the way, Billie Moore was married to Miss Anna Marable.[11] There is a match for you. She is just fifteen years old. I think they are well matched, dont you? She got a likely negro girl, a horse and saddle, and $1500 from her grandmothers estate and that accounts for the whole matter. you know that is a pretty little fortune for a poor boy these hard times. They did not have any wedding. there was none of their kinsfolks there but H. Bugg.[12] She bought a silk dress for the very reasonable price of $150 and Bill went to Augusta for his suit. They will live at Mrs Moores. I expect Bill will have to go to the army soon. his substitute deserted and he got a furlough for a short time.

Well Bud Jimmie, from what you write, the boys must be taking on considerably about the Quincy Ladies. I think the girls about here might just as well prepare for lives of single blessedness, for I reckon the boys wont look at them. I was very sorry to hear about Mr Kinebrew, but I was glad it was not Cousin John. tell him to beware. I was very much amused at the description of that patriotic Miss Ingram[13] that he wrote so much about. I think she was very kind. I do not blame you all for not liking to leave there when you fared so well. I wish you all could get a plenty to eat and would be glad if we had the chance of sending you a box if there is any passing, you must let us know and we will send something to you. we could send you some dried fruit, hams, butter, etc. etc.

Well Ma's gardens are doing tolerably well. cabbage, pees, onions, etc. are looking very well for the season. our irish potatoes have not come up. Aunt Lucy's is as high as my hand. The rabbits have troubled your garden, gnawed holes in the pailings. We have got a good many little chickens. I sit Liza's old goose in the pile of rails behind the hen house, but she was broken up and that is [the] end to raising geese this year. I found my turkeys nest in the back side of the orchard next to the cross fence with 13 eggs. Eliza's sow and pigs are looking very well. Pa has not lost any very lately. I am in hope we will not lose any more.

Aunt Lucy [Lumpkin] made Ma a present of the prettiest white pig you almost ever saw. fat enough for any use. we keep it in a pen by itself for fear it would take the disease from the others. I have not heard from Brother Marshall in some time. I thought some of us would have gone to see them, but have not had the chance. We have gone through a general siege of soap making and candle dipping last week. we dipped over 400. some of them for Sis Lizzie [Elizabeth Jewel Crowley]. Jimmie [Crowley] has not started to school yet. they have the measles in that neighborhood. Mordicai Edwards had several cases.

Bud Jimmie, I must come to a conclusion for I have written enough stuff to tire you with reading as this paper was a present to me I ought to make a good use of it, but I hate to pay 10 cts [postage] on a letter and not write anything. I hope I shall have the chance to go to Mr Colclough's tomorrow, for I want to see all of them and especially that sweet little Mattie. I wish you could see her. She grows so fast and I think she is a pretty good turn to lift, so that much of your dream is so. everybody says she is like me. She is a sweet little creature, it make no difference who she is like. the wind is blowing very hard from the east and I am afraid it will be raining tomorrow. good bye, [it] is bed time. I commenced writing before night and it now [is] nine oclock. You must write all the news. Good bye. I hope these lines may find you enjoying good health. all send their love to you.

I remain Your Affectionate Sister   Sallie

---

1   Mary Gilham was the wife of Thomas D. Gilham (already cited).

2   Sallie probably was referring to the factory at Scull Shoals in Greene County.

3   Cousins John and Mark Jewel are already cited. Edgar [not Edger] Emory Jewel was their older brother. Edgar is listed in the 1860 census as a 27-year-old minister in Morgan County, Georgia, along with his wife Civility C. [Lawrence], age 20, and Diamond, 3 years old. Emily was Emmialy Jewel Meiere, sister to John, Mark, and Edgar Jewel. Emily was married to Dr. William Stark Meiere (cited elsewhere) and lived in Madison, Georgia.

4   Cousin Nannie is unidentified.

5   Cousin Camella [not Camiller] was Susan Camella Jewel Smith, sister of Cousin John Jewel. She married William P. Smith on February 13, 1850. The 1860 Georgia census identifies her as the 31-year-old wife of Smith, age 36, an Oglethorpe County farmer. Her children listed were Emily, 9, Robert, 8, George, 6, Anna, 5, Mary, 3, and Glendora, 1.

6   Berry Bowling has already been identified. Nat G. Brightwell enlisted in the Oglethorpe Rifles May 28, 1861, and served until the end of the war. He is listed in the 1860 Georgia census as 38 years old and living in the household of William G. Brightwell (his brother?), 42, his wife Elizabeth, 42, and five children. Nat and William were born in Virginia and all others in the household were born in Georgia.

 A. Judson Norton joined the Oglethorpe Rifles as a Private on May 28, 1861, and served until the end of the war. Norton was listed in the 1860 Georgia census as a 21-year-old railroad hand living with his wife Anjaline, 18, and their daughter Varonia, 2 months old, in the household of Elizabeth Bell, age 40, in the Falling Creek District of Oglethorpe County. Others in the Bell home were Richard, 13, Martha, 11, and Bonaparte, 8.

7   Emma was Sallie's niece, Emma Crowley, the daughter of her older sister Elizabeth and Benajah Crowley.

8   Laura, Will, Ann, and Dollie are unidentified but may have been Jewel family slaves.

9   This may have been Henry Young, listed in the 1860 Georgia census as a 95-year- old farmer in Oglethorpe County, living near the William Jewel, I family.

10   Mrs. Lumpkin was neighbor Lucy Lumpkin, sometimes called Aunt Lucy by Sallie.

11   Billie Moore and Anna Marable are unidentified.

12   Hamilton C. Bugg is listed in the 1860 Georgia census as a 34-year-old farmer in the Wolfskin District of Oglethorpe County.

13   Miss Ingram is unidentified.

APRIL 8TH 1863

My Dear Brother

    Your letter of the 31st was received Saturday evening, the one dated [the] 26th, and I was so glad to hear from you [and] to know that you are still, through a kind providence, enjoying good health. We are all very well. I do not hear of much sickness now with the exception of colds. I believe this neighborhood is in fine health. The weather has been very cool for three or four days. it is first warm and then cool. the cool weather keeps vegetation back. the late frosts have injured the vegetables some. irish potatoes were bit to the ground, ours were not up yet.

Mary Crowley & I went to Bud's last Tuesday evening [and] staid all night. Mat was a little better when we left there. we went to see Liza Wednesday morning and left there in the evening and came to Cousin James Smith's[1] and staid until the next morning. Mr Colclough's family was tolerably well. John was at home but was [not] able to be up. I did not have long to stay down there as I was riding one of the plow horses. I was sorry I could not stay longer there. Eliza was busy fixing her dresses to put in. she promised me that she would come and stay a week with us as soon as she could get her cloth out. Mattie was as pert as a cricket (and sweet as sugar).

Sis Mary and I went over to see Berry [Bowling] last night. I don't think he is so low spirited as he was when here before. he went to Uncle Billies today. He expects to go back in a week or two. Pa has finished planting corn. I do not think that which was up was injured much by frost. some of the fruit is killed, but I am in hopes we will have plenty left. Sis Mary and Mec. Edwards[2] are going up to Bro Marshalls next Friday on the [railroad] cars. She will stay a week. I have not heard from there in a long time. Brothers family is well or they are not all well. Maggie and Jewel[3] have the mumps. we have no case at all now.

I went to church Saturday and, by the way, we had a beautiful day, the first pretty day for preaching since last fall. Mr Mell came home with us and of course we had a "very pleasant time." I cannot tell you where his text was [from]. he took several verses in different chapters and books. May joined the church, but could not be baptized Sunday, so it was postponed until the 3rd Sunday. We had a good day again Sunday and a large congregation out. Mr Mells text was the 40th vse, 5th chap of Saint John, "and Ye will not come to me that Ye might have life." It was a good sermon and such a one as we need to revive us up. he pointed out the deep responsibilities resting on the professors of religion and plead as ernest for the unconverted to come to Jesus as you ever heard anybody. it seemed like it was enough to move the hardest heart that ever was. after he preached an hour and a half, he gave an invitation to all who wanted him to pray for them to give him their hands and return to their seats. Charlie Davis,[4] Henrietta Asbury,[5] Lizzie Hunter,[6] Sallie Hunter,[7] Shuge Armstead,[8] and Mrs Dr Bell[9] came up, also two negroes.

He said at the judgement day his skirt will be clean for he felt determined that day that he would do everything he could by persuation and argument. his congregation cannot say that he did not faithfully serve and exhort them to flee from the wrath to come. I hope the seed sown will bring forth an abundant harvest. They took up a collection Saturday for the soldiers to buy paper, tracts, etc., and I think they made something over $150, but I do not know exactly how much. I am glad to hear that your company have organized a regular prayer meeting and hope that much good may be done. for if there ever was a time when people ought to live right, I think it is now.

Well Bud Jimmie, I have written all I can this time. I hope we will have the chance to see you before long. write soon. all send their love to you and cousin John. tell him not to die with the blues, but be cheerful and look for a better time in the future. maybe he will get back to Quincy before long to see that Miss "what is her name?" I hope to hear from you soon and I will try to write longer letters next time. I was very much interested in your last letter. I love to read long letters. I remain Your true and Affectionate Sister Sallie

1   James Edwin Smith married Sallie's cousin Martha Jane Campbell in 1838 when she was 12 years old. Martha Jane was the daughter of William Campbell and Elizabeth Jewel Campbell, sister to James Jewel, Sr. The 1860 Georgia census lists the Smiths as residents of the Falling Creek District of Oglethorpe County. Members of the household were James E., 45, Jane, 37, William, 13, Emma, 12, Edwin, 8, Mary, 8, and Sarah, 3.

2   Mec was Harriett America Edwards, listed in the 1860 Georgia census as the 21-year-old daughter of Lemuel and Mary Edwards, farmers in the Wolfskin District of Oglethorpe County.

3   Maggie and Jewel were children of Sallie's sister Elizabeth Crowley and her husband Benajah.

4   Charles A. Davis is listed in the 1860 Georgia census as a 40-year-old merchant in Greensboro.

5   Henrietta Asbury was listed in the 1860 Georgia census as the 15-year-old daughter of Susan Asbury, 42, in the Goose Pond District of Oglethorpe County.

6   This may have been Elizabeth Hunter, listed in the 1860 Georgia census as the 15-year-old daughter of Nathan and Anna Hunter (Nathan already cited).

7   Sallie Hunter is unidentified.

8   This probably was the abbreviation for "Sugar" and may have been the nickname of one of the six children of Jesse M. and Martha Armstead, listed in the 1860 Georgia census as residents of the Bowling Green District of Oglethorpe County.

9   Dr. A.A. Bell, 37, and Ida Bell, 18, were listed in the 1860 Georgia census as residents of Falling Creek District of Oglethorpe County.

APRIL 23RD 1863

Dear Brother

I have taken my pen to write you a few lines in answer to yours of the 16th, but my pen writes so badly I do not know whether I will be able to write much. We are all tolerably well with the exception of colds. The weather changes so much, first warm and then cool. The wind has been blowing cool all day. it rained a little last night, enough to wet the ground. Pa has been replanting corn today. some places it has come up good and others not. the wheat looks very well so far. He planted sugar cane last week and potatoes. Ma has a good many little chickens. Our gardens look very well. we planted irish potatoes on the upper side of your garden next to the gate. they are growing finely. we have set out one square in cabbage plants. Eliza's flowers are in bloom and they look prettier than mine. everything grows better down there than it does up here. I went down there and staid all day to sun the beds and air the house. I was very busy sewing, not thinking about seeing anyone, when somebody says, you are so busy you cant see me I suppose, and I turned around and there was Josephine Davis[1] and before I could get up, she had drawn up a chair and taken a seat. I had been quite lonely, but had a lively time the remainder of the evening.

Maggie went down to Uncle Billies yesterday morning to see about fixing up a box. they have concluded, I believe, to put the victuals in a bag and sew it up. we had the box ready to send, but Uncle Billie thought it would be better to send it in a bag. I do not know how he will fix it. We tried to make some light bread, but could not get it to rise. I reckon we are too anxious. we thought at first we would send some butter, but can't send it in the bag.

I have not heard from Eliza since she was up here until you wrote. Mat was getting better the last account I had. The militia officiers are to be conscripted. I reckon Bud [William Jewel, II] will have to go again. he had several pairs of shoes to make. I do not know why he has not written to you, but I expect he has had a bad chance to write since Mat has been sick. he had not been here but once since he came from Augusta. He came up last Saturday morning and staid until evening. He bought his cowhide up to put in the tanning trough with Pa's. Brother [Benajah Crowley] came over yesterday. his folks are not all well. several of then are complaining. Jewel was quite sick. Malcom Landrum lost a fine negroe boy night before last with Pneumonia. Cousin Sue Moody[2] died last Sunday with the same. She was buried in an old field next to the McWhorter grave yard. they took up her two children and put them all three in one grave. the children were buried down in green Co. Mr Haynes[3] died Monday. he has been sick a long time and got a piece of skin knocked off his hand and he had the eresipelas. it spread over his arm and killed him. Maggie went to the burying Wednesday from Uncle Billies. Mr Mell preached his funeral at Bairds Church[4] at 11 oclock. one of his brothers, Henry Haynes was there. I do not know what will become of the children. I think there is six of them.

Sis Jane came down Friday and went back Monday. Bro Marshall [Edwards] came down on the train and went back Sunday. me and Liza made arrangements to go up there and I could [go] almost any time now if she was ready, but I do not know when I will have the chance to see her. She told me she wanted to come up next first Sunday. write to her and tell her to come and stay a week or two with us. I expect you will have the chance to write before I see her. We all have to stay at home now while they are plowing. Pa has to have Alice all the time, he cannot hold out to walk.

I heard from Mark [Jewel] the other day. he has had a bad spell of sorethroat again. he was at Petersburg. they are on the road to Suffolk expecting a fight. Berry [Bowling] and his crowd left last Monday. I reckon they will be there in time for the battle when it comes off.

I think you are getting on finely with your hats. I wish I had the chance to help you plat some of that nice palmetto. I will send you a piece of wax by Dr Jarrell. we have put in some biscuit, ham, peaches, & we intended sending other things, but could not put them in a bag. I think that Quarter Master had a poor excuse for not giving out rations. it is a pity that such folks as he is should have any office. they had better be in the army.

Well Bud Jimmie, I have scribbled over this page and I expect you will have to put on your spectacles to read it. it is a pity to spoil this paper, but I had a chance to send it. I have used up my pens, so I can hardly write any at all. You must write soon. All send their love to you and Cousin John.

I remain Your Affectionate Sister

Sallie.

1   Josephine Davis was a younger sister of Howell Cobb Davis (already cited). Greene County marriage records show that on December 13, 1863, Josephine married James Shaw of Greene County, Georgia.

2   Sue Moody and her children are buried in a small, fence-enclosed family cemetery with 10 marked graves a few miles south of Stephens, Georgia, in Oglethorpe County. Sue Moody's maiden name was Bell. In the Georgia Census of 1850 she was identified as 17-year-old Susan Moody, along with her husband "Waldama" Moody, living with him in the household of his parents, John W. and Elizabeth Moody. In the 1860 Georgia census she was listed as Elizabeth S. Moody, age 27, and her husband's name was spelled "Waldimere." He was identified as a 34-year-old physician. On his tombstone, Dr. Moody's name is spelled "Waldemar" and the inscription states that he was born July 7, 1826, and died October 26, 1901.

At the time of the 1860 census, the Moodys had three children: Anna E., 7, John W., 4, and Thomas S[ylvanus], 3. The Moodys share a large common tombstone with smaller individual markers alongside. On the tombstone, Sue's name is spelled "susia" and her death date is erroneously given as April 19, 1862 instead of 1863. The children buried with her are identified as Frances B[ell] Moody, born July 29, 1859, died December 20, 1859; and Thomas S[ylvanus] Moody, born October 8, 1857, died 1861.

3   Mr. Haynes and his brother Henry Haynes are unidentified.

4   Bairds Church was the Baptist Church founded June 24, 1802, at Bairdstown, a small community on the Greene/Oglethorpe county line.

MAY 4TH 1863

My Dear Brother.

I have taken my pen to write to you in answer to yours which was received a few days ago. We are all very well. last night was a stormy night. we had a very hard rain. it seemed like it would wash away every thing almost. We had very hard rains two days in succession last week accompanied with hail, however the hail did not do much damage here, but I expect it did in other places. the cloud passed on below and was much heavier than it was here. the ground has been so wet that we could not have much plowing done.

Pa has taken the negroes off to the irish potatoe patch to work this morning. I went to church Saturday. there was only a few persons out. Mr Mell came home with us, took dinner, and then went to Brothers. he had just been to the Convention and had a great many interesting little anecdotes to tell. I rode with him to church Sunday. we had a pleasant ride. He told me what a laborous work he had to do these days. he preaches twice in the month at Antioch, twice at Bairds [Bairdstown], and goes home on the [railroad] cars and is there next with buggy and horse and taken on to the baptist church in Athens every Sunday evening to preach and added to all that, he gives a lecture every Wednesday evening at the [University of Georgia] chapel, so he does not have one bit of time to rest. he is suffering now from a severe cold. he says he does not mind it when he is well, but it goes hard with him now. Mr Jennings[1] has left Athens entirely. They have been trying to get Mr Mell to leave his churches down here and go up there and have offered him $2000 to preach for them, but he has no notion of leaving us yet. He preached a good sermon yesterday. his text was the 55 chap. 1st ver. Isasiah. Lo, everyone that thirsteth, come ye to the waters, and he that hath no money; come ye. buy, and eat; Ye come, buy wine and milk without money and without price.

Brother Marshall come down. Miss Lou & Hat[?] Bulloch[2] and about a dozen other girls came down to Antioch yesterday. Lou and

Hat[?] came with Bro. they did not know the others were coming. I have heard of a great many deaths lately. Mr Christopher died Friday night. Old Mrs Briscoe[3] died too last week, also Joe Reynolds wife.[4]

I suppose you have heard of Becky Colcloughs[5] death. I do not know when I have heard of anything that was as great a shock as that was. it was just two weeks Friday since she left here. she had a very bad cold and looked badly when here, but we never heard anything from there until Tuesday after she was buried. Martha Moore[6] wrote us a note that she was dead and I was loth to believe it, but she sent us word the next day it was certain so I have been wanting to go down there but have not had the chance to do so. Bud was at Antioch Saturday. he told us that she died Sunday evening at two oclock. I did not have the chance to talk with him about it. I am in hope Liza will come up this week and we can hear the particulars. Sue had been sick but was getting better. one trouble after another comes upon them, but there is one consolation to them. the Lord knows what is best and has promised never to leave nor forsake those who trust in him, though I know it is hard for them to think it is for the best, but I have no doubt at all but what she was prepared for death and if that is the case we know our loss is her gain. She is free from the trials of this life.

There has been more sickness for a month or two back than had been in a long time before. most of them have the Pneumonia and are sick only a short time. The news come yesterday that our folks were fighting in three places on the Rhappahannock. the yanks I suppose are having another [move] on to Richmond. I hope they will meet with the same fate they have heretofore. some people are prophesying for peace in three months. would that it was so. I dont think the yankees are willing to give up yet.

Cousin Franklin Campbell[7] came in Saturday. his family is well. Cousin Mattie intended to come but was disappointed. Cousin Matilda[8] told me Saturday at church she was coming and I was thinking I would have the chance to see her and so I was disappointed and I was almost right sick. John Christopher did not go off with Berry. He went to Maxeys and would not go any further. He is not able to walk without his crutches yet. Aunt Betsy told me that they received a letter from Cousin Mark. he was sick again from a march they had taken. I expect they were in the fight.

The people about here have been carrying Provisions to the depot for the government. Pa says there was a great deal more carried in than anybody thought there was to spare. he carried 23 bushels of wheat to the mill last week and sold some of it to the government and the other to Marcum.[9] the wheat still looks very well but the heavy rains will be bad on it I expect. corn also looks well. cotton is coming up. Bud Jimmie I was so sorry you and Cousin John was disappointed about your box. I could have cried good if it would have mended the matter. we had everything ready and Pa and Cousin George went to the depot to fix it off and that man was not there. Aunt Betsy cooked 2 days she said and she was both sorry and vexed about it. She says she wants you and Cousin John to send up a box of palmetto enough to plait 4 or 5 hats and some fans. she wants you to send it by some man that comes up. I told her I thought it would be a bad chance to get it off, but she believes you could send it if you would. She says if you will send her enough to speculate on she will sell enough to pay the expenses.

The conscript has got Tom Martin and he expects to go to your company next Saturday. Mr Mell says he sympathizes with you very much about the sand flies. he says he was raised with them and he knows how bad they are but he says they will soon leave there, their season is almost gone, and I reckon you all wont cry if it is. I was very sorry to hear of your losing one of your company.

Well Bud Jimmie I have scribbled over this paper with my same old pen. I sent to Bairdstown and got this paper and gave $4 a quire. "cheap paper this." If it was good I would not mind it so much, but it is a very inferior quality. it does not write well at all and it being damp makes it so much worse and an old pen that is not worth picking up. I thought I would not write any more until I got some new ones, but have not [had] the chance to do it yet.

Mary will write soon. Brothers family is only tolerably well. Jimmie had the mumps. All send their love to you and cousin John. I hope these lines may find you well. I remain your affectionate sister

Sallie

1   L.R.L. Jennings was a Baptist minister in Athens. He was listed in the 1860 Georgia census as 29 years old, along with his wife, Sarah E. Jennings, 29, and Susan S. Stow, 51.

2   Lou & Hat Bulloch are unidentified.

3   "Old Mrs. Briscoe" may have been Elizabeth Briscoe, the mother of Madison P. Briscoe (already cited).

4   The maiden name of Joe Reynolds' wife was not determined.

5   Rebecca D. Colclough's tombstone in the Colclough family cemetery in Greene County gives her birth date as September 9, 1840, and her death as April 26, 1863.

6   Martha Lumpkin Moore was listed in the 1860 Georgia census as the 30-year-old wife of Burnett Moore, 41, a farmer in the Falling Creek District of Oglethorpe County. Oglethorpe County marriage records show that they were married February 14, 1842.

7   Franklin Campbell was not Sallie's cousin. She called his older brother Andrew "uncle," but they were not related either. Franklin and Andrew were brothers to William Campbell who married Elizabeth Jewel, Sallie's aunt (sister to James Jewel, Sr.). Franklin was the father of Edwin J. Campbell and Martha Campbell. Sallie married Edwin, and her brother William married Martha. The Franklin Campbell family had lived in Oglethorpe County, but at the time of the 1860 census, they were located in Carroll County, Georgia.

8   Matilda L. Campbell was one of the daughters of Franklin C. and Clementine Campbell, who married John M. Gilham, January 1, 1856.

9   This was G.R. Marcum (already cited).

MAY 11TH 1863

My Dear Brother

It has been so long since I heard from you the week seems as long as a month to me and I should think it would seem so to you, for you do not have so much to employ your time as we do who are here at home. I heard Tom Martin was going to start Wednesday and he said he would carry a letter.

We met at Antioch yesterday to organize a sabbath school. we have 26 scholars. Mrs Jane Jones[1] and Miss May Gilham[2] are the female teachers. Columbus Landrum, John Gilham,[3] and Dr Harrison,[4] male teachers. Mrs Landrum,[5] Mattie, Ellis, Sue Bell,[6]

Shug Armstead, and myself are in the older class. They give us the privilege of chosing our teacher. We took Mrs Jane first and then Miss May and neither one of them would accept us and we then chose Mr Landrum. I think our lesson is right hard. You know something about it, I think you studied it. I think a school will be very beneficial. There is so many children about Antioch that need some employment beside doing mischief. we will meet at 9 oclock. They have had the school house at Center[7] enlarged. Mr Landrum has 45 scholars and more want to come.

Cousin George [Jewel] came up to see us Saturday night. I was a little surprised at seeing him. it is so seldom he comes. They heard from Cousin Mark about two weeks ago. I have not heard any of the particulars from the fight, who of our friends were killed and wounded, but I expect there is a many a one. the paper says it was a complete victory and the loss heavy. I wrote to you about Cousin Franklin [Campbell] coming in. He came up to see us today. he has just been to Virginia and had a great deal to talk about. Cousin Billie [Campbell] is courier in the 19th Regiment. Ed[8] is well and is doing finely. Cousin Franklin does not look so well as when here before. He has sold out his land & got the money for it. he is going to live there until christmas and is going to get out of debt. he brought the money to pay you, and Sis Mary and I are going down to Mr Colclough tomorrow to let Eliza know about it so she can send the note to Cousin James Smith and he will be there to settle it Friday. William Smith came in last Wednesday. he is at Cousin Joes.[9] he is coming up here to see us. he is fixing to go to war now soon. [undecipherable] Robert is in the army in Virginia. Willie is just like he used to be.

Pa received a letter from Cousin Mary Norwood[10] saturday evening to meet her at Antioch about the fifteenth of the month which is Friday. She has taken a notion to visit us, she did not say who was going to come with her. Cousin James[11] is living with Aunt Peggie.[12] Richard[13] is working in the government shop in Columbus, Ga. Cousin Mary has a son-in-law in the western army and one was killed and her son is there. Cousin Williams son[14] has put in a substitute.

Well Bud Jimmie it is getting late. I will have to stop writing. the nights are so short and we will have to be up soon to get off to Mr

Colcloughs. I am very anxious to see them. it seems like it has been a long time since I have seen any of them. Bud [William Jewel, II] went up to Athens two days last week on the train. I do not know what for. Mat had not got well the last account I had. Dr Moody[15] was expected to die last week with Pneumonia. they sent up for his mother and Aunt Mary Bell one night last week to come and see him. You must write all the news. Tell Cousin John I think it is time for him to write. we are all well. Bro Marshalls and Bens families are well. The crops are growing finely. wheat is very promising and the seasons are splendid. the weather is cool and clear. Pa says he thinks it is the right kind of weather for the wheat. our garden looks very well. irish potatoes are growing very fast. Ma has some chickens large enough to eat. I have 10 little turkies. I would write more if I had the time.

Good night my dear Brother, may God protect and bless you is the sincere desire of your Sister, Sallie

1   Mrs. Jane Jones is unidentified.

2   Miss May Gilham is unidentified.

3   John M. Gilham is listed in the 1860 Georgia census as a 29-year-old farmer in the household of Margaret Chappell, 67, in the Falling Creek District of Oglethorpe County. Also in the home were Margaret Chappell, 10, Matilda [Campbell] Gilham, 26, and three Gilham children, ages 9 months, 2 years, and 3 years.

4   Dr. T.C. Harrison is listed in the 1860 Georgia census as a resident in the household of William and Narcissus Edwards, farmers in the Wolfskin District of Oglethorpe County.

5   This probably was Elizabeth Landrum, wife of Columbus J. Landrum (already cited).

6   Mattie, Ellis, and Sue Bell are unidentified.

7   Center School originally was Center Meeting House, established in 1813 as the first church in the Antioch Community, and was owned jointly by the Baptists, Methodists, and Presbyterians. In 1828 the Baptist congregation built Antioch Church, the Presbyterian members eventually moved elsewhere, and the Methodists continued there as Center Methodist Church.

8   Ed was Edwin J. Campbell, son of Franklin C. and Clementine Campbell (already cited). Ed Campbell was a Private in Company F, 19th Georgia Volunteers, Colquitt's Brigade. He was wounded in the thigh by a minie´ ball at the Battle of Olustee, Florida, February 20, 1864. Edwin Campbell and Sarah Rebecca "Sallie" Jewel were married after the war.

9   William Franklin Smith was the son of Joseph Benjamin Smith, who was the son of Paschal Smith and Polly Jewel Smith. Polly was a sister of James Jewel, Sr. The 1860 Georgia census lists the Smiths as residents of the Falling Creek District of Oglethorpe County. At the time of the census Joseph Smith was 45 and his wife Harriett Newell McLaughlin Smith was 39. Their son William was 20, and there were seven other children in the household from the ages of 9 months to 15 years old.

10   Mary Ann Norwood was the daughter of Margaret Jewel Mattox, the sister of James Jewel, Sr. Margaret was married to Anthony W. Mattox. The 1860 Alabama census identified Margaret as a 58-year-old farmer in the Southern Division of Chambers County. Mary Ann Norwood is listed in the 1860 Alabama census as the 47-year-old wife of James M. Norwood, 48-year-old farmer in the Southern Division of Chambers County. Both were born in Georgia. Also in the home were Ann America, 21, George W., 18, Richard, 14, Elizabeth, 12, and James, 12. All five children were born in Alabama.

11   Cousin James was James Mattox, son of Margaret Jewel Mattox, sister of James Jewel, Sr. James's age at the time of the 1860 census was given as 35. Also in the home was Richard Mattox, 32. All three were born in Georgia.

12   Aunt Peggy was Margaret Jewel Mattox. See footnote 11 above.

13   This was probably Richard Mattox. See footnote 11 above.

14   John T. Mattox is listed in the 1860 Alabama census as the 22-year-old son of William J. and Elizabeth W. Mattox, farmers in the Southern Division of Chambers County. William J. was probably the brother to A.W. Mattox, who married Margaret Jewel, sister to James Jewel, Sr. The records indicate that John was born in Alabama and both parents were born in Georgia.

15   Dr. Waldemar Moody (already cited) did not die until 1901.

May 21st/63

My Dear Brother

Your letter from the hands of Lieutenant Gibson dated the 14th was received yesterday evening. I was glad to hear that you was well. We are enjoying tolerably good health. I do not hear of as much sickness as there was a few weeks ago. Sis May and I went to see Eliza the day after I wrote to you. Eliza was well, the rest of the family was tolerable. Mattie was very lively, she did not seem to be in any pain. that place on her eye was swollen and looked like a bruise, it looks purple. I thought maybe Addie[1] let her fall, but Eliza said there was no sign of a bruise there until it swelled up. I am in hopes it has got well by this time. I have not heard from there since we were there.

Bud had just received a letter from you the day we were there. Mr Colclough had one very sick negro, Silvy I think is her name. several others were complaining. I wish Eliza could come up and see us but she has a bad chance to get off. Mr Colclough is busy plowing. crops are growing finely. Wheat still looks well, the weather continues cool in the morning. we have not had any rain in some time. we are not suffering for rain though.

I reckon Tom Martin has got to your company but he did not start until Wednesday after I wrote to you. I reckon he staid to see Mit married to William Jones.[2]

Brother Marshall came down last week to get Maggie to cut him a coat and pants, also to get a wheel from Mr Mc Laughlin.[3] he is making [spinning]wheels for $10 a piece. Sis Jane and the children are well. Brothers family is well. he went up to Athens last week. he got one bunch of thread for $5 1/4. they have to draw by lottery. [they] put in blank paper and put [in] some with names and if you draw your name you will get one bunch. it is [a] slow way of getting along. I reckon people wont be clothed fast at that rate if they have to depend on the factories.

I wrote to you about Cousin Mary Norwood sending us word to meet her at Antioch. well we went to work and fixed up for her. Pa went to the depot Friday and Saturday to meet her but she did not come and we have not heard anything from her. I reckon she give out the idea of coming. William Smith has not been up to see us yet. I think he is a poor hand to visit his kinsfolks anyway. He is out here hunting him a horse. he is going to the war with a cavalry company. he will be 18 sometime next month, he is anxious to go.

I went to Antioch to Sunday school and to preaching last Sunday. we have about 32 scholars now. Mr Mells text was 2nd Corinthians 8th chap and 9th verse. I wrote to you some time ago about such a crowd coming down to Antioch from Madison [Georgia]. well, there was 12 or 14 came down Sunday but I did not know any of them. Cousin Franklin staid all night with us Friday. he is lively and well. he has been paying up his debts. he paid off your note to Cousin James Smith for Eliza. he has gone home now.

Well Bud Jimmie, I hardly know what to write. We have had beets and peas to eat and could have some irish potatoes but they are too small to begin to eat yet. We have chickens large enough to eat. We have been thinking perhaps you could get off on furlough and stay with us a few days but that hope like many others has been laid low in the dust. Liza told us when we was down there that she was sorter looking for you. Brother said he dreamed one night you and cousin John had deserted. I hope your box you fixed up will come on safe if you started it. if we get it we will all be much obliged to you and cousin for it.

Bud Jimmie, I must quit writing now and feed my little turkeys and get supper. You must write us [as] often as you can and I will do the same. all send their love to you and Cousin John. tell him his Pa's family is well. tell him he must write when you dont have the chance. Mary will write soon. I will be glad when you can get away from that place for I think it is useless to keep men at any such place. my love to you and friends. I remain your true and affectionate Sister, Sallie Jewel

1   Addie undoubtedly was a slave of the Colcloughs.

2   William M. Jones and Lucinda J. "Mitt" Camp were married May 21, 1863.

3   This probably was George McLaughlin, listed in the 1860 Georgia census as a 62-year-old farmer in the Falling Creek District of Oglethorpe County.

June 4th 1863

My Dear Brother

I came down to Uncle Billies Saturday morning for the purpose of going to Salem[1] Sunday to the union meeting. Saturday evening it rained very hard and then cleared off. Cousin George carried me to Salem Sunday, there was a good many people out. we had several preachers. Mr Coil[2] preached in the forenoon and then Mr Chandler[3] took his text, or rather a chapter, the 4th of Revelations, and explained it. I think it was the drollest sermon I ever heard. well after that Mr John Young[4] preached. they did not give but 20 min. intermission and there was no body hardly that had any thing to eat, so you can imagine how a set of folks hungry and tired would feel a warm June evening.

I came home to Uncle Billies from church and staid until Monday evening and went to Uncle Johns [Bell?] and Tuesday morning I went to cousin Camillas and spent the day. I had a pleasant time, then back to Uncle Johns and intended going to Uncle Joes the next morning but it rained all day and this morning I went to Uncle Joes and I met up with a right smart crowd. Miss Julia Smith,[5] Sue Bell, Cousin Camilla and Aunt Sallie, Lizzie Cramer[6] and cousin Liza. they are all getting on very well. Uncle Joe's Ben runaway Monday. Joe says he never give him any cause to go away. he had not spoken a short word to him. I suppose he got tired of work and concluded he would rest awhile.

I expect you have been looking for a letter from me, but I did not get your letter and cousin Johns. it was sent home and I have been almost crazy to see it. They were all well when I left home. Pa was getting on very well with his crop. We are having fine Irish potatoes & beets now and chickens occasionally.

When I wrote to you that our Alabama kinfolks had not come, well Cousin Mary Norwood, Mary Ann Seals,[7] and Mandy Patrick,[8] all came to see us. Cousin Rich has a substitute. Cousin Mary N. went home today. the girls are going to stay some time. Cousin Mary Ann is a sprightly young widow, very interesting indeed. I have not seen Eliza since I was down there. I do hope she will come up this week. Brothers and Brother Marshalls families are well. Cousin Henry Paris came home sick last week. Uncle Billie was there. this evening he was better. I am in hopes he will be well soon. it is the opinion of almost every body that all the able bodied men will be called out. Mr Mell is going to be Col of a Regiment and is to be ready when called upon to go for state defence.[9] I think it is so hard to have to give him up. I have had the blues ever since I heard it. He will not be at Antioch to preach Sunday. Dr Neeson will be in his place. Oh, I do hate to give him up so much. it seems to me that he is the last man that ought to go. but some have urged it on him and he himself thinks it his duty to go.

Friday. Well Bud Jimmie, I will write a few more lines this evening. it has been raining again today. It has been raining for two or three days. it is a bad time on the wheat. some of it is ripe enough to cut. Tell Cousin John his clothes have never come home yet and we have not heard from your box of Palmetto.

Uncle Billie has made arrangements to send on Cousin Johns substitute, Freeman.[10] he staid here night before last. he wants to get Mark one. Aunt Betsy has sent him a pair of socks some time back. he was well the last they heard from him. Billie Young[11] is at home. Uncle Billie received a letter from Cousin Emily. Dr[12] is quite sick, they think he has the consumption. Cousin Edgar came over a few days ago, he was very well. he did not stay long. I did not have the pleasure of seeing him.

Well Bud Jimmie, I wish I had the chance to write a long letter, but cannot at this time. I will write again as soon as I can get home. I will answer your letters so you must excuse me for not writing sooner. I will have to close this letter as Mike[13] is waiting. these lines leave us all tolerably well and hope they find your Company in good health. Aunt May[14] gave me a letter for Simon from his wife. I hope I shall hear from you soon. All send their love to you and Cousin [John]. I have not received my letter yet, I expect to go home tomorrow. I am so anxious to see it, I can hardly wait until tomorrow comes.

I remain Your Affectionate Sister Sallie.

1   Salem was a very early settlement on the Apalachee River in Oconee County [then Clarke County], Georgia. It now is a "ghost town."

2   James Nicholas Coile was born in Madison County, Georgia, in 1828. He was married to Susan Elvira McCurdy. Coile moved his family to Oglethorpe County in 1860, and he and three of his six sons attended Meson Academy together in Lexington. He was ordained at Cloud's Creek Church in 1862. Coile died in October 1878.

3   Asa Chandler served as pastor of Salem Church from 1851-1865. He is listed in the 1860 Georgia census as a 51-year-old Baptist minister in Elbert County, Georgia, along with his wife L.H., 43, and nine children ranging in age from 1 to 18.

4   Jonathan R. Young is listed in the 1860 Georgia census as a 36-year-old Baptist clergyman in Greene County, along with his wife A.J., 30, and five children.

5   Miss Julia Smith is unidentified.

6   Lizzie Cramer probably was the Elizabeth Cramer listed in the 1860 Georgia census as the 18-year-old daughter of Joseph Cramer, a farmer in the Bowling Green District of Oglethorpe County.

7   Mary Ann Seals was a sister of David A. Patrick (already cited). She was the widow of Enoch Z. [or T.] Seals. At the time of the 1850 census Seals was identified as a 24-year-old merchant and he and Mary Ann, age 16, were living with her parents in the 19th District of Chambers County, Alabama. Mary Ann is listed in the 1860 Alabama census as a 25-year-old resident in the household of her father, R.B. Patrick, 57, farmer in Beat Number 5 of Tallapoosa County, along with her two children, Benjamin P., 8, and Elizabeth A., 6. Other Patricks in the household were Martha A., 30, Martha, 18, Mandre J., 16, Benjamin P., 14, Eliza K., 3, Carrie T., 2, and Frances T., 5 months.

8   Mandy was Mandre J. Patrick, a sister to David Patrick and Mary Ann Patrick Seals and daughter of R.B. Patrick. See footnote 7 above.

9   P.H. Mell did organize a company in June 1863 called Mell's Rifles whose officers and men served for the remainder of the war. Dr. Mell, however, resigned from office on July 24, 1863, and did not serve with the company.

10   This was James S. Freeman. See James Jewel's letter of June 15, 1863, for further information.

11   Billie Young was William T. Young, listed in the 1860 Georgia census as a 22-year-old overseer in the household of his parents, Giles Young, 62, and Mary Young, 64, farmers in the Bowling Green District of Oglethorpe County. Young joined the Oglethorpe Rifles as a Private when the company was formed May 15, 1861, but was later promoted to Sergeant. Young was severely wounded late in the war. He was discharged January 1, 1864, and was elected sheriff of Oglethorpe County.

12   This was Dr. William Stark Meiere, the husband of Cousin John's older sister, Emmialy [Emily] Jewel. Meiere and Emily Jewel were married December 25, 1849. Dr. Meiere is listed in the 1860 Georgia census as a 34-year-old physician in Madison, the county seat of Morgan County. He was born in Virginia. Emily is listed as 29, and their two children at that time were Julius, 9, and Anna, 1.

13   Mike's identity is uncertain, but he may have been a slave of the James Jewel, Sr., family.

14   Aunt May is unidentified but she may have been a slave of William Jewel, I.

[The following is the only surviving letter from James Jewel's wife, Eliza Cordelia Colclough Jewel]

JUNE THE 8 1863

Dear Husband

I received your letter the sixth which was written the first day of June. I was very glad to hear from you and hear that you was well. this leaves me and mattie tolrable well at this time. I am now at your pars [Pa's] siting in the room that we uster to stay in when we was first married, writting. I come up sunday. I found all well. I had not ben up their before in six weeks. they wer all gone to church but mar [Ma] when I got their, but it was not long before they come home. they all say they wer a great many at church. they had old Dr neason[1] to preach fore them and you no it was a pore preaching. John came up at par sadurday eavening before I left, a little while before I got your letter, and told me that he had got a letter from you. I was very glad to hear from you fore I was begining to git uneasy about you. I look fore a letter from you fryday but did not git it. I did not no you had got back to quincy until John came up. I am very glad you have got back to quincy as you all like to stay their so well. I am in hopes you will git to say their all the tim that you have to say [stay] in the wor [war] if you cant git nearer home. I would be so glad if you could be wher I could go to see you, as it is so you cant come home. I want you to try to come home as soon as you can.

I and Sally are fixing to go up to mr edwards. we inten to go wendsday and come back fryday morning. I recon I will go back home next sunday if nothing happens so that I cant. I cant stay away from hom sadisfid long at a tim. it looks like they have ben sick their so much that I am uneasy all the tim fore fear som of them will be sick agin. they all have got well agin except colds. they all have took fresh colds agin and I am aferd some of them will be sick agin.

I wrot to you abou par loosing one of his negros when I wrot you before, but recon you have not got that letter yet. I sent it to St Marks and I recon you will git this before you will git that as I am a going to send this byhand. I never told you which one of the negros it was that did [died], it was Lebron. dide in seventh days ifter he was taken. he was taken very bad when he was first taken and kept giting worse until he did. their has ben seventh cases of the tyford neumonia at pars or that of the kind. their has ben a great eal of sickness about. I dont no as I ever her of as much sickness in my life.

we have had rane a plenty fore the last too or three weeks. we was needing rain very bad before we got it. the corn is growing finly, crops are looking very well. par says his cotton looks better than he ever saw it look fore the time of the yer. I recon their never was such crops of wheat as will be mad this [year]. they are beginning to cut wheat. some are complaing about the smut[2] being in their wheat. gardens are looking very well. our garden looks finly. it [looks] better than I ever saw it. mar has planted the ishpotatoes [irish potatoes] an enlish peas an unions and cone [corn] and all kinds of vetabl. if you could come home we would have a garden if we did not have any thing els.

James maxey[3] has come home and is very sick. they thout last fryday he would not live, but he has got a little better. he has the tyford dirre [diarrhea]. I herd from cousin henry parris. he is on the mend. the box has come that you [sent] but they have not got it from the depo yet. I would be glad to see in it but I dont no as I will have the chance of seeing it before I go home as I dont expect to stay but one wek. I want you to writ soon and let me no how you are giting along. I will now close as sally wants to write some. John saw Jim barrow the other [day]. he says he thinks you will be kept their as they will hev [to] keep men their. no more at present, only I remain as ever your affecttion wife,

Eliza C Jewel I hope to see you soon

<hr />

1   Horrice Neeson [also seen as Horace Neason] is listed in the 1860 Georgia census as a 48-year-old minister from the Bairdstown District of Oglethorpe County, born in Ireland.

2   Smut is a fungal disease of wheat and other grain crops.

3   This probably was the James M. Maxey listed in the 1860 Georgia census in the household of L.M. and Nancy Maxey in the Scull Shoals District of Greene County, along with George W., 14, and Richard, 11.

[JUNE 8, 1863]

Dear Brother

I thought I would write you a few lines while I had a good chance. I do not know why you have not received a letter from me, for I have written three since Tom Martin went down there. I sent one to you Saturday directed to Tallahassee. I do not know when you [will] get it. I came to Antioch Saturday with Aunt Betsy. it was a sad looking day to us all. I felt almost like Mr Mell was dead. we will continue to meet regularly and the old Dr has promised to serve us to the best of his ability. We are going to try to get Crawford,[1] John Young, or somebody, but I doubt very much whether we get either of them, but I hope we will succeed in getting somebody.

The box of palmetto is at the Depot and we will go to work on it as soon as we can get it home. I went Antioch Depot and staid Saturday evening until the cars come with Lou Pass and I saw I. Cheatham, Jim Barrow, and Rufus Moss[2] I have heard that Lucy Barrow will be married in a very short time to John Cobb.[3] I went to Aunt Peggy Chapels to dinner from Church Sunday with Cousin Mary Ann and Mandy Patrick. Liza and I will try and get off Wednesday. Pa says his crop is very good. The wheat is fine. he expects to cut wheat in a day or two. our gardens are fine. Irish potatoes plenty and we have had two messes of beans. Mattie is as fat as a pig and is very lively. her eye is nearly well, it looks a little red. I am glad it was no worse. she has 4 teeth. I have filled up my paper. tell Cousin I will write to him before long.

[Sallie]

1   Nathaniel Macon Crawford was a Baptist clergyman and the President of Mercer University in Penfield, Georgia. Crawford was the son of William Harris Crawford, prominent

resident of Oglethorpe County who had served as a U.S. Secretary of the Treasury for 8 years during both terms of President James Monroe.

2   Rufus Lafayette Moss was born in Oglethorpe County in 1825 and had moved to Athens at age 17. He became a successful businessman in Athens, with interests in several businesses. Moss enlisted in the Confederate Army in 1862 and was assigned to duty on General Howell Cobb's staff in Florida. When Cobb transferred to Athens, Moss also was transferred to Athens as Cobb's Commissary Officer.

3   Lucy Pope Barrow was the daughter of Colonel D.C. Barrow, Sr., and the sister to James Barrow (already cited). The Barrows had been neighbors of the Jewels, but now lived in Athens. John A. Cobb was the oldest son of General Howell Cobb. He and Lucy Barrow were married July 29, 1863.

[Undated, but from content it probably goes here chronologically]

Bud Jimmie

I wrote to you that Meck Edwards was going to marry. the man come and has gone back. I do not know what to think of them. it is reported that this is the fourth time it has been broken off. I think it ought to be forever if they have to break off so many times. those rings you sent me were very nice. I am much obliged to you for them but I can not wear them, they are too small for any of us. I will keep them for Mattie. I am going to send you the measure of my finger so if you get any more guttapercha you can make me one. I have not seen Eliza since she was up here. Mat told me yesterday that Lettie was down there Sunday. they were all well. I want to go to see Eliza but as long as Cousin Sarah is sick one of us will have to go there occasionaly to sit up with her. I am going the first chance. I do hope you will have the chance to come home and see us and get some peaches and figs. Tell Cousin J we have a great many figs. figs are beginning to get ripe enough to eat. the gardens are very good. it has rained two or three times this week. we do not suffer for want of rain at all. You said I must not let that palmetto keep me from writing, I will try not. we keep making hats and orders coming for more. Sallie Stephens saw my fan at church Sunday and she asked me to make her one. I reckon I will have to do it for Cousin Johns sake if I can find time. the freight on the box was five and a half dollars. Evaline came down to Antioch sunday on the cars, she said they were all well. I must close this letter as there is nobody here to string the beans for dinner but me and Maggie. all send their love to you and Cousin John. Write soon all the news

[Sallie]

JULY 3RD 1863

Dear Brother Jimmie

I received your letter and should have answered it sooner, but thought perhaps you would write again this week. I was glad to hear that you was well. We are all tolerably well, some of the little negroes have been complaining but are nearly well now. It is very warm weather. we have not had any real summer weather until this week. last week we had some of the hardest rains that I ever saw and this week has been the driest of any we have had in four. It has been bad on the wheat that was in the field and not capped well. some of it was shocked without caps and before it would get dry enough to take up, it would rain again. several are complaining of it sprouting, but as Pa as generally [was] slow but sure, his was well capped.

Well Bud Jimmie, I have been as busy as I could be plaiting. every body and his folks wants hats, palmetto preferred to straw. I have plaited four and they keep coming in. Sis May and Maggie have been plaiting too. we have only sewed three, and four or five more plaited. I sold the two I made at $2 apiece. it was not the highest price, but I sold them to Aster Smith[1] & John. they are selling at $5 at Antioch, but I have not got that high yet, but may ask some that are able to pay it before I get through. I have also made me a fan. I stripped it up in pieces about half as broad as your finger and then worked it in like a basket bottom, trimmed it round and bound it. Pa made me a nice maple handle for it and I have just finished it off this evening.

Sis Mary went out to see Aunt Sallie [Parris] this morning. she was taken sick yesterday was a week ago and her and cousin Sarah are very sick indeed. Dr [A.A.] Bell is going to see them. they sent word to us by Cousin Joe Smith to Marcum, or he told him to tell us Monday and he never sent us any word at all and we did not hear anything about it until yesterday. aunt Lucy sent us word. They have got the Typoid fever. I dont think she will ever get well. I must stop writing tonight as they are all going to bed and the nights are short.

Saturday morning I am ready to go to church, but it is not time to start. I will write a few lines. Pa and Ma have started to see Aunt Sallie this morning and I will not have any one to go with me but Phil.[2] Brother and the boys are going to the organization of the militia in Lexington and the girls will not have any way of going. we do not know whether there will be any preacher or not.

Old Mrs Powell[3] and Mrs Rebecca Moore[4] are both very sick, they cannot live much longer unless there is a great change. Mrs Moores children have come in to see her. Clem came from Alabama two or three days ago. Mrs Powell has been lying for weeks and all anybody could say [is] she is alive. she is perfectly blind and suffers as much as any old person ever did. the old people cannot stand so much trouble. I think it is what is the matter with a great many of them.

I have got back from church, there was no preacher. 8 old men and 5 women was the crowd. It was quite a lonely looking place to what it generally is. I engaged four more hats, so you may know I will have to be quite buzy. America Edwards is going to marry, or that is the talk. she is going to marry Mr Robinson[5] that used to live at William Day's[6] he has come to Mr Edwards on furlough. the license were taken out last Monday. I have not heard from Brother Marshall in a good while. I thought some of them would have come down before this time. Eliza promised to come up today, but she has not come yet. I would like very much to see her. Mrs Lumpkin was at Mrs Moores Monday and saw Sallie and Mrs Colclough. they were all well.

Bud Jimmie, figs are getting ripe and peaches are turning but there will not be very many forward ones. they are very small and knotty. the june apples are all gone. we have some very nice horse apples but I dont reckon they will stay long, the negroes can get such a good price for them. Mr Edwards says he saw them selling forward peaches at the point $1 a dozen. I wrote to you in my last letter that Cousin Henry was going back Tuesday last. He went up to Mr Taylors[7] last Saturday night and one of Wil Gils[8] negro women went in the room where he was sleeping and was taking out bed clothes and any thing she could carry and she woke him and he called for Mr Taylor and they both started after her. Mr G fell over a chair and hurt himself and Cousin H ran as far as the railroad and broke one of his toes and he cannot go back yet, but they sent and got Burnett Moores[9] dogs and caught her. she ran strait home. she has been going in there several times and taking off bed clothes and they could not find what become of them until they caught her. she had taken some of Shuges nicest quilts Mrs Colclough had given her. they were strewed all over the neighborhood [where she] sold them. they got everything back except a piece of bleached homespun that belonged to Ellen.

I have written my paper full. Pa told me he wanted me to write some about his crop. I will have to wait until he comes home. Pa has come. Aunt Sallie is no better and cousin S. [Sallie] is about the same. Dick Maxey[10] is very sick. He [Pa] expects to make as much wheat as he ever made. he has cut the most of his oats and have them up. has some to cut on the Martin branch. he did not sow a great many. the corn crop is as promising as we ever had and if it will rain soon we will [have a] splendid crop. we have plenty of grass if any body wants any we can supply them. it has been impossible. He is done ploughing the corn and expects to run around the peas, and will have to plow the cotten. taking all things into consideration, we are getting on finely. the first garden corn is beginning to tassle.

I have been expecting a letter all this week from you. I have not heard from you yet. Lizzie Hull[11] told Ma that there was one at Maxeys to cousin John and promised to send it tomorrow. Give my love to Cousin John and accept a large portion for yourself. All send their love. I hope to hear from you soon. [Sallie]

1   Aster Smith is unidentified.

2   Phil was probably a Jewel family slave.

3   The 1860 Georgia census lists Lavinia Powell as an 84-year-old resident of the Falling Creek District of Oglethorpe County, and notes that she was born in Virginia. Others in the household were Elizabeth, 50, Rebecca, 42, and Mary, 40.

4   Rebecca Billings Moore was the widow of Burnette Moore, Sr. Their joint tombstone in the family cemetery in Greene County, Georgia, states that she was born October 30, 1786, and died July 12, 1863. Burnette Moore was born August 22, 1787, and died December 9, 1849.

5   Alexander Robertson and Harriett America Edwards were married December 24, 1863.

6   William Day is listed in the 1860 Georgia census as a 42-year-old stone cutter in the Simston District of Oglethorpe County. Day was born in England. His 36-year-old wife Susan H. and their seven children were all born in Georgia.

7   This probably was John Taylor, listed in the 1860 Georgia census as a 58-year- old farmer in the Falling Creek District of Oglethorpe County, along with Frances, 50, Pope, 19, and Ellen, 17. John Taylor was the father-in-law of William Jewel, II, and Jewel's brother-in-law Thomas F. Colclough.

8   This probably was William Gilham, father of Ben and Thomas Gilham (already cited).

9   Burnett Moore is listed in the 1860 Georgia census as a 41-year-old farmer in the Wolfskin District of Oglethorpe County along with Martha, 30, Lucy, 14, and four other children.

10   This may have been the Richard Maxey listed in the 1860 Georgia census as the 11-year-old brother of James M. Maxey (already cited).

11   Lizzie Hull is unidentified.

July 9th 1863

My Dear Brother,

I received two letters from you Sunday, one by Mr Eberheart[1] was left at Maxeys and Mr Fleming[2] brought [it] to Sunday school, and I received the other at Antioch. I was glad to hear that you are still in good health. I hope you will not have to go down to the Narrows. We are all well.

I am sorry to have to relate to you the sad news of Aunt Sallies[3] death. she died Tuesday night at ten oclock. Maggie left there Tuesday morning and she [Aunt Sallie] had not noticed any thing from Monday night at dark. Dr Bell left there just before she got there monday evening and said she was better, but I dont think he thought so for she seemed to suffer more all day than she had done before. she did not wake but once during the day Tuesday and tried to talk but could not be understood. They said she had not been well in four weeks before she took her bed and she got so bad she was obliged to take her bed. I did not have the chance to go to see her but all the rest went. I went to the burying yesterday evening at five oclock. there was as many as I ever saw at a burying. Cousin Sallie[4] is very sick yet. I think from Dr Bells look he was uneasy about her. he said she was no worse, but she was no better. they carried the corpse in to let her see it. She stood it as well as any one could expect considering she was so weak.

Ma is over at Brothers. she has been there two or three days. Sis Lizzie[5] has another boy. she was tolerably well yesterday. I am looking for Ma at home this morning. Mary staid with Cousin Sallie last night. there is not many to sit up, they are all worn out. Mrs Powell died last Saturday and Mrs Moore they did not think could live through the day yesterday. I saw Uncle Billie, Aunt Betsy, and Cousin George at the burying. Uncle Billie staid at Aunt Sallies all day Tuesday and until the next day. He is not very well but not much worse that he has been all the time. He had found out it is not worth while to try to get substitutes. I suppose they have had a desperate fight in Pennsylvania. I do not think the 8th Georgia was there. from the newspaper account it must have been an awful fight. I hope our troops may still be able to hold Vicksburg, but it seems as if the Yankees are determined to have it.

There are two refugees at William Gilhams from Mississippi, nieces of Mr Gilham, Miss Loubella and Mollie Wise.[6] I saw one of them at church Sunday, their father used to board here and go to school at Herman.[7] I expect you have heard Ma and Pa talking about him. they are orphan girls. they have two married sisters living there but they could not get away.

I forgot to tell you that Cousin Henry went back to Kingston [Georgia] Tuesday. He went to get another furlough to come and stay with his Ma and she died the day he started   Sallie

1   Probably either Nathan Eberhart or his father John (already cited).

2   Thomas Flemming was the Postmaster at Maxeys, Georgia, from December 17, 1853, to May 10, 1866.

3   Sarah "Sallie" Parris, younger sister of James Jewel, Sr. (cited previously).

4   Sarah A. "Sallie" Parris, was a daughter of N.H. and Sarah Parris and was married to David Christopher (cited elsewhere).

5   Sis Lizzie was Elizabeth Jewel Crowley, Sallie's older sister. The baby was Benajale, the last of the 12 children of Elizabeth and Benajah Crowley.

6   Loubella and Mollie Wise are unidentified.

7   Hermon Academy was established near the Jewel home place in 1821. The community in the neighborhood of the school is identified as Hermon or Herman on early maps of Georgia.

Beginning of letter missing

Sunday before she left to hear the Chaplain preach to the soldiers. she enjoyed it very much. they staid to see the soldiers cook. she said the funniest of it all was to see them making biscuit. Cousin Henrys company is stationed there. I reckon you have heard of James Maxeys death by this time. I am sorry for his Mother, he was such a favorite with her. Bud came up yesterday to see us. they were all well at home. I have not heard from Eliza since she went from here. Bud had not heard from there since we had. I hope they are all well, they have been afflicted so much. I want to go down there the first opportunity I have as soon as Pa can get through with his ploughing. the grass will grow fast now.

Mrs Pope[1] and Lucy [Barrow] staid at the plantation last week. they came over to see us. Lucy is as familiar and affectionate as she used to be when we went to school. I had a very pleasant time with her. she went with me over to Brothers and she went around to see all the school girls that was near enough. She was paying me a visit for the last one in a state of single blessedness. She is going to marry John Cobb. they will marry in the latter part of July if nothing prevents. she showed me a ring that he sent her last week. it is the prettiest one I ever saw, it has three diamonds in it. He is in Macon tending to his uncles business. She gave me a full description of the important events. Mary Cochran was married to Lieutenant Bearden[2] of Clarke Co. last Thursday night. he was at home on furlough. he was wounded in the last battle in Virginia at Chancellorsville. I was very much surprised when I heard it.

our Alabama cousins have not gone home yet. they were at Cousin James Smiths last week. Well I have written nearly all the news. we are having vegetables of all kinds to eat except corn. we will have some of that before a great while. Aunt Lucy had some two or three weeks ago. We have had a quantity of cherries nice as I ever saw, but we have had less use than ever for them, for we did not have sugar to sweeten them with. some people are going to make brandy of them. Lemay[3] came down to Antioch yesterday. he said they were all well. Brothers family is only tolerably well. Henry has been sick all last week with something like the measles but I think it is the roseola. it has been all around us here. Sis Mary had it two weeks ago and [I] have it now. it has not made me sick at all but it makes some people quite sick. Pa is busy planting peas. You must write as often al you can. All join me in much love to you and Cousin John.

Mary received your letters and will write soon. I hope you all have the chance to come home and see us before long. I hope you all will try and not be low spirited.

You must not think I have forgotten you because I have not written sooner. Tell Cousin John to write.

I remain your true and affectionate Sister, Sallie

1   This was Lucy Hopson Lumpkin Pope, wife of Middleton Pope and daughter of former Georgia Governor Wilson Lumpkin. She was Lucy Barrow's maternal grandmother. Lucy's mother, Sarah Pope Barrow, died when Lucy was 10 years old and Mrs. Pope raised her.

2   Mary Cochran was listed in the 1860 Georgia census as the 19-year-old daughter of Martha Cochran, 45-year-old farmer in the Falling Creek District of Oglethorpe County, along with an older brother and 5 younger brothers and sisters. Warren Hayes Bearden was listed in the 1860 Georgia census as the 26-year-old son of Parthenia G. Bearden of Athens. He enlisted as a Private in Co. K., 3rd Regiment, Georgia Volunteer Infantry (Athens Guards),

but transferred to Co. L (Clarke County Rifles) in 1862. Bearden was successively promoted to 2nd Lieutenant, 1st Lieutenant, and Captain. He served throughout the war and was wounded at the battles of Chancellorsville, Spotsylvania Court House, and Petersburg.

3   Lemay is unidentified but may have been a slave.

JULY 27TH 1863

My Dear Brother,

I received two letters from you last week and ought to have answered them sooner, but when I give you the reasons you will excuse me I know. one of them I received Tuesday evening and Wednesday we had company. Cousin Richard Maddox and cousin John, William Maddox's son, came up from Uncle Billies. they come Saturday evening before the 3rd Sunday to Uncle Billies. he came with them up here Wed. He seemed to be very low spirited all day. Cousin Rich and John staid all the week with us, or Cousin John left Saturday evening and went to Ham. Buggs, and cousin Rick went with us to Antioch yesterday and then Bugg sent for him yesterday evening and he went there. Friday Cousin Matilda [Campbell Gilham], Mary Gilham, the two Miss Wises and Mrs C Landrum came and spent the day. and day before yesterday Cousin Camilla [Smith], and George [Jewel], Emma Smith[1] and Paschal [Smith], Patty Moore[2] and Becky [Moore] was here and Mr Taylor and Mary Crowley. So you know I had a bad chance to write.

Eliza and Sou [Sue] came up Tues morning. I was very glad to see them, they were all well down there. Mattie is sweet as sugar. she does not look altogether as fleshy as she did. Liza said she had been sick, but she was very lively when she was up here. that is a pretty little ring you made her. she will hold up her hand to show it to any body. Those you sent me were too small. Bud came up yesterday. He come by to see Cousin Sarah. she is very sick indeed. They thought she was mending slowly but I dont think she has ever been any better. Dr B. [Bell] says she cannot live long. she has been bleeding at the gums and nose ever since last Thursday. Bell tells her the symptoms are better but tells other people that every symptom is worse. she has never been able to sit up any since she was first taken sick. They have sent on to try to get Davy[3] home, but if he does not come soon I dont think he will see her.

Jimmie & John went up to Brother Marshalls Saturday but I have not heard the news from there yet. they are coming down Friday if nothing happens. Columbus Landrum is going to have an examination Thursday. I want to go if there is nothing to prevent [it]. I suppose you have heard of the members of the Oglethorpe Rifles that was killed. Mr Gilham went to Virginia after Berry Bowling. they heard he was severly wounded but it was only a slight wound. he had gone back to his company before Mr Gilham left home. he got home with Tom Saturday evening. Tom has been in the hospital a long time. his furlough is 40 days. He looks thin but is able to [get] about.

The drums are beating for more volunteers but they come slowly. I expect there will have to be a draft in some counties. Mr Mell preached for us the 3rd Sunday. he says the counties up above us are promptly responding to the call. Bud has joined a cavalry company[4] in Bairdstown. he bought a horse from Uncle Andy Campbell.[5] They do not know when they will be called upon to go. as soon as there is any probability of a raid being made. some think that will be early. I was in hopes you could have been at home by this time. I think it will certainly be your time to come before long. I would have been glad if you could have seen Cousin John & Richard. I know you could have spent a pleasant time with them. Cousin John sorter half way promised to come here again tomorrow, but I do not know how it will be. He is as much like Cousin John as common for Cousins to be. he is about his size, not quite so tall. everybody that has seen him says they are alike. he is at home any where he goes. He has been in the army nearly a year in Mississippi, Tenesee, and Kentucky. it is very interesting to hear him tell over his travels. his Pa gave $4000 for a substitute for him and Cousin Rich $3500. some how [or] another the report got out that they had come off to keep from being conscripted, and Dr Lumpkin[6] told Ham Bugg at Antioch yesterday that some of their kinsfolks told they were deserters and Ham he could not keep it to

... [remainder of letter missing]

1   Emma Smith was the daughter of James E. and Martha Jane Smith (cited previously).

2   Patty Moore is unidentified.

3   Davy was Davy Christopher, husband of Sarah Parris Christopher (both already identified).

4   William Jewel, II joined Co. D, 7th Georgia Battalion (State Guards), in August 1863 as a Private. Colonel Linton Stephens, half-brother to Alexander H. Stephens, was commanding officer. The unit was formed as a local defense company to serve in the 5th, 6th, and 8th congressional districts.

5   Andrew J. Campbell was not Sallie's uncle. She also called Andrew's younger brother Franklin C. "cousin." Andrew and Franklin's older brother, William, was married to Elizabeth Jewel, sister to James Jewel, Sr.

6   Dr. George Lumpkin is listed in the 1860 Georgia census as a 35-year-old physician in the Bowling Green District of Oglethorpe County, along with Jane, 25, and two young sons.

NO DATE

Dear Brother,

I received your letter last week. We are all very well. It has been raining all day and the wind is blowing cold. I think it will surely be cool weather after this. it is the first rain we have had in a good while. Pa has been quite busy for the last two or three days picking peas. it was so cloudy he was afraid it would be a wet spell. he says he has about half of his peas gathered and half of [his] corn under shelter. our potatoe crop will not be very good, [the] potatoes are small.

Liza intended going home today. Pa was going with her but the rain prevented [it]. She is anxious to get off. she wants her Pa to see [Alexander H.] Stephens about getting you off. she has been low spirited this week for fear you would have to go to Maryland. little Martha is well and fat as a pig. she will laugh a little and play. she has got to be a right good baby. she is the sweetest little creature that ever was.

Berry [Bowling] has been over to see us this week. he is very low spirited. he expects to go back before a great while.

Monday. It is still cloudy & disagreeable weather. it rained all day yesterday. I think the ground is thoroughly wet. the negroes are shucking corn this morning. Pa is going with Liza home if it does not rain again. I wish she could have staid longer with us, it will be very lonesome without her.

it was reported a few days ago that your company was ordered off, but we did not hear where to. but as we have not heard anything of it anymore we will have to wait and see if there will be another [report]. somebody about here keeps very well posted about here. Tom Martin & Gus Hurt, I understood, were going up to Randolph. Tom says he cannot walk any distance on his foot or step suddenly off anything. I [reckon] he has forgotten about dancing so much. I reckon he will get in with Dr Lumpkin and manage some way to get off. I have not seen or heard from George Martin since he came home. I do not know when he will go back. I heard that Jim Hurt had come but I have not seen him. his Mother had the measles.

Some of the people in this neighborhood are going down the country after salt. they are going to carry their kettles and wagons down there. William Raidens,[1] Col Nichols, Nat Hunter, Uncle John, and several others are making up their company. Brother, I think, is about getting out of [the] idea of going, it is too great an undertaking for him. As for our part, I do not know what we will have to do, without we dig up the smokehouse.[2]

Bud Jimmie, I have written all the news. I heard from Brother Marshall last week. they were all well. all of our friends are well as far as I know. All send their love to you. I remain your affectionate Sister

Sallie

---

1   William R. Raiden [not Raidens] is listed in the 1860 Georgia census as a 31-year-old farmer in the Falling Creek District of Oglethorpe County.

2   During the War Between the States many farmers dug the soil from beneath the outbuildings where hams and bacon had been salt-cured annually for many years and leached the salt from the dirt with water. The salt was recovered by boiling and evaporating the water.

UNDATED NOTE

My Dear Brother

As Mary has written a letter I thought it would be useless for me to write this time. Sis May has the mumps and has been right sick with them. Bud and Mat came up Sunday night, they were well. they saw John at Atkinsons,[1] he said Liza and all the rest were well. You must write soon. Cousin John offered to take any thing we wanted to send you but we did not know what you needed and we thought he would [have] a right smart to carry besides. I hope these lines may find you well. Good bye my dear brother. Your true and affectionate sister, Sallie

1   Atkinsons is unidentified.

AFTERWORD

It is unlikely that anyone could spend as much time as I did reading and transcribing the Jewel letters and researching the family history without forming some sort of emotional bond with certain individuals. On reading and rereading their correspondence, I became attached to James, Sallie, and other family members and their friends. I acquired a strong desire to learn what happened to certain people after the war, especially to James's parents, sister Sallie, wife Eliza, baby Mattie, brother William, and Cousin John.

James's mother died December 28, 1866, at age 64. His father lived $11^1/_2$ years longer and died July 12, 1878, at age 90. Sallie remained at home with her widowed father and unmarried twin sisters until, at age 26, she married Edwin J. Campbell on November 23, 1871. Edwin Campbell was the son of Franklin C. and Clementine Campbell and was the brother to Martha C. Campbell, who was married to Sallie's brother, William Jewel, II. Sallie and Edwin had four children, two of whom survived infancy. Lizzie May was born September 8, 1872. James Norwood (called Nord) was born October 17, 1879. Lizzie May never married and died March 26, 1930. After Lizzie May died, Nord married Claudia Estelle Thomas, a sweetheart from his youth, on October 12, 1930, when he was 51 years old. Nord and Claudia had no children, and Nord died April 27, 1959, at age 79.

James's older brother William, II, married Martha B. Taylor in 1857. It was not determined what happened to her but in 1867 he married Martha C. Campbell. William had no children by either wife. After just over 40 of marriage, Martha Campbell Jewel died January 22, 1908. William survived $2^1/_2$ years more and died July 30, 1910, at age 80.

Cousin John married his longtime sweetheart Sara F. Stevens March 3, 1864, and eventually had four children: William B., Annie Elizabeth, Kattie Bell, and Lilla M. John died June 30, 1925.

When James did not return home, Eliza and $2^1/_2$-year-old Mattie remained with Eliza's family in the Penfield District of Greene County. Mattie never married and preceded her mother in death by almost 14 years, dying of typhoid fever on August 11, 1897, just 3 weeks before her 35th birthday. Eliza did not remarry and was 78 when she died July 30, 1911. Her will, dated 4 days before her death, declared that she was "of sound and disposing mind and memory" but further stated that she was blind and had signed her name with an X before witnesses. Although the War Between the States had been over for 46 years, the memories of the personal grief that it brought must have been with her to the end. In the space of just $2\frac{1}{2}$ years, from August 1862 to March 1865, Eliza lost two brothers and her husband to the war, and her younger sister and grandmother died of sickness at home. The list does not include numerous other relatives and close friends who died during that time. Eliza and Mattie are buried among family members in the Colclough family cemetery near the home place of her parents, 4 miles west of Penfield on the North side of Fishing Creek.

Most of James's family are buried in the family cemetery at the home place in Oglethorpe County (33⁰49'09" 83⁰12'00"). The old house has been gone for many years. All that remains are the chimneys and a scattering of wild daffodils that beautify the surrounding woods each spring. The headstones marking each grave site also serve as footstones for huge white oak trees which now claim the area.

Of literally millions of letters written by soldiers on both sides during the War Between the States, relatively few are extant and even fewer reach the printing press to be shared with enthusiasts of that period. James's and Sallie's letters are among the survivors that were cherished and passed down to the present. Sallie retained the letters until her old age, at which time she gave them to her son Nord. When Sallie died in 1927, Nord gave them to a cousin (Sallie's niece) who was the great-granddaughter of Sallie's sister, Jane Jewel Edwards. Sometime in the 1930s a collector from Atlanta acquired eight of James's letters from Sallie's niece and they eventually were deposited in the Special Collections Department in the Robert W. Woodruff Library at Emory University in Atlanta (Confederate Miscellany Ia 4). These letters are included with the permission of Emory University and each is identified as it appears in the text. Sallie's niece owned the remainder of the letters until the early 1980s and, having no children, passed them on to me. And I will cherish and protect them until they are passed on to the next steward.

Gary L. Doster

APPENDIX A
GENEALOGICAL TABLES

The following genealogical tables were originally developed as "work sheets" to help sort out and identify various family members as they were encountered in the letters and identified in the footnotes. There was no intention to include the tables in the book. However, because they may also help the reader to better understand how everyone fits in, and because there is some information here that some readers will value, I decided to include them. I am positive of the accuracy of most of this information; however, the reader is cautioned that some of this information must be considered tentative, and some tables are quite incomplete. The tables are presented alphabetically.

JOHN BELL FAMILY

John Bell m. Mary (it is not known if she was the mother of his children)

His children (listed in the order they were named in his will):

1. John A. m. Mary Ward
2. James
3. Rebecca b.1802 m. 1819 **James Jewel, Sr.** b. 1788
4. Elizabeth b. 1808 m. **William Jewel, I** b. 1800
5. Sylvanus
6. Nancy m. Joseph Cramer
7. Patsy m. Beasley Whitlock

WILLIAM CAMPBELL FAMILY

William Campbell – wife's name unknown

His children (listed in the order they were named in his will):

1. Andrew Campbell m. Nancy Patrick

2. William m. Elizabeth Jewel (**sister to James Jewel, Sr.**)
   a. Martha Jane Campbell m. James E. Smith

3. Franklin C. m. Clementine [?]
   a. William M. Campbell m. Docia Sheets
   b. Edwin J. Campbell m. **Sarah Rebecca (Sallie) Jewel**
   c. Joseph Campbell m. Lizzie Eidson
   d. Matilda Campbell m. John M. Gilham
   e. Martha C. Campbell m. **William Jewel, II**
   f. Mary R. Campbell m. John A. Christopher
   g. "Sis" Campbell m. Will Ellis

4. Bailey A. m. Mary A. Betts

5. Peggy m. [?] Johnson

6. Polly m.[?] Varner

7. Jane m. Simeon Cramer

8. Betsy m. [?] Johnson
   a. William A. Johnson
   b. Rufus M. Johnson
   c. Eliza L. Johnson m. [?] Timmons
   d. Martha A. Johnson m. [?] Spearman

JOHN & NANCY COLCLOUGH FAMILY

John Colclough, b. Dec. 8, 1800, d. March 13, 1868 (son of Charity d. 1846) m. Nancy Nelms, b. Feb. 11, 1812, d. Feb. 14, 1892 (daughter of Sallie Nelms, d. Nov. 1862)

Their children (listed in the order of birth):

1. William A., b. May 9, 1827, d. June 10, 1896, m. Matilda J. Moore Nov. 12, 1854, b. May 20, 1833, d. Feb. 18, 1919
   - a. Tallulah
   - b. William A., Jr.
   - c. John
   - d. Margaret
   - e. Matilda
   - f. Julia
   - g. Peter
   - h. Burnette C.

2. Thomas F., b. Aug. 22, 1829, d. Aug. 21, 1862, m. Aug. 11, 1859 to Sarah F. Taylor
   - a. Laura
   - b. Sallie

3. Sarah Ann, b. Feb. 22, 1831, d. April 26, 1914, not m.

4. **Eliza Cordelia**, b. April 15, 1833, d. July 30, 1911, m. Dec. 1, 1859 to **James Jewel, Jr.**
   - a. Martha Elizabeth (Mattie)

5. Charity Elizabeth, b. Nov. 16, 1835, d. Oct. 11, 1841

6. Franklin W., b. May 1, 1838, d. Sept. 16, 1862, not m.

7. Rebecca D., b. Sept. 9, 1840, d. April 26, 1863, not m.

8. Susan Elizabeth, b.Sept. 8, 1842, d. Nov. 8, 1876, not m.

9. John Martin, b. Dec. 17, 1845, d. July 6, 1930. m. Feb. 5, 1874 to Frances Josephine Boswell
   - a. John Ernest
   - b. Susan Estelle
   - c. Clarence
   - d. Lila
   - e. Annie
   - f. James Howard
   - g. Hattie Irene
   - h. Unnamed infant
   - i. Fannie Etta

10. James D., b. 1849 or 1850, d.1907, m. Sarah R. Durham,
 b. 1857, d. 1914

   a. Mavis S.

   b. John L.

   c. Walter James

   d. Charles Paul

   e. Robert

   f. Jewel

   g. John

   h. Sarah

   i. Richard

11. Daniel W., b. 1852, d. 1938, m. Ruth Champion,
 b. 1876, d. 1914

   a. Mary M.

JOSEPH & JANE JEWEL FAMILY

Joseph Jewel m. Jane [?]

Their children (listed alphabetically):

1. Elizabeth m. William Campbell

2. **James, Sr.** b. 1819 m. **Rebecca Bell** b. 1802

3. Margaret m. Anthony W. Mattox

4. Martha not m.

5. Polly m. 1809 Paschal Smith

6. Sarah m.1819 Nathan H. Parris

7. **William, I** b. 1800 m. **Elizabeth Bell** b. 1808

James & Rebecca Jewel Family

James Jewel, Sr., b. March 15, 1788, d. July 12, 1878, m. Feb. 3, 1819, to **Rebecca Bell** b. Aug. 6, 1802, d. Dec. 28, 1866

Their children (listed in the order of birth):

1. Martha, b. Nov. 5, 1820, d. Nov. 22, 1851, not m.

2. Rebecca Elizabeth, b. Oct. 4, 1822, d. May 11, 1895, m. Jan. 7, 1841 to Benajah Crowley b. Sept 30, 1816, d. Jan. 12, 1865
   a. Rebecca Susan d. age 12
   b. Martha J. m. Joseph N. Bird
   c. Mary E. m. D.B. Fitzgerald
   d. James T. m. Nancy Susan Spratlin
   e. John Bell m. Mary E. Thomas
   f. William Jewel m. Fannie Tribble
   g. Joseph Franklin m.1st Mittie Eidson 2nd Mary Virginia (Mrs. Ed) Martin
   h. Sarah P. not m.
   i. Emma m. W.W. Maples
   j. Ella m. 1st Frank D. Eidson 2nd M.F. Drake
   k. Maggie
   l. Benajah M. m. Margaret M. Vaughn

3. Jane, b. Sept. 28, 1824, d. May 26, 1910, m. Dec. 12, 1841 or 1844 to Rev. Marshall Washington Edwards b. Nov. 18, 1821 d. Feb. 12, 1890.
   a. Lemuel J. m. Elizabeth Ann [unknown]
   b. Mary Rebecca m. Landrus R. Eidson
   c. George M.
   d. Martha J. m. [unknown] Young
   e. Benjamin C. m. 1st Sallie Moore, 2nd Nellie Marshall, 3rd Loubelle McCollum

4. John, b. Jan. 8, 1826, d. Jan., 1827

5. & 6. Twins, Mary & Margaret, b. Nov. 23, 1827. Mary d. Feb. 24, 1887, and Margaret d. Sept. 1, 1912 - neither m.

7. William, b. Jan. 5, 1830, d. July 30, 1910, m. 1st Martha B. Taylor, Nov. 17, 1857, 2nd Martha C. Campbell, Oct. 8, 1867, no children

8. **James, Jr.**, b. July 29, 1834, d. March, 1865, m. Dec. 1, 1859, to **Eliza Cordelia Colclough**, b. April 15, 1833, d. July, 30, 1911

   a. Martha Elizabeth (Mattie) b. Sept. 1, 1862, d. Aug. 11, 1897, not m.

9. **Sarah Rebecca (Sallie)**, b. March 15, 1845, d. March 31, 1927, m. Nov. 23, 1871 to Edwin J. Campbell, b. Oct. 6, 1845, d. Feb 12, 1909; 2 of 4 children survived infancy:

   a. Lizzie May b. Sept. 8, 1872, d. March 26, 1930, not m.

   b. James Norwood (Nord) b. Oct 17, 1879, d. April 27, 1959, m. Oct. 12, 1930 to Claudia Estelle Thomas, no children

WILLIAM & ELIZABETH JEWEL FAMILY

Willilam Jewel, b. 1800, d. July 24, 1866 (brother to **James Jewel, Sr.**), m. to **Elizabeth Bell**, b. 1808, d. June 21, 1871, (sister to **Rebecca Bell**, who m. **James Jewel, Sr.**)

Their children (listed in the order of birth):

1. George Hughey – not m.
2. Edgar Emory, m. Civility C. [unknown]
   a. Dianna E.
   b. Laura
   c. Bessy
   d. Cornelius Judson
   e. Edgar
   f. Emma
   g. Crawford
   h. Ida May

3. Emmilay, m. Dr. William Stack Meiere
   a. Julius
   b. Anna

4. **John Anderson** (**Cousin John**), m. March 3, 1864, to Sarah F. Stephens, b. Mar. 24, 1846, d. Sept. 17, 1917
   a. William B.
   b. Annie Elizabeth
   c. Kattie Bell
   d. Lilla M.

5. Marcus de Lafayette, m. Nancy Susan Arthur
   a. James William
   b. Mattie Elizabeth
   c. Willie Mae
   d. Edgar Emory
   e. Joseph Lee

6. Susan Camilla, m. William P. Smith
   a. Emily
   b. Robert
   c. George
   d. Anna
   e. Mary
   f. Glendora

APPENDIX B
OBITUARIES

Available obituaries of some family members of James Jewel and Eliza Colclough Jewel. Cited alphabetically.

Edwin J. Campbell
From the *Oglethorpe Echo*, Lexington, GA, February 19, 1909

Death of Mr. Ed Campbell

The spirit of Mr. E.J. Campbell was called to the great beyond last Friday night about eight o'clock. His remains were laid to rest Sunday by the side of his sister, Mrs. J.A. Christopher, in the Jewell cemetery, after funeral services were conducted by Rev. John D. Mell. Mention was made of his serious illness in last week's issue. He was a Confederate veteran and a member of the Baptist church. The vast number of friends and relatives attending his burial spoke the esteem and respect in which he was held in life.

Sarah Rebecca Jewel Campbell
From the *Oglethorpe Echo*, Lexington, GA, April 8, 1927

Aged Lady Goes Hence

Mrs Sallie R. Campbell, who had just passed her eighty-second birthday, died at her home near Stephens Thursday of last week after five years of invalidism. As Miss Sallie R. Jewell she was married to Mr. Edwin R. Campbell November 30th, 1871, he having preceded her to the beyond eighteen years ago. She is survived by one daughter and one son, Miss Lizzie May Campbell and Mr. James Norwood Campbell, to whom deep sympathy of hosts of friends is extended in their bereavement of truly a mother in Israel. While quite young she united with Antioch Baptist church and for more than half a century had been a consistent member and a consecrated Christian. After impressive funeral services conducted by her former pastor, Rev. W.M. Coile, Friday morning, her remains were laid to rest by the side of those of her husband in the family cemetery within a few yards of her birthplace, the old James Jewel place, pall bearers being nephews of the deceased, Ed J. Crowley, B.M. and R.E. Edwards, W.F. Gilham, Edward Earl and Henry B. Morris. A large concourse of friends and relatives were present to pay the beloved deceased a last sad tribute and the floral offerings were many and beautiful. Truly a good woman has gone to her reward.

John Colclough
From *The Christian Index and South-Western Baptist,*
Atlanta, GA, April 16, 1868

Colclough – Died, at his residence in Greene County, Ga., on the night of the 13th of March, 1868, John Colclough, in the 68th year of his age.

About the first of March he was prostrated by a violent pneumonia, which, in spite of attentive nurses and skillful physicians, continued to make steady progress until death – to him a kind messenger - came to his relief.

Brother C. was born the 8th of December, 1800, in Warren County, North Carolina, but was removed when a child, to Middle Georgia, where spent the rest of his life. He was a man of steady, industrious habits, and had, by careful attention to his own business, accumulated a considerable estate, and though the greater portion was swept away by the recent political tornado, yet a sufficiency was left to make his family comfortable, so far as property can do it.

Among the many noble traits which adorned his character, were those of honesty, candor, and truth. About the year 1830, he was baptized into the fellowship of the Baptist church at Shiloh, Greene County, but subsequently changed it to what is now the Macedonia Baptist church, of the same county, about the year 1839, at which time he was elected deacon, which office he not only continued to hold, but actively and faithfully continued to discharge in said church, the many duties of said office as long as he lived.

His loss is sensibly and sadly felt by neighbors, relatives, church, his former servants – in fact, by the whole community, but most keenly and sorely by his greatly distressed widow and weeping children and grand-children.

And now he is dead, there is solid comfort in the thought that he died the death of the Christian. His mind, to the last, was cool, calm, clear, composed, sensible of every passing thing, of the progress of the disease, of the giving way of his frame, of the nearness of death. He forgot nothing, he omitted nothing, but seemed more like one in perfect health arranging for the dissolution of some one else. And *finally*, calling up his family, he gave them, one at a time, a final farewell, and a parting admonition to meet him again, and then gently closed his eyes on earthly things and fell asleep in Jesus. Heed, dear children, a sainted father's dying admonition.

W.A.O.

John M. Colclough
From *The Herald-Journal*, Greensboro, GA, July 11, 1930

John M. Colclough Dies at Penfield
Prominent Penfield Citizen Passes Away After Long Illness

Mr. John M. Colclough, one of the oldest citizens of the county passed away Sunday afternoon, at his home in Penfield.

A pioneer citizen of Greene, he had a large share in the county's growth, holding many places of honor and trust.

He was converted at an early age and throughout his life he served the Baptist Church, at Penfield, in every capacity afforded a member. His influence as an upright citizen and consistent Christian was powerful in shaping the religious life of the community.

Appreciative but never boastful of his ancestry, which was his, he reflected the worth while things in every phase of his life in a simple unobtrusive manner.

Mr. Colclough was a man of deep conviction and was not swayed by popular opinions. He reached his own conclusions and dared to stand by them. He lived and died among people who had known him all his life. He had been in failing health some time, due to his advanced years.

The funeral was held Monday. Rev. R.L. Robinson, of the Union Point Baptist Church and Rev. M.A. Macdonald, pastor of the Union Point Presbyterian Church, officiated.

Mr. Colclough is survived by his daughters, Miss Estelle Colclough, Mrs. T.W. Cannon, and J.H. Colclough of Penfield; Mrs. Irene Paschal, of Atlanta; Mrs. R.F. Whelchel, of Decatur, and Mrs. J.E. Colclough of Columbia, S.C.

The pall bearers were Hon. F.E. Boswell, Mr. Ralph Boswell, Mr. E.R. Boswell, Mr. Ben Colclough, Mr. A.J. Boswell.

Matilda Colclough
From *The Herald-Journal*, Greensboro, GA, February 21, 1919

Aged Lady Passes Away at Penfield

The death of Mrs. Matilda Colclough occurred Tuesday at Penfield. The deceased was eighty-six years of age and lived an exemplary Christian life. She was the consort of the late William Colclough.

The following sons and daughters are left to mourn the going away of this splendid woman: Mrs. Lula Geer, Miss Jimmie Colclough, Messrs John T. Colclough, Peter Colclough, William Colclough.

The funeral occurred Wednesday from the Penfield Baptist Church. Rev. R.E.L. Harris officiating.

Sarah Ann Colclough
From *The Herald-Journal*, Greensboro, GA, May 1, 1914

Death at Penfield of Miss Sallie Colclough

Miss Sallie Colclough passed away Sunday at noon at the home of her brother, Mr. John M. Colclough at Penfield.

The deceased was 83 years of age at the time of her death. She had lived a consistent christian life and has now gone to reap her reward.

The funeral occurred Monday. Rev. John S. Callaway officiating. Interment was in the family cemetery near Penfield.

Benajah Crowley
From *The Christian Index*, Macon, GA, April 6, 1865

Died in a military hospital in Augusta, on the 12th of January, 1865, Benajah Crowley in the 49th year of his age.

Bro. C. was baptized by the venerable Jack Lumpkin, and united with the Antioch church, Oglethorpe County, where his membership remained to the time of his death. His quiet demeanor, punctuality and faithfulness in the discharge of duty, genial temper and consistency of christian conduct secured him the affection of his brethren and the confidence of his acquaintances. He was one of those rare characters whom, though marked with strong individuality, men felt no disposition to disparage. When the time came for those of his age and position to take their places in the ranks of the country's defenders, he unhesitatingly obeyed the call. In vain did friends urge that he should plead physical disability of long standing, and appeal to a Medical Board for exemption. His country had called for him, and he was prepared to *do what he could*, leaving the event with God. It pleased the Lord that his term of service should not be of long duration, and that he should die thus away from wife and children; but His rod and His staff they comforted him: Thus has fallen another victim of this atrocious war.

P.H.M.
[Patrick Hues Mell]

Rebecca Elizabeth Jewel Crowley
From the *Oglethorpe Echo*, Lexington, GA, May 11, 1895

An Old Lady Dead.

Saturday morning last at 8:30 o'clock at her home in the Big Creek neighborhood, Mrs. Elizabeth Crowley, aged seventy-three years, peacefully breathed her last after a short illness. Mrs. Crowley was truly a mother in Israel. Being left a widow during the war, she reared by her own efforts a family of eleven children and lived to see them all good and useful citizens. She was beloved by a large circle of acquaintances, a consistent member of the Baptist church. Her remains were laid to rest at Herman church Sunday, Rev. J.F. Cheney conducting the services. She leaves a large family and connection to mourn their loss.

From *The Christian Index*, Macon, GA, June 6, 1895

Crowley – Mrs. Elizabeth Crowley (nee Jewell) was born October 4, 1822; baptized at Antioch Baptist church, Oglethorpe County by Billington Sanders August 1842. Joined Corinth church by letter Feb. 9, 1890. She was married to Benajah Crowley, Jany. 7, 1841, who died in the Confederate service, leaving her a widow with six daughters and five sons to be reared, all of whom are living to-day, and each of whom is a credit to the mother, being consistent members of the church and worthy members of the communities in which they live.

Sister Crowley was a remarkable woman possessing marked individuality, having fine common sense, strong convictions, expressing herself fluently yet forcibly. She was a devoted mother, an earnest Christian, never neglecting the duty of family prayer, a close student of the Bible, liberal and regular in her contributions for missions. She was a regular subscriber to the Index from the time it was called the Columbian Star until the day of her death. She was an inspiration to her pastor, quick to detect error, ready to endorse the truth, convincing all with whom she came in contact that she was a Christian. Her children, her church, her pastor, and her community have sustained a great loss. While her children are bereaved indeed, they ought to rejoice that the Lord gave them such a mother, and they should endeavor to imitate her patient, faithful, godly example. Though dead she yet speaketh, through her children and in the many good works that follow her devoted Christian life. A large crowd of relatives and friends followed her remains to Herman where her body was deposited in the silent tomb, each feeling that truly a mother in Israel had gone to her final reward.

In looking back over her past life her pastor wishes to say, that in every department of life, at home, in the community, and in the church, in the midst of duties and trials it could be said of her in simple truth, "She hath done what she could."

John F. Cheney.
Crawford, Ga., May 23, 1895

Jane Jewel Edwards
From the *Oglethorpe Echo*, Lexington, GA, June 3, 1910

Death of Excellent Lady

The sad death of Mrs. Jane Edwards last week at the home of her daughter Mrs. L.R. Eidson, on Big Creek, brought sorrow to the hearts of many relatives and a host of friends. She was eighty-five years of age and during her long life had usually enjoyed the best health. Her advanced age had brought feebleness and on the tenth of May she suffered a fall, dislocating her hip, which injury was the immediate cause of her death. She was the relict of Rev. Marshal Edwards, who was an ordained Baptist minister, and who preceded her to the grave a number of years. She was the mother of five children, Mr. George Edwards, whose home is near Atlanta; Mr. Ben Edwards of Decatur; Mr. Lemuel Edwards of Winterville; Mrs. Eidson, at whose home she was living at the time of her death; and Mrs. Mattie J. Young, who died some years ago. Before her marriage, Mrs. Edwards was a Jewell. She was a member of the Antioch Baptist church, joining when she was twenty years old, being the oldest member of that church and had lived a most exemplary life. The funeral services were conducted last Saturday by her pastor, Rev. Jno. D. Mell, and the body was laid away in the family burying ground.

Marshall Washington Edwards
From *The Christian Index*, Macon, GA, March 13, 1890

Edwards – Rev. Marshall W. Edwards, was born November 18, 1821, joined the church at Antioch, Oglethorpe County, GA., December 11, 1841, and died a consistent member of the same, after a long, upright, and useful life, on February 12, 1890, in the 69th year of his age.

He was ordained to the Gospel ministry June 3rd, 1871. Though not many times pastor of churches, yet he did a considerable amount of preaching during the nineteen years of his ministerial life in destitute places where, by him alone, "the poor had the gospel preached to them."

He was pastor of Pleasant Grove, in Madison county, for a number of years, where he was greatly beloved and did much good.

He was punctual in compliance with all his business and religious engagements; successful in life, and very thoughtful in praying for his children, and teaching them the importance of being Christian.

He leaves a wife and five children – all members of the church – with a large number of relatives and friends to mourn his loss. But the bright hope and earnest faith of him who has gone before, will ever admonish us all who knew him, to come up higher.

W.M. Coile
Winterville, Ga.

Eliza Cordelia Colclough Jewel
From *The Herald-Journal*, Greensboro, GA, August 18, 1911

Mrs. Eliza Jewell Dead.

Penfield Correspondent

Mrs. Eliza Jewell died at her home in Penfield, Sunday afternoon, July 30, and was buried, after the services in the Baptist church, at the old home cemetery about four miles from town.

Mrs. Jewell had been a great sufferer of rheumatism, neuralgia and a complication of diseases for several months previous to her death.

Mrs. Jewell was married to Mr. James Jewell, of Oglethorpe County, during the Civil War. He was called away to defend his country, leaving her and an infant. He never returned to tell the horrors of war in all of its cruelties.

Many, many times she watched and waited, hoping to hear of him some where on his return home. After many years she gave up all hope of his return, and devoted her life to her young daughter, Mattie, whom she reared to womanhood, when just at the brightest and most useful period of life, she died of typhoid fever. Mrs. Jewell continued to live with her only sister until the time came.

She was a consistent member of the Baptist church, her life was long and useful, always the happiest while denying herself for the pleasure of others.

She was the sister of Miss Sallie A. Colclough, Mr. John M. Colclough, and Mr. D.W. Colclough, all of Penfield. The other brother and sister preceded her to the great beyond.

John A. Jewel

From the *Oglethorpe Echo*, Lexington, GA, July 8, 1925

Veteran John A. Jewell Answers Last Roll Call

After a gradual decline from old age of more than a year, Mr. John A. Jewell, in his eighty-fifth year, peacefully breathed his last at home in Crawford Monday morning at four o'clock. Mr. Jewell was a native of the county, having been born near Stephens in 1840 and had spent his entire life in our midst. No citizen of the county was more widely or favorably known than he, he having ever taken a prominent part in public affairs.

On March 4th, 1863, he married Miss Sarah Frances Stevens, their happy united life lasting until eight years ago, when she passed away. To this union were born four children, two of whom survive – Mrs. Bell Barnes, who had for many years given her father and mother devoted care, and Mrs. Lilla Houser, of Meridian, Miss. Mr. Jewell had been a devout member of the Baptist church since early life and it was at his church in Crawford that his funeral was conducted Tuesday afternoon at four o'clock by his pastor, Rev. Y.T. Shehane. His remains were afterwards laid to rest besides those of his wife in the Crawford cemetery.

Mr. Jewell was one of the few remaining veterans of the Civil War, having been among the first to enlist in defense of his beloved Southland and serving valiantly almost the entire four years of the struggle. His death takes from amongst us one of the oldest and most highly honored citizens. That he is at rest from the worries of a long and quite active life and infirmities of old age can be accepted as true.

To the bereaved ones goes out the sympathies of many friends, especial condolences being offered the devoted daughter, Mrs. Barnes, in whose loving care the father had been for so long a time. Their consolation is that he has but rejoined their sainted mother on the righter shore where they too may go and all again be united in the happy family that they were while in life.

Martha Elizabeth Jewel
From the *Oglethorpe Echo*, Lexington, GA, August 13, 1897

Miss Mattie Jewell, quite well known in this county, died at her home in Greene county Wednesday evening. She was about twenty-five years old [actually she was 35] and had many friends. Her death was unexpected as she had only been ill a few days with fever.

From *The Herald-Journal*, Greensboro, GA, August 13, 1897

At 12 o'clock on Wednesday last, Miss Mattie Jewell passed from this life. She was a lady of unsurpassable character, and a member of the Baptist church, and deserved the admiration of all who knew her. Her home was in 4 miles of this place, and she will be buried in the family cemetery. We extend to the bereaved family our sympathy in their sore affliction.

Penfield, Ga.
C.B.B.

Rebecca Bell Jewel
From *The Christian Index and South-Western Baptist*, Atlanta, GA, February 14, 1867

Jewell – Died, in Oglethorpe County, Ga., Dec. 28th, 1866, in the 65th year of her age, Mrs. Rebecca Jewel, wife of James Jewel. She was for many years a consistent member of the Baptist church

Another circle on earth is broken; another glorified spirit has entered Heaven! God saw fit grievously to afflict her ere she was called hence; but Jesus was with her as she passed through the valley of death, and her faith failed not. We shall never meet her again on earth; but may we all mingle with that happy throng in that purer clime where death and sorrow never come!

M.

APPENDIX C
ROSTER OF
ECHOLS LIGHT ARTILLERY

This roster was constructed with information from several sources. The primary reference is the Compiled Military Service Records of the Echols Artillery, which was assembled from the following six original muster rolls in the National Archives, Washington, DC. (National Archives Microfilm Publications, Microcopy no. 266, roll 115):

> July & August 1862 – Atlanta, GA
>
> September & October 1862 – Atlanta, GA
>
> March & April 1863 – Camp Brokaw, FL
>
> July & August 1863 – Quincy, FL
>
> March & April 1864 – Camp Leon, FL
>
> November & December 1864 – Ft. Johnson, SC

Also consulted was the original roster of Echols Artillery, dated March 4, 1862, which is located in the Georgia Department of Archives and History, Atlanta.

Additional information came from a reconstructed roster of Echols Artillery made between 1904 and 1931 under the direction of the Georgia Soldiers' Roster Commission. The original copy of that roster is located in the Oglethorpe County Court House, Lexington, GA.

Additional information, such as individuals' names instead of initials, was added from other sources.

All individuals were privates, except those whose higher ranks are noted after their names. Enlistment date follows name or rank.

Amason, Manoah Bolton (also Amerson), Cpl, May 3, 1862. Sent to hospital in Tallahassee, FL, July 28, 1864; no further record.

Appling, James, March 4, 1862. Discharged Dec.1, 1862, by hiring Wilson Cantrell as a substitute.

Armstrong, Joseph W., May 3, 1862.

Banks, Henry D., June 1, 1862. Paroled at Greensboro, NC, April 26, 1865.

Banks, James, March 4, 1862.

Banks, John L., March 4, 1862. Died of "congestive chill" in the hospital in Tallahassee, FL, Dec. 10, 1863.

Banks, W.T., March 4, 1862. Died of "dropsy" Dec. 8, 1863, in Oglethorpe County.

Barnes, C.R., March 1, 1863. Hired as substitute for Joshua Lester; died of "fever" July 28, 1863, in Jackson Co., GA.

Barnett, David A.F., May 3, 1862.

Barnett, E.H., March 4, 1862.

Bell, Frederick, Oct. 7, 1863. Transferred to the Confederate Navy April 25, 1864; died of yellow fever in Charleston, SC, Oct. 26, 1864.

Bell, Jonathan Edward, March 4, 1862. Surrendered at Tallahassee, FL, May 10, 1865, and paroled there May 15, 1865.

Bell, Matthew T., March 4, 1862. Discharged in Tallahassee, FL, March 29, 1864, because of disability due to "Bright's disease and general dropsy."

Billingslea, William A., Sgt, March 4, 1862. Paroled April 28, 1865, in Greensboro, NC.

Bishop, D.G., Jan. 1, 1863. Hired as substitute for William W. Lester; reportedly later transferred to another unit.

Bolton, James L., May 3, 1862. Paroled April 28, 1865, in Greensboro, NC.

Bowers, J.E., Aug. 20, 1862. Transferred to the Confederate Navy April 25, 1864.

Bowers, John R., Aug. 20, 1862. Hired as substitute for William G. Ham

Boyle, Phelix, (also Boil, also Felix), Sept. 2, 1862. Hired as substitute for C.H. Mattox. Reported to have deserted Sept. 4, 1862, but apparently later rejoined the company and was captured in Cheraw, SC, March 6, 1865. Boyle was sent to Washington, DC, where he took the oath of allegiance to the Union and was furnished transportation to West Pittsburgh, PA.

Broach, Charles Willis B., Cpl, March 4, 1862.

Broach, James Alexander, March 4, 1862. Paroled April 28, 1865, in Greensboro, NC.

Brooks, Robertus Glover, March 1, 1862. Not listed in the Compiled Military Service Records as having served in the Echols Artillery, but the March 4, 1862, roster of the Echols Artillery reveals that he was an original member of the company. The reconstructed roster of the Echols Artillery also lists Brooks and discloses that he was discharged later in 1862 with a physical disability. Brooks' Confederate Pension Application also shows that he served in the unit.

Bulloch, R.H., May 3, 1862.

Bunting, John, Cpl, March 4, 1862. Paroled at Tallahassee, FL, May 12, 1865.

Burroughs John C. (also Borroughs & Burrows), March 4, 1862. Paroled April 28, 1865, in Greensboro, NC.

Burt, Emsley Parks, Nov. 1863.

Burton, E.T. Not listed in the Compiled Military Service Records as having served in the Echols Artillery, but Burton is included on the reconstructed roster of the Echols Artillery, which states that he joined the Echols Artillery in Nov. 1863 but transferred to an another unit in 1864.

Cantrell, Wilson, Dec. 1, 1862. Hired as substitute for James Appling; died from wounds in battle at Bentonville, NC, March 19, 1865.

Carter, Elbert B., March 4, 1862.

Carter, William, March 4, 1862.

Chandler, John S., March 4, 1862.

Cheatham, John Isham, Dec. 18, 1862.

Childers, Edward Thomas (also Childress), May 3, 1862.

Childers, J.A. (also Childress), March 4, 1862.

Clancy, Michael C., Feb. 12, 1863. Detailed to Clerical Dept.

Coil, E.M., March 4, 1862. Recorded as absent without leave as of Dec. 12, 1864; no further record.

Colclough, John M. Not listed in the Compiled Military Service Records as serving in the Echols Artillery, but Colclough's Confederate Pension Application states that he served in the unit.

Collier, Frank P., May 3, 1862. Paroled April 28, 1865, in Greensboro, NC.

Colquit, Hopson Hope Hull, March 4, 1862. Paroled April 28, 1865, in Greensboro, NC.

Cooper, J.B., Aug. 1863. Captured in Hartwell, GA, and paroled there May 20, 1865.

Cooper, Jonathan, Aug. 18, 1863. Died of "congestion" in Monticello, FL, Oct. 19, 1864, on his way home on sick furlough.

Cooper, K.R., Cpl, March 4, 1862.

Cooper, Winston Oliver, Bugler, March 9, 1862. Recorded as absent without leave as of Dec. 3, 1864; no further record.

Culbreth, J.P., Blacksmith & Artificer, March 4, 1862.   Paroled in Tallahassee, FL, May 12, 1865.

Cunningham, George Washington, March 4, 1862.

Cunningham, John William, Oct. 10, 1863. Transferred in 1864 to Co. E, 38th Reg. GA Vol. Inf.

Cunningham, Thomas Seborn, May 3, 1862. Paroled April 28, 1865, in Greensboro, NC.

Daniel, John Chesley, May 3, 1862. Transferred to Co. K, 6th Reg. GA Vol. Inf. Nov. 1, 1863, in exchange for Walter W. Stevens.

Davis, Howell Cobb, Sgt, March 4, 1862.   Paroled April 28, 1865, in Greensboro, NC.

Davis, Malachi R., March 4, 1862. Paroled April 28, 1865, in Greensboro, NC.

Deadwyler, Martin, Sgt, May 3, 1862. Died of disease at Ft. Gadsden, FL, Aug. 11, 1863.

Downer, Thomas P., Aug. 4, 1862. Paroled April 28, 1865, in Greensboro, NC.

Dunn, D.T., Aug 10, 1863. Reportedly transferred to another unit in 1864.

Eberhart, Jacob W., March 4, 1862. Paroled after surrender.

Eberhart, Nathan M., March 4, 1862. Killed in the Battle of Averasboro, NC, March 16, 1865.

Eberhart, P.S., May 9, 1862. Paroled April 28, 1865, in Greensboro, NC.

Edwards, Benjamin Franklin, May 3, 1862.

Edwards, Thomas Jefferson, Jr., March 4, 1862. He was not the son of T.J. Edwards, Sr. Paroled April 28, 1865, in Greensboro, NC.

Edwards, Thomas J., Sr., Bugler, May 3, 1862. He was not the father of Thomas Jefferson Edwards, Jr.

Esco, Martin Marshall, May 3, 1862. Recorded as absent without leave as of Dec. 8, 1864; no further record.

Evans, N.H., March 4, 1862. Paroled April 28, 1865, in Greensboro, NC.

Evans, William, Nov. 18, 1863.

Faust, James A., March 4, 1862.

Faust, J.B., Sept. 29, 1862. Died of "brain fever" April 3, 1865.

Faust, William D., March 4, 1862.

Fitts, James M., March 4, 1862. Died of "fever" Dec. 4, 1862.

Furcron, Henry C. (also Fircron), May 3, 1862. Recorded as absent without leave as of Dec. 17, 1864; no further record.

Gaulding, William D., Aug. 27, 1863. Served in Co. I, 15th Reg. GA Vol. Inf. from July 15, 1861, to Oct. 31, 1861, and was discharged due to disability. Later enlisted in Co. E, 66th Reg. GA Vol. Inf but subsequently transferred to the Echols Artillery. There is some evidence that Gaulding also served in Co. D, 9th Reg. GA Vol. Inf. during the war.

Gibson, Jonathan Christopher, Dec. 8, 1862.

Gibson, John Glenn, 1st Lt, March 4, 1862.

Gibson, Robert H. Joined Co. E, 19th Reg. GA Vol. Inf. June 26, 1861. Received a leg wound at Cold Harbor, VA, June 27, 1862, and declared disabled for further infantry service. Transferred to the Echols Artillery Oct. 1, 1863. Reportedly later transferred to an AL unit in 1864.

Glenn, Alex H.S., March 4, 1862.

Glenn, George Rockingham Gilmer, Cpl, March 4, 1862. Paroled April 28, 1865, in Greensboro, NC.

Glenn, George Washington, Sgt, May 3, 1862. Reported absent without leave as of Dec. 31, 1864; no further record.

Glenn, John T., March 4, 1862. Died of "fever" Nov. 11, 1863, in hospital in Quincy, FL.

Glenn, Dr. James Mallory, 2nd Lt, March 4, 1862.

Glenn, Joseph (also Joe) Matthew William, March 4, 1862. Paroled April 28, 1865, in Greensboro, NC.

Glenn, Robert Howard, March 4, 1862.

Glenn, Robert Richard, March 4, 1862. Paroled April 28, 1865, in Greensboro, NC.

Glines, T.A., May 1, 1863. Hired as substitute for T.R. Watkins; died of "fever" in 1864.

Goolsby, Andrew J. Not included in the Compiled Military Service Records as having served in the Echols Artillery, but according to James Jewel's letter dated April 16, 1863, Goolsby apparently was obligated to serve, but hired Shimer John Tiller as a substitute.

Goolsby, Jefferson W., May 3, 1862. Paroled April 28, 1865, in Greensboro, NC.

Graham, John William, March 4, 1862.

Gresham, J. Scott, Sgt, March 4, 1862. Not listed in the Compiled Military Service Records as a member of the Echols Artillery, but the March 4, 1862, roster of the Echols Artillery reveals that he was among the original members of the company. Gresham also is listed on the reconstructed roster of the Echols Artillery, which notes that he was discharged due to consumption, no date given.

Grier, J.H. (also Greer), Nov. 1863. Reportedly transferred to another unit in 1864.

Griffith, Crawford B. Originally joined Co. H, 31st Reg. GA Vol. Inf. as a Private Nov. 14, 1861. Relieved from duty on May 13, 1862, by the Conscript Act and enlisted in the Echols Artillery Nov. 23, 1863. Reportedly later transferred to an AL unit in 1864.

Ham, Dr. William G., March 4, 1862. Discharged Aug. 20, 1862, by hiring John R. Bowers as a substitute.

Hardman, Ezekiah F. (Also Hardeman), March 4, 1862.

Hardman, Wilson S. (Also Hardeman), May 3, 1862. Paroled April 28, 1865, in Greensboro, NC.

Hargrove, Richard L., Sgt (also Hargroves), March 1, 1863. Paroled May 3, 1865, in Greensboro, NC.

Harrison, C.E., May 3, 1862.

Harrison, James K., Aug. 4, 1863.

Hartsfield, Robert F., Jan. 23, 1864. Transferred to Co. K, 6th Reg. GA Vol. Inf. later in 1864. Captured April 13, 1865, while hospitalized in Raleigh, NC. Died there May 22, 1865, and is buried in Raleigh.

Hartsfield, S.R., May 3, 1862. Died of "fever" Aug. 27, 1863, in camp at Quincy, FL.

Haynie, William B.P. (also Hainey), March 4, 1862. Discharged on or about Aug. 31, 1863, in Quincy, FL, with disability, "tumor on shoulder."

Herring, Alfred (also Alpheus), Oct. 29, 1862. Hired as substitute for John H. Mattox. Discharged June 16, 1864, in Tallahassee, FL, "by reason of persistent intermittent fever."

Hitchcock, William C., Cpl, May 3, 1862. Paroled April 28, 1865, in Greensboro, NC.

Holmes, Ira H., March 4, 1862. Transferred March 19, 1864, to Co. K, 6th Reg. GA Vol. Inf..

Hopper, Wiley Brooks, March 4, 1862.

Howard, Robert Groves, Cpl, March 4, 1862. First joined Co. B, 4th Reg. TX Volunteers; transferred to Echols Artillery; then transferred back to the Texas unit and was killed in battle May 10, 1864.

Huff, Joseph Terrill H., March 9, 1863.

Huff, Jacob Eberhart, March 4, 1862.

Huff, Thomas Pool, Oct. 11, 1863. Reportedly transferred to 6th GA Reg. in 1864.

Hurt, James L. (or C.), March 4, 1862. Assigned to Quartermaster Dept. in July 1864 on account of being physically unfit for field duty due to "Endo Carditis of eight months standing."

Jarrell, Jesse Lewis, April 27, 1863. Paroled April 28, 1865, in Greensboro, NC.

Jarrell, John Warner, Sgt. Joined Co. K, 6th Reg. GA Vol. Inf. in June 1861, and transferred to the Echols Artillery June 12, 1862. Paroled April 28, 1865, in Greensboro, NC.

Jarrell, Dr. William H., 1st Lt, March 4, 1862.

Jennings, Thomas C. Not listed in the Compiled Military Service Records as having served in the Echols Artillery, but Jennings' Confederate Pension Application and the reconstructed roster of the Echols Artillery show him to be a member.

Jewel, James, May 3, 1862. Missing after fight at Averasboro, NC, March 16, 1864.

Jewel, John Anderson, May 3, 1862.

Johnson, E.W., Jan. 26. 1864. Reportedly transferred to another unit in 1864.

Johnson, James Butler, March 4, 1862. Paroled April 28, 1865, in Greensboro, NC.

Johnson, James I. or T., March 4, 1862. Paroled April 28, 1865, in Greensboro, NC.

Johnson, J. Winston, March 4, 1862. Paroled April 28, 1865, in Greensboro, NC.

Johnson, M.A., March 4, 1862. Paroled April 28, 1865, in Greensboro, NC.

Johnson, Middleton Witt. Originally joined Co. K, 6th Reg. GA Vol. Inf. May 28, 1861, and served as Sgt. Transferred to Echols Artillery as Pvt June 12, 1862. Discharged April 1, 1863, by hiring W.L. Padgett as substitute. Reenlisted in the Echols Artillery Jan. 3, 1864.

Kidd, Charles W., March 4, 1862. Paroled April 28, 1865, in Greensboro, NC.

Kidd, J.N., March 4, 1862. Discharged Nov. 14, 1862, due to sickness.

Kidd, John M., March 4, 1862. Deserted Dec. 23, 1864, at Hardeeville, SC; no further record.

Kidd, Josiah (also Joe), Aug. 12, 1863. Reportedly deserted Dec. 23, 1864, at Hardeeville, SC, however records show that he was present and paroled at Greensboro, NC, April 28, 1865.

Kidd, W.B.N., Dec. 28, 1863. Transferred to Co. E, 38th Reg. GA Vol. Inf. in 1864.

Kinnebrew, John H., Sgt, March 4, 1862. Sent to hospital in Savannah Dec. 17, 1864; no further record.

Kinnebrew, Marcus B., May 3, 1862.

Lester, Joshua, May 3, 1862. Discharged March 1, 1863, by hiring C.R. Barnes as substitute.

Lester, Robert, May 3, 1862.

Lester, William W., March 4, 1862. Discharged Jan.1, 1863, by hiring D.G. Bishop as a substitute.

Martin, A.D., Oct. 8, 1863.

Martin, Elijah Thomas, April 30, 1863. Discharged April 26, 1864, after being elected Constable of Oglethorpe Co.

Martin, George Wynn, May 3, 1862. Died in April 1865 of "brain fever."

Martin, Joseph E., March 4, 1862. Discharged Oct. 13, 1862, due to "disease of the tongue & general disability."

Mathews, Augustus David, May 3, 1863. Paroled April 28, 1865, in Greensboro, NC.

Mathews, James T., March 4, 1862. Sent to the hospital in Lake City, FL, Oct. 15, 1864; no further record.

Mathews, John Posey, March 4, 1862.

Mathews, Oliver Walton, May 3, 1862. Died of "Typhoid" in Oglethorpe Co., Oct 25, 1863.

Mathews, Richmond Butler, Cpl, March 4, 1862.

Mathews, William Sanford, March 4, 1862. Discharged Sept. 9, 1862, due to sickness.

Mattox, Christopher H., May 3, 1862. Discharged Sept. 2, 1862, by hiring Phelix Boyle as substitute.

Mattox, John Henry, Cpl, May 3, 1862. Discharged Oct. 29, 1862, by hiring Alpheus Herring as a substitute.

McCannon, Alfred S. (also McCanon), March 4, 1862.

McCannon, Woodson M. (also McAnnon & McHannon), May 21, 1863.

Mealor, James Asberry (also Mealer), Nov. 15, 1863. Transferred to Co. E, 38th Reg. GA Vol. Inf. in 1864. Wounded in battle in Oct. 1864 and remained at home on wounded furlough until the end of the war.

Mobley, W.D. (also Moblie), March 4, 1862. Transferred to Co. K, 6th Reg. GA Vol. Inf. March 19, 1864.

Murray, F.H. (also Murry), Artificer, March 4, 1862.

Noell, James S. (also Nauel, Noel, and Nowell), March 4, 1862. Died of "typhoid" in Atlanta Sept. 25, 1862.

Noell, James T. (also Nauel, Noel, and Nowell), Aug. 4, 1863. Father of James S. Noell. Compiled Military Service Records reported that Noell was absent without leave as of Dec. 13, 1864, and show no further record; however, the reconstructed roster of the Echols Artillery states that James T. Noell transferred to another unit in 1864.

Noell, Upson C. (also Noel), March 4, 1862. Discharged Sept. 9, 1862, due to sickness.

Norton, James M., March 4, 1862.

Pace, John Howard, Artificer, March 4, 1862. Pace was listed as absent without leave as of Dec. 17, 1864; no further record.

Padgett, W.L. Hired as substitute for Middleton Witt Johnson April 11, 1863. Died of "typhoid" in Quincy, FL, Sept. 10, 1863.

Parr, Thomas, March 4, 1862. Compiled Military Service Records reported that on the Muster Roll for Nov.-Dec. 1864, Parr was absent without leave, however, the reconstructed roster of the Echols Artillery states that he died of "fever" in 1864.

Pass, Matthew J.H., May 3, 1862. Compiled Military Service Records reported Pass absent without leave as of Dec. 13, 1864; no further record.

Patman, William Thomas, Sgt, March 4, 1863. Paroled April 28, 1865, in Greensboro, NC.

Patton, Allen David, March 4, 1862. The reconstructed roster of the Echols Artillery states that Patton died in 1864.

Patton, George W., Jr., May 3, 1862. Died of pneumonia Oct. 23, 1863, in the hospital in Quincy, FL.

Patton, George W., Sr., March 4, 1862. Paroled April 28, 1865, in Greensboro, NC.

Patton, Jacob T., March 4, 1862.

Paul, Archibald M., Aug. 4, 1862. Sent to hospital in Savannah Dec. 17, 1864; no further record.

Paul, John William, March 4, 1862. Compiled Military Service Records reported that Paul was absent without leave as of Nov. 25, 1864, however, the reconstructed roster of the Echols Artillery states that he died of "fever" in 1864

Paul, Richard Marion, March 4, 1862. Died of "fever" at home Oct. 24, 1863.

Paul, Thomas Jefferson, Jr., May 3, 1862. He was the nephew of T.J. Paul, Sr. Compiled Military Service Records reported that Paul was absent without leave as of Dec. 8, 1864, however the records further show that he was present and paroled April 28, 1865, at Greensboro, NC.

Paul, Thomas Jefferson, Sr., March 4, 1862. He was the uncle of T.J. Paul, Jr. Paroled April 28, 1865, at Greensboro, NC.

Peek, William J., Sgt, March 4, 1862. Captured in Cheraw, SC, and paroled there March 5, 1865.

Phelps, William , March 4, 1862. Paroled April 28, 1865, at Greensboro, NC.

Porter, W.T., Oct. 11, 1863.

Powers, J.D., Oct. 23, 1863.

Powers, W.B., Jan. 29, 1864.

Powers, W.D., March 4, 1862.

Raines, Benjamin Vaughn (also Rains), Sgt. Enlisted in Co. K, 6th Reg. GA Vol. Inf., as Cpl May 28, 1861, and transferred to the Echols Artillery March 4, 1862.

Reed, Robert N., March 4, 1862. Discharged Feb. 1, 1863, by hiring John P. Tiller as a substitute.

Robertson, Pleasant P., March 4, 1862. Transferred to Co. I in M.A. Hardin's Mountain Rangers in Sept.1862, and was discharged soon thereafter by furnishing a substitute.

Scroggins, J.W. (also Scoggins), March 4, 1862. Reported absent without leave as of Dec. 12, 1864; no further record.

Shaw, A.J., March 4, 1862. Wounded in battle defending Savannah in Dec. 1864.

Sims, Charles W., Cpl, March 4, 1862. Discharged November 24, 1862, by hiring D.E. Stinson as a substitute.

Smith, Daniel C., 2nd Lt, March 4, 1862. Resigned Feb. 7, 1863, upon being selected by Col G.W. Lee to form a cavalry company in Atlanta. The original roster of the Echols Artillery gives Smith's name as Dewitt instead of Daniel. There was a man named Dewitt Smith in Oglethorpe County at the time, but there is no further evidence that he served in the Echols Artillery.

Smith, George B., Feb. 9, 1864. Reportedly transferred to another unit in 1864.

Smith, George K., May 3, 1862.

Smith, Henry Clay, March 4, 1862. Paroled April 28, 1865, at Greensboro, NC..

Smith, J.D., March 4, 1862. Deserted at Hardeeville, SC; no further record.

Smith, J.W., May 3, 1862. Paroled April 28, 1865, at Greensboro, NC.

Smith, S.J., March 4, 1862. Sent to hospital in Monticello, FL, Oct. 12, 1864; no further record.

Smith, Thomas L., Cpl, March 4, 1862.

Smith, William M., 1st Lt, March 4, 1862. Resigned Dec. 5, 1862, with a medical disability, "Because of varicose veins of both legs, preventing free locomotion conjoined with chronic bronchitis and great general disability."

Sorrow, George W., March 4, 1862. Transferred to the Confederate Navy April 24, 1864.

Stevens, Columbus Augustus, March 4, 1862. Paroled April 28, 1865, at Greensboro, NC.

Stevens, John Cilvainus Gibson, March 4, 1862. Stevens was listed as absent without leave as of Dec. 10, 1864; no further record.

Stevens, Walter W. Was in Co. K, 6th Reg. GA Vol. Inf and transferred to the Echols Artillery in 1863 in exchange for John Chesley Daniel but died of diarrhea March 21, 1864, before arriving at the unit.

Stinson, David E., Hired as a substitute for Charles W. Sims Nov. 24, 1862. Deserted in Atlanta Jan. 12, 1863; no further record.

Thaxton, Henry, Nov. 1863. Reportedly transferred to another unit in 1864.

Thornton, John Boykin, Oct. 11, 1863. Transferred to Co. K, 6th Reg. GA Vol. Inf. in 1864. Hospitalized with chronic diarrhea in Greensboro, NC, in January 1865; no further record.

Tiller, Frank Tolliver, May 3, 1862. Sent to hospital in Savannah Dec. 17, 1864; no further record.

Tiller, Hopson R., May 3, 1863.

Tiller, John H., Jr., March 4, 1862. He was a 1st cousin to J.H. Tiller, Sr. Wounded at the Battle of Averasboro, NC, March 16, 1865.

Tiller, John Hopson, Sr., Capt, March 4, 1862. He was a 1st cousin to J.H. Tiller, Jr.

Tiller, John P. Hired as substitute for Robert N. Reed Feb. 17, 1863; died of "congestion" in the hospital in Tallahassee Aug. 11, 1864.

Tiller, Joseph Thomas, March 4, 1862.

Tiller, Joseph William, March 4, 1862.

Tiller, Shimer (Shimmie) John, May 3, 1862. According to James Jewel's letter of April 16, 1863, Shimmie Tiller was hired as a substitute for Andrew J. Goolsby. Tiller died of pneumonia April 19, 1863.

Tiller, William Martin, March 4, 1862. Compiled Military Service Records reported that Tiller was absent without leave as of Dec. 17, 1864, however, the records further show that he was present and paroled April 28, 1865, at Greensboro, NC.

Tiller, Woodson (also Wootson), May 3, 1863. Died of "fever" Jan. 11, 1864, in the hospital in Tallahassee, FL.

Tison, J. (or T.?) A., Nov. 25, 1863. Identified as Thomas Tison on the reconstructed roster of the Echols Artillery and reportedly transferred to another unit in 1864.

Turner, George Washington, Aug. 4, 1863. Paroled April 28, 1865, at Greensboro, NC.

Turner, Valentine M., Cpl, March 4, 1862.

Vaughan, R.H. (or R.T.) (also Vaughn), March 4, 1862. Sent to hospital in Lake City, FL, Oct. 15, 1864; no further record.

Wade, James Bolton, 2nd Lt, April 15, 1862.

Waller, T.J., Cpl, March 4, 1862. Paroled April 28,1865, in Greensboro, NC.

Watkins, Thaddeus Reese, Sgt., March 4, 1863. Discharged May 1,1863, by hiring T.A. Glines as a substitute.

Webb, Horatio James (Horatius on tombstone), May 3, 1862.

Webb, Isham Hamilton, May 3, 1862. Wounded at the Battle of Averasboro, NC, March 16, 1865.

Webb, W.P. (or W.T.), March 4, 1862. Died of jaundice in the hospital in Lake City, FL, Aug. 5, 1864.

Wheless, Pleasant Lafayette (also Wheelis), May 3, 1862.

Whitehead, George W., Cpl, March 4, 1862. Wounded in battle defending Savannah in Dec. 1864.

Williams, Harrison B., March 4, 1862.

Willingham, William T., March 4, 1862. Paroled April 28, 1865, at Greensboro, NC.

Wise, Dr. Joseph, Sgt, March 4, 1862. Discharged due to consumption April 7, 1864.

Wise, Robert, Sgt, March 4, 1862.

Witcher, Charles McElroy, Cpl, March 4, 1862. Paroled April 28, 1865, in Greensboro, NC.

Wood, Samuel J., Oct. 11, 1863.

Wood, William B.J., May 3, 1862. Died Oct. 1, 1863, in Quincy, FL.

Wright, John H., May 3, 1862.

Young, James C., March 4, 1862. Discharged Sept. 9, 1862, "on account of physical disability."

Young, Wiley (also Wyley), May 3, 1862. Paroled April 28, 1865, in Greensboro, NC.

References

Armor, E.H. *The Cemeteries of Greene County, Georgia.* Athens, GA: Agee Publishers Inc., 1987.

Avant, David A., Jr. *Illustrated Index, J. Randall Stanley's History of Gadsden County, 1948.* Tallahassee, FL, 1985.

Barnwell, V.T. *Atlanta City Directory and Strangers Guide,* Vol. I. Atlanta, GA, 1867.

Boyd, Mark F. "Events at Prospect Bluff on the Apalachicola River, 1808-1818." *The Florida Historical Quarterly,* Vol. XVI, No. 2, pp. 55-96. Tallahassee, FL,1937.

Bryan, T. Conn. *Confederate Georgia.* Athens, GA: University of Georgia Press, 1953.

Carroll, John M. *List of Staff Officers of the Confederate States of America.* Mattituck, NY, 1983. Self-published.

Coleman, Kenneth. *Athens, 1861-1865, as Seen Through the Letters in The University of Georgia Libraries.* Athens, GA: University of Georgia Press, 1969.

—. *Confederate Athens.* Athens, GA: University of Georgia Press, 1967.

Confederate Military History, Extended Edition. Vol. VII Georgia. Original Edition: Confederate Publishing Company, Atlanta 1899. Wilmington, NC: Reprint: Broadfoot Publishing Company, 1987.

Coulter, Ellis Merton. *Lost Generation: The Life and Death of James Barrow, C.S.A.* Confederate Centennial Studies, W. Stanley Hoole Editor-in-Chief. Tuscaloosa, AL: Confederate Publishing Company, Inc., 1956.

Crute, Joseph, H., Jr. *Confederate Staff Officers 1861-1865.* Self-published, Powhatan, VA, 1982.

Davis, William Watson. *The Civil War and Reconstruction in Florida.* New York: Columbia University Press, 1913.

Dixon, Sara Anderson and Mary Jane Dixon. *Newton County Cemeteries.* Self-published, Starrsville, GA, 1972.

Ellis, Mary Louise, William Warren Rogers, and Joan Perry Morris. *Tallahassee Favored Land.* Norfolk/Virginia Beach, VA: Donning Publishing Company, 1988.

Faz, Carolyn Bryant. *The History of Salem Baptist Church 1789-1989.* Salem Baptist Church Bicentennial Committee. [Oglethorpe County, GA, 1989].

Ferry, Richard J. *Soldiers of Florida in the Seminole Indian - Civil - and Spanish American Wars.* Self-published, Macclenny, FL, 1893.

Frier, Joshua Hoyt, II (1847-1903). *Reminiscences of the War Between the States by a Boy in the Far South at Home and in the Ranks of the Confederate Militia.* Transcribed by J.W. Hart. M76-134 Florida State Archives.

Garrett, Franklin M. *Atlanta and Environs: A Chronicle of its People and Events.* 2 Vols. Athens, GA: University of Georgia Press, 1954.

Henderson, Lillian, comp. *Roster of the Confederate Soldiers of Georgia, 1861-1865.* 6 vols., Georgia Confederate Pension and Record Department, 1959-1964. Hapeville, GA: Longino and Porter.

Heritage Papers. *The Hills of Wilkes County, Georgia, and Allied Families.* Vol. 2. Danielsville, GA: Reprint Company, 1987.

Hewett, Janet B. Arranged by Joyce Lawrence. *Georgia Confederate Soldiers 1861-1865. Name Roster Vol. I A-J, Vol. II K-Z.* Wilmington, NC: Broadfoot Publishing, 1998.

Historic Oglethorpe County, Inc. *Cemeteries of Oglethorpe County, Georgia.* Fernandina Beach, FL, 1995.

Hudson, Frank Parker. *A 1790 Census for Wilkes County, Georgia, Prepared from Tax Returns with Abstracts of the 1790 Tax Returns.* Spartanburg, SC, 1988.

Jewel, James. Letters deposited in the Special Collections Department in the Robert W. Woodruff Library at Emory University in Atlanta (Confederate Miscellany Ia 4).

Kinsland, William S. "The Dahlonega Mint: A Civil War Mystery." *North Georgia Journal,* Vol. I, Summer 1984, pp. 39-46. Dahlonega, GA, 1984.

Lunceford, Alvin Mell, Jr. *Taliaferro County, Georgia, Records and Notes.* Spartanburg, SC, 1988.

Maddox, Joseph T. and Mary Carter. *37,000 Early Georgia Marriages.* Self-published, Irwinton, GA, 1975.

Maddox, Joseph T. and Mary Carter. *40,000 Early Georgia Marriages.* Self-published, Irwinton, GA, 1977.

McRee, Fred W. *Oglethorpe County, Georgia Marriage Records 1853-1963.* Self-published, Dahlonega, GA, 1999.

Mohr, Clarence Lee. *Oglethorpe County, Georgia During the Formative Period, 1717-1830.* Unpublished M.A. Thesis, Athens, GA: The University of Georgia, 1970.

Montgomery, Horace. *Johnny Cobb: Confederate Aristocrat.* Athens, GA: University of Georgia Press, 1964.

Moore, Albert Burton. *Conscription and Conflict in the Confederacy.* New York: MacMillan Company, 1924.

Paisley, Clifton. *The Red Hills of Florida, 1528-1865.* Tuscaloosa, AL, and London: University of Alabama Press, 1989.

Procter, Samuel, ed. *Florida A Hundred Years Ago.* Florida Civil War Centennial Commission, 1960-1963. Florida Library and Historical Commission 1963, State Library, Tallahassee, FL.

Rainer, Vessie Thrasher. *Henry County, Georgia: The Mother of Counties.* Privately printed by the author. Undated.

Rice, T.B. *History of Greene County, Georgia 1786-1886.* C.W. Williams, ed. Macon, GA, 1961.

Rodgers, Ava D. *The Housing of Oglethorpe County, Georgia, 1790-1860.* Tallahassee, FL: Florida State University Press, 1971.

Sheppard, Peggy. *Andersonville, Georgia U.S.A.* Andersonville, GA: Sheppard Publication, 1973.

Smith, Florrie Carter. *History of Oglethorpe County, Georgia.* Washington, GA: Wilkes Publishing Company, 1970.

—. *History of Oglethorpe County, Georgia, Supplement I.* Washington, GA: Wilkes Publishing Company, 1972

—. *History of Oglethorpe County, Georgia, Supplement II.* Washington, GA: Wilkes Publishing Company, 1979.

Stegeman, John F. *These Men She Gave: Civil War Diary of Athens, Georgia.* Athens, GA: The University of Georgia Press, 1964.

Turner, Maxine. *Navy Gray: A Story of the Confederate Navy on the Chattahoochee and Apalachicola Rivers.* Tuscaloosa, AL, and London: The University of Alabama Press, 1988.

United Daughters of the Confederacy, Georgia Division, Oglethorpe County Chapter, No. 1292. Gussie Reese, ed. *This They Remembered.* Washington, GA: Washington Publishing Company, 1964.

U.S. War Department. *War of the Rebellion: A Compilation of the Official Records of the Union and Confederate Armies.* 130 vols. Washington, DC: U.S. Government Printing Office, 1880-1901.

White, Virgil D. *Index to Georgia Civil War Pension Files.* Waynesboro, TN, 1996.

Wise, Lena Smith. "A History of Oglethorpe County." M.A. Thesis, The University of Georgia, Athens, GA, 1953.

Womack, Miles Kenan, Jr. *Gadsden, A Florida County in Word and Picture.* Quincy, Florida: Gadsden County Bicentennial Commission, 1976.

GOVERNMENT DOCUMENTS

Barbour County, AL, 1860 census.

Campbell County, GA, 1850 and 1860 census.

Carroll County, GA, 1860 census.

Chambers County, AL, 1850 and 1860 census.

Clarke County, GA, 1850 and 1860 census.

Cobb County, GA, 1860 census.

Confederate Pensions and Records Department. Pension Application Files, Greene and Oglethorpe counties. Microfilm in Georgia State Archives.

Elbert County, GA, 1860 census.

Fulton County, GA, Deeds and Morgages, 1854-1871.

Greene County, GA, 1840 census, 1850, 1860, and 1870 census.

Greene County, GA, Will Book 6, 1877-1921. Will of Eliza C. Jewel probated 1911.

Henry County, GA, 1860 census.

Lee County, GA, 1860 census.

Leon County, FL, 1860 census.

Morgan County, GA, 1860 census.

Oglethorpe County, GA, Administrators and Guardians Bonds, 1821-1830.

Oglethorpe County, GA, Bench Dockets for the Ordinary, Commenced July Term 1829 [to 1855].

Oglethorpe County, GA, Bonds, Administrators, Guardians, and Temporary Administrators, 1812-1820.

Oglethorpe County, GA, 1800, 1810, 1820, 1830, 1840, 1850, 1860, 1870, 1880, 1890, and 1900 census.

Oglethorpe County, GA, Confederate Roster. Reconstructed Roster of Co. K, 6th Regiment, GA Vol. Infantry (Gilmer Blues); Co. K, 8th Regiment, GA Vol. Infantry (Oglethorpe Rifles); Capt. Tiller's Battery, GA Light Artillery (Echols Artillery); Co. E, 38th Regt. GA Vol. Infantry (Tom Cobb Infantry).

Oglethorpe County, GA, Indigent Soldiers Pension Roll (also contains sections entitled Disabled or Invalid Soldiers Roll; Widows of Deceased Soldiers Roll; and Indigent Widows Roll).

Oglethorpe County, GA, Inventories and Appraisements, Returns, and Sales 1808-1829.

Oglethorpe County, GA, Inventories and Annual Returns on Estates, 1811-1826 and 1815-1831.

Oglethorpe County, GA, Letters of Administration, 1856-1901

Oglethorpe County, GA, Marriages 1794-1831 Vol. II.

Oglethorpe County, GA, Marriage Book C 1828-1863.

Oglethorpe County, GA, Marriage Book D 1863-1877.

Oglethorpe County, GA, Marriages 1891-1897.

Oglethorpe County, GA, Marriage Book J April 1923-December 1952.

Oglethorpe County, GA, 1860 Slave Schedule.

Oglethorpe County, GA, Tax Digests, 1863.

Oglethorpe County, GA, Widows' Allowance 1856-1903.

Oglethorpe County, GA, Will Book D 1833-1866. Will of John Bell probated 1849. Will of William Campbell probated 1844. Will of John Martin probated 1864. Will of Joseph B. Stevens probated 1865.

Oglethorpe County, GA, Will Book E Part I 1866-1886. Will of Emily Meire probated 1869. Will of James E. Smith probated 1882. Will of Joseph Smith probated 1871.

Spalding County, GA, 1860 census.

Stewart County, GA, 1850 census.

U.S. Dept. of Defense. Compiled Service Records of Confederate Soldiers in Georgia Units. Capt. Tiller's Co. (Echols Artillery). National Archives Microfilm Pulications. Microcopy No. 266, roll 115.

Warren County, GA, 1860 census.

Wilkes County, GA, 1860 census.

Yazoo County, MS, 1860 Census.

Yazoo County, MS, 1860 Slave Schedule.

NEWSPAPERS

The Christian Index, Macon, GA.

Christian Index and South-western Baptist, Atlanta, GA.

Herald Journal, Greensboro, GA.

Oglethorpe Echo, Lexington, GA.

Southern Confederacy, Atlanta, GA.

INDEX

Because of frequency of reference, not all page numbers are listed for some family members after they are initially identified.

Langston, Crane, & Hammock's
Store, 20

Laura (slave?), 233

Lawrence, Evan H., 23

Leathy (slave), 68

Lebron (slave), 255

Lee, Col George W., 34, 42, 43, 52,
57, 68, 69, 70

Lee, Gen Robert Edward, 15, 22, 138

Lee County, GA, 111, 277

Lemay, 264

Leon Cavalry, 95

Lexington Depot, 119, 142, 146

Lexington, GA, iii, vii, 5, 7, 8, 12, 18,
20, 25, 35, 47, 54, 60, 77, 107,
119, 120, 142, 146, 158, 204,
220, 223, 225, 227, 252, 259,
270, 281

Lexington Militia District, Oglethorpe
County, GA, 35, 60

Lexington, KY, 47

Libby Prison, Richmond, VA, 59n

Lincoln, Abraham, xvii, 59n, 181

Lofton, John T., 7n, 35

Lookout Mountain, TN, 43

Louisville, KY, 24n, 55

Lumpkin, Anna R., 85n

Lumpkin, Callendar Cunningham
Grieve (Mrs. Joseph Henry
Lumpkin), xxi

Lumpkin, Edward P., 81

Lumpkin, Dr. George, 277, 279

Lumpkin, Hopia N. ("Hope," Mrs.
Middleton W. Johnson), 214n

Lumpkin, John, 65

Lumpkin, Joseph Henry, xxin, 82n

Lumpkin, Lucy Deupree Johnson (1st

Mrs. James Johnson, 2nd Mrs.
Samuel Lumpkin), 11, 13n, 96n,
234, 245, 246, 270, 275

Lumpkin, Marion McHenry (daughter
of Joseph Henry Lumpkin, wife
of T.R.R. Cobb), xxin, 82n

Lumpkin, Reverend Jack L., 85n

Lumpkin, Samuel, 13n

Lumpkin, Wilson, 51, 275n

Macclenny, FL, 218n

Macon, GA, 28, 73, 75, 125n, 152,
275

Macon and Chattanooga Railroad, 41

Madison, FL, 190, 208, 210, 225

Madison, GA, 68, 246, 260, 264

Madison County, FL, 109n

Madison County, GA, 33n, 69n, 71n,
183, 215, 263n

Malone, Adaline C. (Mrs. John
Franklin Martin), 43n

Manassas, VA, Battle of, 45, 47n,
48n, 174, 187

Mapp, Dr. J. Lawson, 101n

Marable, Anna, 232, 245

Marable, Frances, 232

Marcum, George R., 3, 255, 270

Marianna, FL, 224

Marietta, GA, 44, 61

Martin, Adaline C. Malone (Mrs.
John Franklin Martin), 43n

Martin, Elijah Thomas, 3n, 43n, 62,
111, 119, 120, 123, 130, 137,
139, 140, 152, 153, 169, 256,
260, 267, 279

Martin, George Wynn, 2, 6, 10, 13,
17, 23, 25, 26, 28, 34, 43n, 46,
49, 55, 57, 58, 61, 63n, 65, 80,

About the author

Gary L. Doster, a native of Athens, Georgia, is the author of *From Abbeville to Zebulon, Early Post Card Views of Georgia* and *A Post Card History of Athens, Georgia*. He is a certified wildlife biologist and has worked for the Southeastern Cooperative Wildlife Disease Study at the University of Georgia since 1965. Gary has a lifelong interest in Georgia history and has ancestors from Oglethorpe County, Georgia, dating back to the 1790s. He is married to the former Faye Ann Thomas of Oconee County, Georgia.

Cover and book designed by William Reeves

www.ingramcontent.com/pod-product-compliance
Lightning Source LLC
Chambersburg PA
CBHW060414030726
47495CB00003B/569